Brandi,
Never is
Being you

Ride the Waves

How to take control of your life
one emotion at a time

Tracy

Tracy Friesen

Copyright © 2013 by Tracy Friesen
First Edition – March 2013

ISBN
978-1-4602-0437-5 (Hardcover)
978-1-4602-0436-8 (Paperback)
978-1-4602-0438-2 (eBook)

The author does not dispense medical advice or prescribe the use of any technique as a form of treatment for physical, emotional, or medical problems without the advice of a physician, either directly or indirectly. The intent of the author is only to offer information of a general nature to help you in your quest for emotional and spiritual well-being. In the event you use any of the information in this book for yourself the author and the publisher assume no responsibility for your actions.

Produced by:

FriesenPress
Suite 300 – 852 Fort Street
Victoria, BC, Canada V8W 1H8

www.friesenpress.com

Distributed to the trade by The Ingram Book Company

I dedicate this book to:

- my loving husband Kevin; I am so grateful for his presence in my life
- my good friend Miss Tammy Gunn; she is my guiding light at the end of the tunnel
- my biggest fan, Mr. Lee; always remember that you ROCK, my friend
- and Tom – without him I would still be sitting and waiting for my life to change

Foreword

After more than thirty years of passionately studying personal development I have found that you can study an entire book, more than once, and grow with each and every reading experience. This is such a book!

With Tracy's Ride the Waves there is a different type of reading experience available to you because of the brilliant way she has designed this book. Inspiration can be found on the first few pages or in one of the powerful quotes or in Tracy's daily inspiration. You will find wisdom and inspiration on pretty much every page you turn.

In fact, you may get so much profound wisdom from the opening words, that you may not even be drawn to read any more … but you will.

When I wrote my New York Times Best Selling Book Your Destiny Switch (a book about understanding the nature and power of our emotions – and how to master them) many readers wrote to me. The readers made comments similar to: "thank you so much for reminding us that we are human and have emotions that do go up and down" or "I appreciate that you do not expect us to be positive ALL of the time but show us how to manage the hills and the valleys" plus many other similar comments.

When I first started getting this type of comment I remember thinking "well, of course, we're all human and our emotions will go up and down". We will feel fear. We may feel doubt, worry, anxious, sad and/ or frustrated. But, at the end of the day, awareness is key. Pay attention to where your emotions are, at which end of the scale they are on, and consciously choose to raise up the emotional level. There is an opposite emotion to all negative emotions. The opposite of fear is faith. The opposite of hate is love. The opposite of worry is calm. When you do learn to master your emotions, you will experience a positive response because you'll be in a vibration of creation.

Tracy reminds you to stay in the positive side of the emotions. She shares ideas for you to consider a new way (a better way) of looking at life and situations. Her experience has and is a beacon of light for others to follow. Her words are inspirational. Her insights are transformational and her guidance can change your life for the better.

Make Ride the Waves your emotional resource guide. Share it with others. My advice to you is to invest in another copy and give it away to someone you care about. They'll be glad you did. And remember to enjoy the "ride"!

By Peggy McColl – New York Times Best Selling Author

Preface

I started writing these messages out of emotional necessity. I was going through a difficult time in my life and I needed that release. I needed to feel I was connected to something. My friends at the time were always coming to me with what was going on in their lives so that I could help them see the good in what was happening. But I had no one to talk to myself, to help *me* see the good, the reason, for what was going on in my own life, so I just started talking to the page. I committed myself to write something every day to help myself get to the next day.

I suggest reading this book like a calendar—one message per day—or just flip the book open to any random page. You never know what you may find for yourself along the way. Please use the blank spaces throughout the book to jot down your own thoughts and ideas that you may have while you are living out the message of each day. Keep in mind, the messages are just my own self-talk to help me ride out my own emotions. Below is an example of what you can expect to find throughout the book:

Pay attention to your emotions

"Emotions are the next frontier to be understood and conquered. To manage our emotions is not to drug them or suppress them, but to understand them so that we can intelligently direct our emotional energies and intentions…It's time for human beings to grow up emotionally, to mature into emotionally managed and responsible citizens. No magic pill will do it." – Doc Childre

"By starving emotions we become humorless, rigid and stereotyped; by repressing them we become literal, reformatory and holier-than-thou; encouraged, they perfume life; discouraged, they poison it." – Joseph Collin

Isn't about time you learned how to ride the waves of your emotions? We all have the power to be the best emotional surfers! You just may have to learn how to use your board more often…because if you are not swimming in your emotions you most likely are drowning in them, and how's that working for you so far in your life to bring about your wishes and dreams? Hmmm…Yeah, that's what I thought. If you learned to get the story out of your head and stopped taking things *so* personally all the time, you might realize that you really do know how to surf!

Think about it…

Tracy Friesen CEMP, CLLE, Reiki Master

Here's a little bit about me:

I came from a background in Computer Programming and Web Design. Using this lopsided logical-thinking approach to everything all the time left me feeling that I was missing something. Although I loved what I did, I just did not like how I had to play the corporate game to move up the ladder, especially the part about stepping on others to get where I wanted to go. After my daughter was born I realized that some things are more important than a paycheck and I left a six-figure salary behind to become a full-time Mom. Once my daughter was older I became bored with my life, so I started working on myself to help heal my emotional state, thinking that something was always wrong with me. Though at the time I didn't realize I was healing myself, I took course after course and read book after book. I now come from a place in my heart of unconditional love. I believe that no one is broken and no one needs to be fixed; we are all in a constant state of Self Evolving. We are all perfect in each moment because we are being the best we can be with the knowledge and know-how we have at every given moment. We make choices in our lives that create consequences and we are continuously evolving who we are by learning from our consequences. We are safe in every moment because we can always make a different choice. We are all made of the same energy. No one is better than or greater than anyone else. Energy is never created or destroyed; it just is. I live by a philosophy that "Everything is OK in the end. If it's not OK, then it's not the end!"

I now work as a Certified Energy Medicine Practitioner specializing in the program Life Lessons through Energy Medicine. We all need help at times in our lives to release the energies and blocks that are no longer serving us to move us forward on our path. I work with the Energy Systems of humans and animals to find and release those energy blocks by reconnecting flow. By doing this it can relieve stress and pain as well as bring clarity and understanding to your Physical, Mental, Emotional and/or Spiritual well being.

Find me on the web at www.crystalcovecenter.com

"Until you make the unconscious conscious, it will direct your life, and you will call it fate." - Carl Jung

Thinking of poverty or wealth?

"Being poor is a frame of mind." – Mike Todd

"The law of abundance is that everything replicates after its own kind. Like is attracted to like. If you want more wealth, concentrate on wealth; think thoughts of abundance and wealth." – Delfin Knowledge System

You can apply the above statement to anything you want to welcome into your life. More LOVE, more ROMANCE, more HAPPINESS, more JOY, more EXCITEMENT, more PEACE, more ADVENTURE, more SUCCESS, more of ANYTHING… It is true that whatever you are thinking about you will BE. Words are powerful, especially the ones you say to yourself in your mind's eye. Our minds do not hear the negative words we use, as in "No Worries"; it may seem that we are saying something good but in reality our minds just hear the word "worries" so that is what we are creating. I invite you to explore the possibilities for one day to only say words of directness and positivity and remove any negative expletives, especially words like no, not, and/or don't, and see what you are able to create for yourself! The more direct and clear you are with what you want to welcome in your life the easier it is to manifest them!

Think about it…

Love and Sunshine,
Tracy

January 2nd

Labels limit us

"When I let go of what I am, I become what I might be."– Lao Tzu

"As long as I am this or that, I am not all things."– Meister Eckhart

"Your only limitations are those you set up in your mind, or permit others to set up for you." – Og Mandino

How many of us define who we are by what we do? I have been caught in the game of "I am"—a woman, a mother, a sister, a daughter, a wife, a lover, a friend, a teacher, a business woman, a business owner, a computer programmer, a web designer, a gemstone retailer, a certified energy medicine practitioner…thinking that these things are who I am. Really, these are just labels to describe a "role" I may or may not play. In reality "who I am" is loving, caring, smart, intelligent, skillful, lovable, successful, funny, thoughtful, honest, compassionate, empathetic, forgiving, desirable, passionate, sexy, and sensual, just to name a few. These are all things that I can BE. Now that I have had a baby I will always be a mother whether I am with my kids or not. That does not define me. What defines me is what kind of mother I am being. Am I a caring mother? A graceful mother? A loving, educating mother? Not just a mother. Do you see a difference? If we continue to pigeonhole ourselves in a "what" we will never be happy in "who" we really are because we will not allow ourselves to truly BE. Allowing is everything. Forgive yourself…know that you are a perfect being in every moment as you are doing the best you can with the knowledge you have on hand in this moment.

I invite you to make your own lists of "What you are" and "Who you are." Email them to; me@tracyfriesen.com and I will help you discern when you are "seeing" yourself through the eyes of what you are rather than who you are.

Think about it…

Love and Sunshine,
Tracy

Happiness is a choice

"Happiness cannot be traveled to, owned, earned, worn or consumed. Happiness is the spiritual experience of living every minute with love, grace, and gratitude."
– Denis Waitley

"It is not easy to find happiness in ourselves, and it is not possible to find it elsewhere." – Agnes Repplier

"You wander from room to room hunting for the diamond necklace that is already around your neck!" – Jalal-Uddin Rumi

Have you ever been caught in "I'll be happy when…"? Did you notice that when "when" happened, you still were not happy and you just created another "I'll be happy when…"? We create so many stories around our own unhappiness, which allows us to continue to use our circumstances to control our happiness. If we take the "have to's" out of our life and insert "want to's" we may begin to live a different life. I recently saw a movie that has impacted me greatly. I am surprised that part of the experience still remains with me today, when I saw it almost two months ago. The movie was *Into the Wild*. If you haven't seen it, go outside your usual comfort zone of laughter and car chases and watch it. I would love to describe what I got out of it but then I may spoil the movie for those who have yet to see it.

Happiness is a CHOICE—period. There is no refuting that point. If you choose to not be happy in any situation, I invite you to go to your mirror and look at yourself and ask the hard questions to take back your life.

It is never in the WHY that we may regain our power; it is always in the HOW! When you cannot be grateful and accepting of your current situation then maybe it is a good time to examine your resistance and objections to what you are experiencing. They may reveal to you the terms and conditions you are dictating for how your reality "should" appear.

Here is a quote by Frederick Langbridge that I have often thought about when I am in over my head in the story of my own life: "Two men look out the same prison bars; one sees mud and the other stars." Which one are you?

Another story comes to mind that has helped me: Two twin boys were brought up by an alcoholic father who used to beat them every day. When it was time for the boys to leave home and take on their own life, one of the twins turned out to be exactly like his father: a drunk who beat his wife and kids. When asked why he thought he turned out the way he did he replied, "With a dad like mine how would you turn out?" The other twin took on his life and became a very successful business-man who gave to charities and helped out the less fortunate. He created a loving, caring relationship with his wife and kids. When asked why he thought he turned out the way he did he replied, "With a dad like mine how would you turn out?"

Happiness is CHOICE. Who are you going to be today?

Think about it…

Love and Sunshine,
Tracy

Be here now

"This moment is the moment of reality, of union, of truth. Nothing needs to be done to it or to you for this to be so. Nothing needs to be avoided, transcended, or found for it to be so." – Da Avabhasa

"Each today, well-lived, makes yesterday a dream of happiness and each tomorrow a vision of hope. Look, therefore, to this one day, for it and it alone is life." – Sanskrit poem

"You must live in the present, launch yourself on every wave, find your eternity in each moment." – Henry David Thoreau

Where are you? Are you sure that you even remember pouring that second cup of coffee? Have you ingrained your routine so deeply that you are mindlessly wandering about your day? I do not believe that we have a subconscious mind. To me, that would mean there is a part of me that I cannot control. I strongly believe I am in control of everything I do. I like to think I have a habitual mind. It is here that I have created an automatic response to certain criteria. I do not do anything without awareness. This brings me to the above statements. If we can be present with what is happening in and around us, we can perhaps remove ourselves from that habitual part of us. If in this moment you are pouring that second cup of coffee, relish it…smell the aroma of a freshly brewed pot, listen to the calming sound of the liquid going into your cup, see the sparkle of the beautiful deep brown color. Enjoy what is available to you at this moment. There is good in every moment. Just as in yesterday's message we learned that Happiness is a CHOICE, so is being present. If you are in this moment thinking about yesterday in an "I shoulda…" kind of way, know that there is nothing you can do to change what has already happened. If you are thinking about tomorrow in a "What if…" frame of mind, you have no idea what is going to happen in the next five minutes so why waste energy in trying to figure it out? The more present you are in this moment, the more happiness you may be able to bring into your life. You gain more focus by being present and you can then learn to turn off that monkey brain of yours and just remain in the present.

The past is history, the future is a mystery, today is a gift that is why we call it the PRESENT!

Think about it…

Love and Sunshine,
Tracy

Look for the gifts

"When it is dark enough, you can see the stars." – *Charles Beard*

"The period of greatest gain in knowledge and experience is the most difficult period in one's life." – *Dalai Lama*

"Out of clutter, find Simplicity. From discord, find Harmony. In the middle of difficulty lies opportunity." – *Albert Einstein*

Everything happens for a reason. Sometimes it takes us years to figure it out, but in the end it all evens out and you may realize the reasons behind it all. I may have said this before but it sure does fit today. I live by the philosophy that "Everything is OK in the end. If it's not OK, then it's not the end."

We may feel challenged to take on our life from time to time, and that's OK…it's called life. Just know that you are doing the best you can with the knowledge you have. Allow yourself to just be who you are in every moment. If you choose to be sad, mad, angry, and/or frustrated, do it with awareness. If we honor our emotions we will find that the ones that feel good will stay longer and longer. The only way you will ever feel like you have a choice in how you feel about any situation is to become aware of your feelings. Awareness is the key. If you are mindful that you are angry in a certain situation you may then be able to be more objective and figure out for yourself what is the trigger in that situation for you. So when the same kind of situation shows up again in your life, you can then choose the same behavior or choose a new behavior. It truly is up to you to decide how you are going to feel.

Once you let go of trying to control the outcome, you may find that the reasons why things are happening in a certain way are right in front of your face.

Think about it…

Love and Sunshine,
Tracy

You are enough

"We tell ourselves so many lies and half-truths…We listen and are duly impressed by these inner voices that turn into unseen judges that nag at us. We give each of these judges a seat of honor in our minds, all the while hating their guts and their never-ending supply of judgments…We give the judges permission to accompany us on each journey of life, never daring to realize that we can park them, at least momentarily."– Eloise Ristad

"The Inner Critic makes each of us a child. As we become the child in our relationships, we lose our sense of self. We are no longer self-contained, self-respecting adults. We look to others for validation. Our self-worth is based upon their opinion of us. Thus, everyone around us becomes a mother or a father whose support and approval is desperately needed to protect us from the constant criticism of the Inner Critic." – Hal and Sidra Stone

Forgive yourself…Love yourself. We are all doing the best we can in every moment. No one else can ever make you happy or glad or joyful. These are things that only you can decide to BE. Words are powerful. Stop telling yourself you are stuck. Imagine you are moving forward. Have faith that you will know what to do. The answers are not in the WHY; the answers are in the HOW. The why just creates an excuse or story to an event. The how will always move you forward. Validation of self is the only thing that matters as you are the only one who can decide if you are worth it. You must love yourself first. How are you ever going to know how to share love if there is no love there in the first place? Be strong in who you are. Why be uncomfortable in someone else's ignorance? It's time to take a stand for your own life and just be you.

Think about it…

Love and Sunshine,
Tracy

Nothing needs to be fixed

"Tolerance does not…do anything, embrace anyone, champion any issue. It wipes the notes off the score of life and replaces them with one long bar of rest. It does not attack error, it does not champion truth, it does not hate evil, it does not love good." – Walter Farrell

"Wherever you are is always the right place. There is never a need to fix anything, to hitch up the bootstraps of the soul and start at some higher place. Start right where you are." – Julia Cameron

I'm a fixer, a problem solver, a solution finder. This has at times gotten me into trouble because I have come to the realization that nothing needs to be fixed. Sometimes people just want to vent and no one is broken. As the quote says, right where you are is the perfect place to be and you can start being whomever you want in this moment. If something isn't going well in your life—that's life, oh well—if you do not like it then change it. If you want things to be different then make it so. It really is that easy. We use our reasons, excuses and stories to remain stationary. Change is the only constant thing in our life. If things didn't change we would all meld together into one big pile of sameness. If you are always thinking that something isn't going to happen…well guess what? It isn't going to happen. Start thinking that it IS going to happen. Think how you want things to be, even if you have to fake it in the beginning. There is no better place to start than right here in this moment.

Think about it…

Love and Sunshine,
Tracy

January 8th

Problems or solutions?

"If you expect the best, you will be the best. Learn to use one of the most pow-erful laws in this world; change your mental habits to belief instead of disbelief. Learn to expect, not to doubt. In so doing, you bring everything into the realm of possibility." – Dr. Norman Vincent Peale

"No pessimist ever discovered the secrets of the stars, or sailed to an uncharted land, or opened a new heaven to the human spirit." – Helen Keller

As I have said in the past, our minds cannot decipher our negativities. Remember, words are powerful. If you keep saying "no problem," how are you then surprised that things show up to you as problems? If you want something, then do not think you do not want it because then you will never have it. Think that you already have it and your Prover will make it so. (I believe you have two parts to your mind: a Thinker and a Prover. Your Thinker thinks and your Prover proves. Your Prover proves what your Thinker thinks.) So again, you must think that you already have it and your Prover will make it happen. It also has to do with your integrity. What are you committed to in regards to your own life? You are the only person who can look at yourself in the mirror at the end of the day and be complete and satisfied that you did as you said you would. I'd rather be an optimist and be wrong than a pessimist and be right!

If you expect problems you will encounter problems; if you expect hap-piness you will encounter happiness. Reread the 2nd quote. It's OK, I'll wait . . . If you still want to be a pessimist, do not ever be surprised that your life is filled with complainers, cynics, defeatists, downers, killjoys, party poopers, prophets of doom, sourpusses, wet blankets, and/or worri-ers…and perhaps you are the worst one. Hmmm…Still want to be right? Or would you rather be happy?

Think about it…

Love and Sunshine,
Tracy

Create the possibility!

"I like thinking of possibilities. At any time, an entirely new possibility is liable to come along and spin you off in an entirely new direction. The trick, I've learned, is to be awake to the moment." – Doug Hall

"Persons and societies do not submit passively to surroundings and events. They make choices as to the places where they live and the activities in which they engage—choices based on what they want to be, to do and to become. Furthermore, persons and societies often change their goals and ways; they can even retrace their steps and start in a new direction if they believe they are on a wrong course. Thus, whereas animal life is prisoner of biological evolution which is essentially irreversible, human life has the wonderful freedom of social evolution which is rapidly reversible and creative. Wherever human beings are concerned, trend is not destiny." – Rene Dubos

Create the possibility of having the life you want and then…

Think about it…

Love and Sunshine,
Tracy

Listen to your heart

"You got to look at things with the eye in your heart, not with the eye in your head." – Lame Deer, Medicine Man of the Oglala people

"Only in quiet waters things mirror themselves undistorted. Only in a quiet mind is adequate perception of the world." – Hans Margolius

Have you ever wanted something soooo bad and received it, and then when you had it you realized it was something you really didn't want after all? This could be because you were looking at your want of it from your head instead of your heart. Sometimes in life we make choices that we really do not want because we need to hold some sense of control in our life. If we didn't make up these reasons to feel a different way from our heart, then we would go crazy. And this kind of crazy is not good...it affects us to our core. As the quote says, quiet your mind, stop your monkey brain and listen to your heart. It really does know what you want.

Think about it...

Love and Sunshine,
Tracy

Not knowing is a gift

"If you see your path laid out in front of you—Step one, Step two, Step three—you only know one thing…it is not your path. Your path is created in the moment of action. If you can see it laid out in front of you, you can be sure it is someone else's path. That is why you see it so clearly." – Joseph Campbell

"To know how to choose a path with heart is to learn how to follow intuitive feeling." – Jean Shinoda Bolen

Life is not a destination; it is a journey! Have you ever been caught in "What do I do next?" Or "I want this to happen but how will I make it so?" The beauty of it is that you do not need to know how; you just need to have faith and know that you will. If it is your path, then make it happen. What comes to mind is a scene from *The Secret*. Jack Canfield talks about driving from one side of the country to the other in the dark. As we drive, all we can see is how far our headlights reach out, and yet we still know we are going to safely make it to the other end. This too can be applied to your life. It's OK to have feelings of "now what do I do?" In that feeling, quiet your mind, stop the monkey and listen to your heart. You do know what to do. Not knowing is a story to have you remain where you are and give you a reason to not move forward. Feel the fear and do it anyway! That is my philosophy. Fear is nothing but a made-up scenario that never happens. Perhaps, look at your not knowing as a gift. If you do not know then ask yourself, "What do I know?" If you are open to your heart and intuition you may be surprised at what you actually *do* know.

Think about it…

Love and Sunshine,
Tracy

Everybody hurts

"Only the weak are cruel. Gentleness can only be expected from the strong." –
Leo Buscaglia

"For every minute you remain angry, you give up sixty seconds of peace of mind." – Ralph Waldo Emerson

Have you ever noticed that "hurting" people hurt people? So the next time you find yourself in conflict with someone, instead of bringing out your defenses why not bring out your arms? Most likely the other person is feeling that they are not being heard or validated. Or they are sad or unhappy about something that is happening in their life; they may feel out of control or misunderstood. Even though that it is their story you can still make a difference in their life. Why not try something different and rather than fulfilling your own need to be right, give them some love instead? As an alternative to meeting anger with anger, next time why not ask, "Hey, what's going on with you?" or better yet HUG them. Let their anger dissipate before it hits you because it has nothing to do with you anyway and everything to do with themselves.

We are all walking mirrors. The negative emotions we create in ourselves that we think others "make us feel" are just a reflection of what we do not like in ourselves. It is easier to point our finger at someone else and say, "You make me feel this way" rather than realizing, "I feel this way because…" You give up every sense of your own control when you give your power over to someone, when you let yourself be taken down the path of "you make me feel." If you are caught in a "you make me feel" moment I invite you to go look at yourself in your mirror instead of attacking the first person who comes along. Ask yourself the hard questions: "What was it that happened that I didn't like and how can I relate that to me?" If you think about the last time you were "hurting," were you yourself just looking for some understanding? Wasn't what you really wanted was for someone to be there for you, to listen, to give you hug and/or share some love to let you know that you are OK? If you ask my daughter ,"What is the answer to everything?" she will tell you "LOVE!" The Beatles really did know what they were talking about. All you need is love—unconditional love. Love of LIFE! Love of every moment and every person around you. We are all linked together and if we all connected to love then, perhaps, there would never be another "hurting" person to hurt you.

Think about it…

Love and Sunshine,
Tracy

How do you define success?

"He who has achieved success has worked well, laughed often and loved much."
– Elbert Hubbard

"Too often, people focus only on results. But getting results without learning something or without having fun are incomplete. So is having fun without getting the results, or having fun without learning something new to help and empower you in the future. Accomplishment is all three: the result, personal growth and having fun." – Peter L. Hirsch

"There are many aspects to success; material wealth is only one component… But success also includes good health, energy and enthusiasm for life, fulfilling relationships, creative freedom, emotional and psychological stability, a sense of well-being, and peace of mind." – Deepak Chopra

"You don't have to stay up nights to succeed; you have to stay awake days."
– Unknown

If you continually focus on the fruits of your labour and wonder why nothing changes, it may be because the fruits or your results will always remain the same if you do not look at the roots. This can be applied to any area of your life. Have you ever been upset about something that just didn't matter? It may be that your upset is/was just a symptom of a much greater matter. It may be a time to take a good look at yourself and get to the root of "what is". If you can identify why you created a situation in your life, you can then change the outcome. Nourish the roots of any situation and you may see that your fruits will always be plenty.

Success is different for everyone. Find your passion and your path will illuminate.

Think about it…

Love and Sunshine,
Tracy

Be an all out!

"It is never about how good your voice is; it is only about feeling the urge to sing, and then having the courage to do it with the voice you are given." – Katie in True to Form, by Elizabeth Berg

"Be an all-out, not a hold-out." – Norman Vincent Peale

Be proud of who you are. What I realized is that the opposite of courage is not weakness; it's conformity! If you have the urge to sing then sing at the top of your lungs! I do this most of the time. I have stopped caring what other people think of me, except for my husband—I am still in the state of caring what he thinks of me. Then I have to ask myself, "Why be uncomfortable in someone else's ignorance?" Why is it that we try to be something we are not for those people we hold the most dear? What happens for me is that I fall into this box that he has created for me, and then I am who he created me to be. I get frustrated at myself every single time that I am not my true self when I am around him. I know I have so much to offer but when it's like hitting a brick wall there is nothing you can do but take a half-step back, buck up and have the courage to just be yourself. I have resolved in my life to be an all-out instead of a hold-out and it's scary. Courage at times can be a scary thing to experience, but that's OK. As I have said in past messages: Feel the fear and do it anyway. My happiness is worth it! My life is worth it! I am worth it! I AM ENOUGH! And so are you!

Think about it . . .

Love and Sunshine,
Tracy

Get rid of the old

"The world situation that life is presenting us with in the 21st century is a natural outcome of the state of consciousness that has created it.

Because people have an internal system for understanding life that is based on limited thought processes and hold a view of themselves as separate and insecure individuals, this naturally creates a world full of conflict and fear.

But consider that this may also be part of a perfect unfolding!

This may be how life works, that each stage of consciousness along the way in our development brings with it its own crisis.

Each crisis forces individuals to question their current reality system, and to try to find a new stability by stretching into new versions of themselves with fuller capabilities and by outgrowing any old habits that no longer support them.

Life creates situations that cannot be solved at their own level because the ways of seeing and knowing that have brought us to this point aren't working anymore. Our old paradigms and models are failing us and we are forced to let go of our old ways of constructing reality and look again to see what we have missed." – the Universe

In order to get to your solutions you must evolve and get rid of your old patterns and paradigms, because you cannot come to the resolution of whatever it is you are facing in your life using the same thinking as you did to create the problem.

Think about it…

Love and Sunshine,
Tracy

Your POWER is your CHOICE

"Freedom of choice is more to be treasured than any possession earth can give."
– David O. McKay

"The truest characters of ignorance are vanity, and pride and arrogance." –
Samuel Butler

*"What man wants is simply independent choice, whatever that may cost and
wherever it may lead."* – Fyodor Dostoyevsky

Just because you have made a choice does not mean that, with new
information or not, you cannot now make a different choice. That's the
beauty of our creation. We do have the ability to create whatever life we
want to live all through our own choices. We can BE whomever we want
in any given moment. If we continually put our past into our future we
will always create the same results whether we mean to or not.

A good friend of mine reminded me of a few things that I have forgotten.
She said to me if you act like you are defeated, out of communication
and wait for the world to change before you go live it, you may be stuck
waiting for someone else to be responsible for your life so you don't have
to be. Hmmm...

There is a difference between being present and just sitting and waiting
for things to happen. If you are just sitting and waiting, you stop living
your life and you give up your power to choose. You can live with that
sense of just waiting until the cows come home—or you can live your
life and whatever shows up for you then it shows up for you and you can
deal with it when it shows up!

Sometimes I find myself in waiting to see someone else make a first move,
but I know that is not how to live my life. I must choose for myself what
it is that I want. I get the logic of it but I still feel that way sometimes...
and it's not to avoid being responsible for my own life. I think I fear
total rejection. It sounds silly but that is what came up for me. This, I am
reminded, is perfectly normal. What is fear? False Evidence Appearing
Real. Fear is just a made-up story that never happened. You can always

regain your power and remember, power is just the ability to do something. It does not make you greater than or better than anyone else. Your POWER is your CHOICE.

Think about it…

Love and Sunshine,
Tracy

January 17th

Remember

"Never forget what you need to remember." – Garrett Bartley

"Memory is the cabinet of the imagination, the treasury of reason, the registry of conscience, and the council chamber of thought." – Basile

We can remember anything that happened to us in our lives and we can attach any meaning to it that we want. The memory can be a negative or a positive…it's your choice. I do believe that everything happens for a reason and that there is good in every event that happens to us. If you haven't found the good yet, then maybe not enough time has passed for you to see it or maybe a certain circumstance hasn't happened yet to reveal why something had to happen.

If you are trying to forget something, you are just creating more of what you are trying to forget. Memory is a powerful thing. It can create the life you want to live or destroy it with a single thought about what you remember.

Live in this moment and you can always be happy!

Think about it…

Love and Sunshine,
Tracy

How do you play your roles?

"What concerns me is not the way things are, but rather the way people think things are." – Epicetus

"Risk! Risk anything! Care no more for the opinion of others, for those voices. Do the hardest thing on earth for you. Act for yourself. Face the truth." – Katherine Mansfield

Hmmm…seems we have a theme going on here. I must not be totally listening—are you?

Risking anything can be a scary place to be in the middle of…but I know I'd rather be scared than stationary. If you really do want something to occur in your life, that fear of rejection may be necessary for you to get what you want, perhaps. Or you can make a choice powerfully and just accept the consequences. For me, it's the denial of my request that I fear the most. I still have issues with accepting it on the first thought of dealing with not getting what I want. This is where we can bring into our life the "care no more for the opinion of others…" because it is just that, their opinion, and not your reality. I have been on such a roller coaster these past few weeks—but why? Because I allowed myself to live in a state of fear of making the wrong choice. That is when my friend reminded me about being stuck waiting for someone else to be responsible for my life so I don't have to be. What I forgot is that when you leave out your story about the past and be who you want to be in the present you can always be happy.

Think about it…

Love and Sunshine,
Tracy

It's your stuff that stops you

"Self-contempt never inspires lasting change." – Jane R. Hirschmann and Carol H. Munter

"When we stop opposing reality, action becomes simple, fluid, kind, and fearless." – Byron Katie

Didn't we learn from *The Secret* that what you resist persists? If you add your own brutal critical tapes on top of that do you really think that you will get a different result? When we are able to accept the situation that we are in without meaning, that is when simplicity of life sets in. Our lives almost become easy because everything is just flowing. Just be like Dori: "Just keep swimming…just keep swimming…just keep swimming…"

Expecting your path to follow a certain route such as wanting a certain job, having a particular someone fall in love with you, or insisting upon this idea, that diet, or the other thing to be your deliverance can severely limit your options. You leave nothing to possibility and stuff everything into a box so small that when you look at the box you can no longer see what's inside. All you see is the "stuff" surrounding that box. You may lose focus on creating what's inside the box…then your focus turns to resisting all the "stuff" surrounding the box, therefore creating more of the "stuff" you do not want. When we take away the need to control our outcomes all that is left is just BEing—so why not choose happiness?

If you get rid of your "stuff" then maybe there is no need for the box?

Think about it…

Love and Sunshine,
Tracy

January 20th

Recognizing abundance

"If your everyday life seems poor, don't blame it; blame yourself; admit to your-self that you are not enough of a poet to call forth its riches; because for the creator there is no poverty and no indifferent place." – Rainer Maria Rilke

"Not what we have but what we enjoy, constitutes our abundance." – John Petit-Senn

"Abundance is not something we acquire. It is something we tune into." – Wayne Dyer

This rings so true for me. Based on certain events in my life, I have come to the realization that it's what makes us happy that makes us abundant. Walls do not make a home. Things and stuff will never love you back, make you any richer or make you any more joyful. It's how you feel about what is happening in your life that will create your abundance. When you find something that you enjoy it is never a "job" or a "have to." When you find satisfaction and happiness in what you are doing the abundance is inevitable, whether it be abundance of money, abundance of joy, or abundance of LOVE. If you enjoy what is happening in your life your abundance will return to you tenfold and as long as you remain happy your abundance will keep flowing to you.

Think about it…

Love and Sunshine,
Tracy

Are you thinking or feeling?

"Our deepest need is for the joy that comes with loving and being loved, with knowing we are of genuine use to others." – Eknath Easwara

"We are able to be of service to those who suffer only to the extent that we have been able to transform fear in our own lives." – Robert Sardello

This is what has come up for me. When you are liking what is happening in your life and it makes you think you are happy…makes you think it's what you want…makes you think that it's what you need…but yet it doesn't feel quite right, we try to make it fit because it feels good at the time. In the end we are left with that same hole, maybe even bigger now, that we were trying to fill in the first place. This may be because the want, the need, the happiness it brought you all came from your head and not your heart. If it came from your heart and not your ego it would ring true every time. Our heart only knows how to sing its true song; that is why I have said in the past, "Listen to your heart, it does know what you want." I know, I know, sometimes this is hard because our egos can be very LOUD in trying to get us to "think" that we really want something. Sometimes our egos can be like a three-year-old having a temper tantrum, so we just listen and follow it to stop the nagging. Hey, sometimes we need certain things in our lives to help us get through what it is that we are going through and this is perfectly normal—but recognize that it is just a "think" and not a "feel." Sometimes the ego can even trick you by creating a new feeling but if that feeling seems to hold you back or prevent you from moving forward, it still is a "think" from your head and not the true "feel" from your heart.

I believe that in our heads we have a Thinker and a Prover. Our Thinker thinks and our Prover proves. Our Prover proves what our Thinker thinks…so if you are in a situation that makes you think you want it and/or need it, your Prover will create situations that will "prove" to you that you need it every time. This allows us to be right in our own minds. If we weren't we would go crazy.

So next time you are feeling vulnerable and you are in a situation that you "think" feels good…close your eyes, go inside and check in with your heart. Truly listen…you may be surprised at what is actually there for you.

Think about it…

Love and Sunshine,
Tracy

Living in harmony

"Peace comes not from the absence of conflict, but from the ability to cope with it." – Unknown

"Peace is not won by those who fiercely guard their differences, but by those who with open minds and hearts seek out connections." – Katherine Paterson

When we are fighting to be right all sense of peace and happiness goes out the window. When you find yourself in a battle of "no, it's this" and the other person is caught in the same game have you ever thought that both of you are right? It's all in our perception. If someone is fighting you tooth and nail, even though you know in your heart that the information they are giving you isn't correct, it just doesn't matter. The other person truly believes that they are right and will not change their perception of it so why waste your time? Just "know" in your own heart that you are right, agree with them and move on. I'd rather be HAPPY than be right —well OK, most of the time...lol. If you agree with the other person who is opposing you there is nothing left to fight about. As the quote says, open your mind; who knows, you may not have the same information as the other person. If you find yourself in a "no, I'm right" situation, then maybe it's time to check in on your happiness meter.

Here is an example that I use a lot: Two people are sitting across the table from each other in a open sunny room. There is a shiny ornament sitting in the middle of the table. One person says it's black; the other says it's white. Because everything comes from our own knowledge base and our own perception, both people are right. If one person got up and went over to where the other person was sitting and saw from their perspective, they might then see the ornament differently. The key is to be able to put yourself in the other person's shoes, not as yourself but as them, because if you saw from their shoes using your own perception nothing would change or be different. By putting yourself in their shoes using their perception you will be able to get a different perspective on things and, perhaps, see things in a different light.

Conflicts will come up, that's life. It's in how you deal with them that will determine your peace of mind.

Think about it...

Love and Sunshine,
Tracy

Listen for your heart's song

"Always listen to your heart, because even though it's on your left; its always right!" – Unknown

One thing that I've realized is that if you do not do things that make you happy, you will remain in a state that prevents you from moving forward in your life. If the things that you are doing only make you think you are happy then it will create the same "stuck" feelings that you've been experiencing. If your heart is singing, then you know that what you are doing is making you truly happy. An example may be that if you think you are in love and your heart hurts, that means, as I've said before, it's all in your head because your heart will always sing its true song and not ever hurt you. If you are in love and you have an odd feeling in your gut that is about your true feelings as that is where we hold our relationships and our emotions.

Think about it…

Love and Sunshine,
Tracy

Create your happiness

*"Happiness cannot be traveled to, owned, earned, worn or consumed. Happiness
is the spiritual experience of living every minute with love, grace, and gratitude."*
– Denis Waitley

Wow…here's that message again. It's not hard to believe that since I've
started talking about being present and just being happy in the moment,
so many things have been directed to me that give me the same message.
I must be listening…lol.

Happiness is a state of being that permeates from your very existence
when you are truly doing the things that make you happy. One thing
that may be missing from the mix is that unless you share that happiness
with those around you, how will you ever know that you are happy?
Sometimes we get caught in the "I'll be happy when…" scenario but
really, if you think about it, the last time you were truly happy what did
you do? Did you not actually feel the happiness when you shared your
feelings with someone else? Being happy or joyful or excited by yourself
is still good but remember how much more of those feelings you created
for yourself when you shared your experience with others. You actually
raised your energy tenfold by expanding your BEing to affect another…
how exciting!

Sharing is the key to change—although I like to think of it as improving
because who really "wants" to change? "Changing" makes us think that
there is something wrong with us. If we approach ourselves in the way
that we need to change then we are admitting that there IS something
wrong with us. And of course there is absolutely nothing wrong with any
of us so we never need to change. It can be a vicious circle and that is
why I created my Crystal Cove Center—the center for self evolution—
and I describe its function as:

"No one is broken and no one needs to be fixed. We are in a constant
state of Self Evolving. We are perfect in each moment because we are
being the best we can be at every given moment. We make choices in
our lives that create consequences. We are continuously evolving who
we are by learning from our consequences. We are safe in every moment

because we can always make a different choice. We are all made of the same energy. No one is better than or greater than anyone else. Energy is never created or destroyed it just is…"

If you really want to take on your life you will get that self evolving is the change that constantly creates our improvement and that improvement will create your happiness.

Think about it…

Love and Sunshine,
Tracy

January 25th

Value the process

"If the doors of perception were cleansed, everything would appear…as it is, infinite." – William Blake

"You watch your mind to see who you are not. I watch my mind to gain a sense of its content, which has always been my pain. As I watch it, I get a sense of its impermanence. Thoughts come and go as part of a process. I see how content dissolves into process and begin to see the patterns in the process. Realizing it isn't MY suffering, MY pain, it becomes THE pain. I've gone from the tiny, the small, and the individual to the universal. I feel OUR pain. When we do, we go from fear to compassion. Fear is MY pain, compassion is THE pain." – Stephen Levine

Oh William…how true is that? If we cloud our perception with trying to control the outcome we then make everything definite. We remove choice from ourselves and get upset when we get a different result and perhaps wonder why. We may put ourselves in a cage that prevents us from moving forward and again wonder why we feel so stuck all the time. If we remove our want or need to control the outcome, we can become open and available to what's possible. If we remove our choice by pigeonholing ourselves into only accepting one perception, what may come up for us is the fear or pain we create around "What if we do not get the outcome that we are after?" If we do cleanse our perception and remove the limitations we may, perhaps, open ourselves to seeing from someone else's perception and accepting that perception as a possible reality. When we see the world from someone else's shoes this may bring up compassion for that person because we can get what they are going through, and when we get what another may be going through we see our own impact on them thus creating another possibility for our own improved BEing.

What I get out of the above quotes is once you get out of the "what's in it for me" power struggle and focus on what you can offer others, that is when you may have released your FEAR (which is just False Evidence Appearing Real) and moved into compassion by helping others with THE pain.

Tracy Friesen

What would you be able to create in your life if you wiped your perception clean and released it from all judgment?

Think about it…

Love and Sunshine,
Tracy

January 26th

Hope gives you strength

"Always do what you are afraid to do." – Ralph Waldo Emerson

"If you do not hope, you will not find what is beyond your hopes." – St. Clement of Alexandra

If you feel stuck in whatever you are going through it may be because you lost your sense of hope for whatever it is that you may be wanting to manifest in your life. In my life I have faced a lot of things that I have been afraid of doing. As you may already know, my philosophy is to feel the fear and do it anyway. For me the more I am afraid of something the more I want to do it to prove to myself that I am capable of handling anything. One thing that has come up for me is that I may have been approaching things in a way that only allows me to deal with things on a surface level. If I just do them to do them, then there really is no purpose to doing them…make sense? I realized that I am ENOUGH and I do not have to do anything to prove myself to anyone, especially myself. I did lose hope in my life and was wandering around lost just to prove to people that I am strong enough to handle things. Well, I am not. I am tired of pretending that things do not get to me and that I do not need help at times. I have been looking at my life and I did not have to make it so difficult. Giving up hope put me in a superficial state of being someone I'm not for everyone else, rather than just being me in who I am.

The second quote struck me right in my heart today. For me what came up was that if I do not hope then I may be always searching but never discovering what's truly there for me…or for you for that matter.

Think about it…

Love and Sunshine,
Tracy

It takes action

"You cannot plough a field by turning it over in your mind." – Unknown

"Do not wait to strike till the iron is hot; but make it hot by striking." – William B. Sprague

"Nothing will ever be attempted if all possible objections must first be overcome." – Samuel Johnson

We've been talking a lot about being "stuck" in whatever is going on in your life and these quotes remind us that if you remain in your "story" of what's happening and do not ever "do" anything about it, then nothing will ever change. Plus if you have to go through every possible reason why it won't happen, then you will continually get the same result.

Life is about taking action towards actually getting what you want in your life. If no action is taken then you will remain stationary and potentially never be happy and who wants that?

The more you play your story over and over in your head without doing anything to change it, the more you will get caught up in it. I have lived by the words "It's easier to ask for forgiveness than permission." In these words I have found that I was able to make decisions whether I knew they were the right ones or not. You can always make a different choice if your first choice doesn't work for you. You can always clean up any mistake and learn from it. Remember LOVE is the answer to every question!

Instead of playing your horrible critical tapes in your head why not just go buy yourself a plough?

Think about it…

Love and Sunshine,
Tracy

You can change your destiny

"You cannot dream yourself into a character; you must hammer and forge your-self one." – Henry David Thoreau

"Reputation is what men and women think of us; character is what God and angels know of us." – Thomas Paine

"Sow an act, and you reap a habit; sow a habit, and you reap a character; sow a character, and you reap a destiny." – George Dana Boardman

What comes up for me when reading the above has integrity written all over it…well, the first two anyway. Maybe throw some commitment in there too.

If we remain dreaming about who we want to be, we may never actually BE. It's one thing to "think" about who we want to be but who we are in the moment is another reality. Our character is developed through our actions. If you do not like who you are in this moment then it may take a different action to improve your character. Nothing about our character is permanent because we have the ability to make a different choice – ALWAYS! If you want to be or act a certain way then do it or be it, instead of just thinking about it. I've heard so many people say, "I wish I could be like you or them." Question: Why can't you be? What's holding you back? Fear? Insecurity? Other people's opinions? What block have you created to being the character you really want to be? Sometimes in our life we use our situations to our advantage so that we do not have to be responsible for what is happening to us. It is so much easier to point fingers at everything and everybody else and maybe say, "Well, you would do the same." Really? Maybe if I was you, yes I would do the same thing, but everyone has their own perception and everyone is right in their own mind and we will all react differently to the same situation. The key is our ability to not take things personally because we all do have our own per-ceptions. It does not matter what others think of us because that is their perception of us. If you can look at yourself in the mirror at the end of the day and be happy with who you are—great! If not, this may be a time to look at your actions. Did you have the integrity to do the things you said you would do? If you didn't do them, did you have the integrity to clean it up? What does John Maxwell say? "Integrity when other people are watching is easy, but it is TRUE integrity that shows in what we do when no one is watching." and what is commitment? Commitment is doing the things you said you were going to do long after the feeling you said them in has left you.

The last quote shows me that we all can change our destiny by improving our actions. It does not matter what you did yesterday; what matters is what action are you going to take in this moment. Remember awareness is the key to being whomever you want to be. If a certain action in a certain situation did not get you the results you wanted, then maybe the next time that situation comes up again you can then, through your awareness, choose a different action – and as a result change your character and therefore change your destiny.

Think about it...

Love and Sunshine,
Tracy

January 29th

Honey is better

"Kind words are the music of the world." – F. W. Faber

"Arguing with a fool proves there are two." – Doris M. Smith

I may have said this before, but if you have gotten out of your own head and paid attention to your surroundings you may realize that "hurting" people hurt people. The next time you are confronted by someone who is totally on you about something why not try some kind words? Words like "I am sorry for whatever it is that you are going through in your life to make you think you have to act this way…just know that I care about you and I am here to support you." Then be open to listening without solving. Most of the time people just want to be heard and accepted for who they are in whatever they are going through. This has been a challenge for me in my past because I am a fixer, a solution finder. I never did realize until a short bit ago that I was making things worse for people by trying to "fix" everything. Even though I know I was coming from love it wasn't landing with love on the other person. I now know that often it made them feel that there was something wrong with them or they may have felt less than enough. Of course, this was not my intent but remember, everyone has their own way of processing any information that comes to them. I would sit and wonder why I didn't get the results I thought I would get, results of appreciation and acceptance of my "help." The key to effective communication is being a good listener; that is why we were born with two ears and only one mouth, perhaps.

Why not do some random acts of kindness today in your words and actions? Even if it's just a simple smile, you may be able to help someone believe that there still is good in this world. I have said before that offering a simple smile to someone may then in turn make them smile, which may make someone else smile, and it could, by a chain reaction, affect the whole world one smile at a time.

Think about it…

Love and Sunshine,
Tracy

Just let it go

"Do not anticipate trouble, or worry about what may never happen. Keep in the sunlight." – Benjamin Franklin

"The mind that is anxious about future events is miserable." – Seneca

"It is the trouble that never comes that causes the loss of sleep." – Chas. Austin Bates

What comes up for me is some advice that a good friend and teacher once gave me about dealing with fear. She said "Tracy, is there anything that is happening in this moment that you should be fearful about? Is there anything right now that is endangering you?" Of course I had to tell her no. So she said, "Then why be afraid?" Good point, I told her. I have used her advice more than not. Why do we stop ourselves from living in happiness for fear of things that may never happen? Our thoughts are powerful. This past week I have gone through a lot of unnecessary internal strife because the things that I was thinking didn't happen. It helped that a safe place was created for me to share what was up for me in the moment. It was impactful for me to have a listening ear. I was brought back to BEing present in this moment and to just being happy. The future is a mystery, so why be fearful of events or situations that may never happen? The key to happiness is being able to process what comes up for you in the moment and then thank it and just let it go.

Think about it…

Love and Sunshine,
Tracy

January 31st

Make time for yourself

"What is it that makes all of us end each day with the sense that we have not lived our time, but have been lived, used by what we do?" – Jacob Needleman

"Why has time disappeared in our culture? How is it that after decades of inventions and new technologies devoted to saving time and labor, the result is that there is no time left? We are a time-poor society; we are temporally impoverished. And there is no issue, no aspect of human life, that exceeds this in importance. The destruction of time is literally the destruction of life." – Jacob Needleman

Time is a made-up thing that we have allowed to control us on a daily basis. You hear so many people say there's not enough time to accomplish the things that they really want to do. At the end of the day, they may feel jilted because they feel that they are doing things just to get by, perhaps. The words "I'm busy" is a cop-out. It is just an excuse to allow yourself to remain in a stationary overwhelming state of not striving for what you really want in your life. Remember, words are powerful. I have changed my description of time to allow myself to have "more than enough time" to do the things I want to get done, including those things that I really do not want to do like clean the kitty litter…lol. All our dreams are attainable. You may just have to dust off the ideas and recreate the possibility that you will get what you want.

If we all just made the time by pure intent to do something completely for ourselves each day, whether it be something that takes five minutes or five hours, we might realize that we are not trapped in our lives. We can accomplish and create all that we want and just be happy in the moment.

Think about it…

Love and Sunshine,
Tracy

Tracy Friesen

Feel the fear and do it anyway

"The only way of finding the limits of the possible is by going beyond them into the impossible." – Arthur C. Clarke

"The best way out is always through." – Robert Frost

"Our greatest glory is not in never falling but in rising every time we fall."
– Confucius

I live by the philosophy that "Everything happens for a reason." Robert says it best above. What comes up for me is that sometimes we must go through whatever it is that we are going through so that when we come out on the other side we may see why things had to happen the way they did. Another thing that comes up for me is *Rocky*! I love most of those movies. The third one and the last one are my favorites. I get sooo inspired watching them. I know you are singing the song right now too…lol. *Rocky* teaches us that it doesn't matter how many times you get knocked down, what counts is that you always get back up again. I hear so many people say, "I've failed" and for me the only way that anyone ever fails is when they give up on achieving what it is that they want. Also, if you keep "trying" at something you are just giving yourself a reason or an excuse to fail and to be OK with it. Take Yoda's advice: "Do or do not; there is no try." Give yourself credit when you do not know how to do something. One thing that I've always asked people when they get caught in their "I'm stupid and don't know how to do that" is this: "Hey, were you born with that knowledge?" I didn't think so… Do something different and go outside your comfort zone. GROW yourself. If you do not ask, the answer is always no. Take it from IMPOSSIBLE; even it says…I – M – Possible

Think about it…

Love and Sunshine,
Tracy

February 2nd

Are you out of tune?

"Align your personality with your soul. Until that happens, you won't be able to give the gifts you were meant to.

Remind yourself daily of the following:

1. You are a soul first and a personality second.

2. You are worthy. You are not on this Earth by accident. You have a reason to be here. There's a difference between accepting that in your mind and accepting it in your heart.

3. It's not an "it" that you're looking for—it's your life that you're living.

You are here to create an authentically empowered life. There is no guarantee you will do it. It's up to you." – Gary Zukav

Your soul is what makes your heart sing…your personality is the chord that you play to make the song come into tune. If you align your personality to your heart song, your soul song, then the only thing that you can create is true happiness and pure bliss because you will be in true alignment with your purpose.

Life is your choice in what you want to create for yourself. Do you want to create happiness or drama, happiness or being right, happiness or story, happiness or upset? It is what it is and that is all that it is…nothing more nothing less.

Think about it…

Love and Sunshine,
Tracy

Let go of blame

"My days of whining and complaining about others have come to an end. Nothing is easier than fault finding." – Og Mandino

"Take your life in your own hands and what happens? A terrible thing: no one to blame." – Erica Jong

"Life appears to me too short to be spent in nursing animosity or registering wrong." – Charlotte Bronte

When we take a good look at our own lives we may realize that we are a product of our choices. You are the only one to look at when your life isn't going the way you want it to. Whether someone gives us new information or not, ultimately, we ALWAYS make the final decision to do anything. It may be easier to point the finger elsewhere but remember, there are always three fingers pointing back, so majority rules...lol. I may have said this before but when you find yourself saying, "I do not like it when..." this is a perfect time to go look at yourself in the mirror and ask yourself some hard questions. You can ask yourself: "Why does this bother me so much?" Other people are just a mirror reflection of what we do not like in ourselves. It may be hard to grasp but it is true. When we take responsibility for our choices we take full control of our own life. It doesn't mean that you are right or wrong. If you do something in full awareness, there is no loss of control. We are only human. If you want to be upset be upset, but do it in awareness. You can always go back and clean up any impact that you may have created in that upset.

Remember, AWARENESS is the key to remaining in control of your own life.

Think about it...

Love and Sunshine,
Tracy

Celebrate your fear!

"Courage is resistance to fear; mastery of fear – not absence of fear." – Mark Twain

"Courage is almost a contradiction in terms. It means a strong desire to live taking the form of a readiness to die." – G. K. Chesterton

"Perfect courage is to do without witnesses what one would be capable of doing before all the world." – La Rochefoucauld

If you are faced with a fearful situation, what is your pattern? You should know by now that my philosophy is to feel the fear and do it anyway. I know that I have in the past been caught in doing something just so I could say I did it to prove something, and this goes without purpose. I like to throw myself into the fire—a lot—and one thing I've learned over the years is how to deal with my fearfulness and nervousness over doing things. This may sound silly but what works for me is that I celebrate my fear. When I feel the nervousness or fear start to boil and churn, I give a loud "Whoohoo! This is awesome! I love this feeling!" Give it a try… oh come on, now let's hear you: "WHOOHOO!!" What happens is that you can start to train your brain into thinking that these lower vibration feelings are actually enjoyable.

I started celebrating my nervousness and fear when I had to do a lot of public speaking. I would get myself so wound up that my whole body would shake, starting with my voice…how embarrassing. After celebrating my fear and nervousness a few times I was able to get behind the podium still full of fear, but no one knew it because they could not see that my knees were shaking…lol. People would say to me, "Wow, I wish I could do what you do." The thing is you CAN!! I would tell them that I was so scared and nervous and they would be amazed that it seemed so easy and natural for me. I tell you, "WHOOHOO!!" works. So the next time you are faced with fear, nervousness, anger, frustration or any lower uncomfortable feeling, celebrate with a loud "WHOOHOO!!" You never know what may happen.

Think about it…

Love and Sunshine,
Tracy

Go with ease and grace

"Strength does not come from winning. Your struggles develop your strengths. When you go through hardships and decide not to surrender, that is strength."
– Arnold Schwarzenegger

"But there is suffering in life, and there are defeats. No one can avoid them. But it's better to lose some of the battles in the struggles for your dreams than to be defeated without ever knowing what you're fighting for." – Paulo Coelho

"If you succumb to the temptation of using violence in the struggle, unborn generations will be the recipients of a long and desolate night of bitterness, and your chief legacy to the future will be an endless reign of meaningless chaos." – Martin Luther King, Jr.

I get the above quotes but why do we have to "struggle" to get what we want? Words are powerful. Sure, we may be presented with some conflict or an obstacle here or there but why struggle? If you look inside your mind's eye what picture are you creating by using the word struggle to get to your goal or preferred outcome? Honestly, are you really in a struggle to do what you want to do? Is there really something that is physically holding you back? Look at what you are creating for yourself to get to where you want to be. Instead of struggle imagine yourself being moved forward with a gale force wind. I just imagined everyone blowing by my window, tumbling along, feet in the air…lol…so maybe that's a bit too strong of an image! Instead of seeing yourself as stuck in something, see yourself moving forward with ease and grace. Think of yourself as surrounded by a force field that nothing but good can get through and everything else either bounces off or slips around you. Obstacles are good to come by…mistakes are needed…how else are you ever to learn and grow? You are an AMAZING powerful being that can accomplish anything that you put your mind to so why not, instead of struggle, do it with ease and grace? You may find that your life isn't so hard after all.

Think about it…

Love and Sunshine,
Tracy

Nothing needs to be fixed

"It's always helpful to learn from your mistakes because then your mistakes seem worthwhile." – Garry Marshall

"Freedom is not worth having if it does not include the freedom to make mistakes." – Mahatma Gandhi

Oh boy…today I sure do feel like something needs to be fixed. I came clean with something that I did that I am not too proud of. A part of me is wishing that I had just kept it in because of the consequences I am now facing. Another part of me is happy that I am no longer hiding anything. My past BEing would have me stuck in "damned if do, damned if I don't so why bother?" This time I decided to do something different and I am still not too sure about the consequences that it may have triggered, although I am happy that I decided to tell the truth. It really made me look at myself and what I am capable of in a not-so-positive light. All I could do is show that I knew the impact that I created, say I was sorry and ask for forgiveness. It makes me look at the words that I've written and I have said, that no one needs to be fixed because we are perfect in every moment because we are making decisions with the knowledge that we have in that moment. It's like I create different rules for myself. What comes up for me is that if I just had faith, I would not have had to do what I did because the information would have been given to me with love and not through unjust ways. It has been a life lesson for me that I have put in my heart and I have learned from my mistake. I am thankful that a safe place was created for me to be who I was in that moment. Thank you SP. :)

From this experience I realize that no matter how much I want to believe it, I am not always right. Something for me to think about…

Love and Sunshine,
Tracy

February 7th

Don't avoid the void

"When we feel stuck, going nowhere – even starting to slip backward – we may actually be backing up to get a running start." – Dan Millman

"Every positive change – every jump to a higher level of energy and awareness – involves a rite of passage. Each time to ascend to a higher rung on the ladder of personal evolution, we must go through a period of discomfort, of initiation. I have never found an exception." – Dan Millman

When I first read the above quotes they triggered a memory of a poem that I wrote many years ago. It was titled "The Discernment of Nothing." The gist of the poem is that I could not find an excuse to stop me from doing what I really wanted to do, so I created "Nothing." I find it interesting that I am once again in that very same spot. I am an information gatherer and now that I have all the information that I thought I needed I went into anxiety mode because I didn't have anything to "wonder" about anymore. My future was opened up to every possibility and I once again created nothing to prevent myself from moving forward. This time it only lasted one day…whoohoo! I remember last time it was months, even years that I remained in a state of "Nothing" holding me back. This time I have more wisdom, not only in my own understanding but in the form of information coming to me from my "Heart Family." I have learned that I am not going backwards; it's something I am doing in order to propel myself forward. What a relief! We all get struck in our blind spots from time to time, myself included. I am fortunate and grateful that I have people who love me enough to tell it like it is and support me in getting back on track rather than living in my story. The only constant thing IS change. It's how you are able to accept what's happening and the meaning you put behind it that will affect your daily life. We can all live happy with everything that goes on in our lives just by not allowing our stories to control our actions. I'm not saying that you have to like it; just accept it as it is what it is, nothing more.

Think about it…

Love and Sunshine,
Tracy

The push & pull of relationships

"It's surprising how many persons go through life without ever recognizing that their feelings toward other people are largely determined by their feelings toward themselves, and if you're not comfortable within yourself, you can't be comfortable with others." – Sydney J. Harris

"The purpose of relationships is not happiness, but transformation." – Andrew Schneider

I like what Andrew says because isn't that why we create relationships with people? Do we not see in them what we'd like for ourselves? We aspire to be like them. We transform our BEing to be in alignment with their BEing. Alternatively, the same goes for the people we do not like. I have said this before; the way we feel about them is just a mirror reflection of what we do not like in ourselves. If you are unable to love or even like yourself, how would you ever be able to love or just be with someone else? You are the most important thing in this world. If you understand yourself and love yourself there is nothing to search for because what will show up for you is your true happiness, which comes from your core BEing and not from someone else. It will come from your heart and not your thought that this person "makes me happy."

One thing that comes up for me is that the purpose of relationships is not to create happiness but to share happiness. If you are not already truly happy with who you are, the purpose of the relationship that you created may be for reasons that will not serve you in the end. If a relationship that was once awesome turns to being not so awesome, maybe the first place to look is where you stopped being happy within yourself? You are responsible for the choice to stop being happy. No one else… ALWAYS you.

We create relationships to learn and grow. Some last for five minutes and others can last a lifetime. Check in with yourself: Are you doing things to make yourself happy or are you doing things to make someone else happy? If something doesn't work for you then do not do it. It is not personal. It is as simple as that.

Think about it…

Love and Sunshine,
Tracy

Don't let your excuses stop you

"The reasonable man adapts himself to the world; the unreasonable one persists in trying to adapt the world to himself. Therefore all progress depends on the unreasonable man." – George Bernard Shaw

This brings me back to when I attended a training course as a guest. I walked in with it already started and the lady on stage was talking about being unreasonable. At that time in my life I looked at being unreasonable as a negative stubborn trait that I did not like in other people. (lol... yeah, right, other people...lol) But as I listened to what she was saying it clicked for me and I gained a deeper understanding of how being "unreasonable" could work in your life.

What I got out of it was that if you want to live your life with integrity, the more unreasonable you can be about whatever you said you were going to do, the easier it will be for you to accomplish it, because you will have put no reason in front of it for it to not happen. Capiche?

What comes up for me when thinking about this is that as long as you stay out of your story and follow through, no matter what happens, with what you said you were going to do, you will live an unquestionable life because you have upheld your integrity.

Here's an example: Let's say you made an appointment to meet someone and along the way your car breaks down. Most people would use that as a reason to cancel the appointment, but if you were being unreasonable in what you said you were going to do you would do whatever it takes to get to that appointment on time.

We as a society have made it OK to get out of the things we said we were going to do, and people block themselves with excuses and reasons all the time. As an example, just by using the simple words, "Oh, I got busy and couldn't do such and such..." we have accepted that as being OK. What does "busy" mean, exactly, anyway?

How are you going to get out of your reasons and excuses today and become unreasonable with the things that you said you were going to do?

Think about it…

Love and Sunshine,
Tracy

Open your eyes

"Do not spoil what you have by desiring what you have not; remember that what you now have was once among the things you only hoped for." – *Epicurus*

"What is not started today is never finished tomorrow." – *Johann Wolfgang von Goethe*

Have you ever been caught in a want of something that almost consumed your life? So much that it caused you to put blinders on to what amazing things are already available to you? Were you happy in that want? Or did it just create more upset for you? This is another example of why it's awesome to live in the present moment. I'm not saying do not desire or dream – this is where the second quote comes in. If your desire for something doesn't trigger you into stepping into action, then is it really something that is in your heart? Look around you…what do you see?

Could it be that what is right in front of you IS your desire? How have you blocked yourself from being happy with what you have in this moment? I have said that awareness is the key to great communication but what about acceptance? This doesn't mean that you should settle for anything less; I am saying really look at what you have without the story around it. I bet that you'll see things in a different light. If you find that what you have is not making you happy then step into action and change it. Maybe it's an improvement on your part, applying for a different job or just finding a new place to live? You always have the ability to choose what makes you happy. If you live your life in a fantasy world consumed with what you do not have, you may shut yourself down from all that is available to you in this moment.

Think about it…

Love and Sunshine,
Tracy

February 11th

Loneliness

"When humans find themselves surrounded by nothing but objects, the response is always one of loneliness." – Brian Swimme

"Loneliness is caused by an alienation from life. It is a loneliness from your real self." – Maxwell Maltz

"No soul is desolate as long as there is a human being for whom it can feel trust and reverence." – George Eliot

Whoa…have I been there, and not that long ago either. This totally reminds me of one of my favorite songs by Blue October: "Have you ever been so lonely, there's no one there to hold?" That song, if you want to get into the story of it, is quite desolate, about feeling abandoned by friends or by hope. Wow…I now look at it in a different way. It's about reaching out to someone so that the loneliness that you created does not take over your life. Loneliness is just a story anyway. When I was in it, I felt like I would never have someone special in my life ever again. How silly is that? For Pete's sake…I am a beautiful, smart intelligent, funny, caring, sensual, sexy woman. Who wouldn't want to be with me? Open your eyes! Look in that mirror and who do you see? This is where I think about happiness. Happiness is meant to be shared. Have you watched *Into the Wild* yet? Come on what are you waiting for?

Happiness does not come from "things." If you had a gazillion dollars it wouldn't change a thing unless you had true happiness in your heart… and that true happiness comes from you and only you.

I invite you to check in with yourself and see what words come up for you when you think about your own happiness. If you start describing your happiness by using the words "He/She makes me…" then it is not your true happiness because it is coming from someone else. As soon as you start any statement by using the words "He/She makes me…" you are giving your power away and may be leaving yourself in a state of being out of control in your own life. These words go both ways, for lack of better words, both the negative and the positive. I suggest you start using "I feel" statements. "I feel happy when…" "I feel angry when…" "I feel frustrated when…" "I feel joyous when…" You may be surprised at

Tracy Friesen

how your life will quickly shift when you are taking responsibility for it. Dooo eeet! I dare you!

So the next time you go into your story about being lonely, stop. Look in the mirror and tell yourself that you love yourself. Know that I love you unconditionally for who you are in every moment. That way you can always have that sense that there is at least one person out there in this world who you can trust and know that you are not alone.

Think about it...

Love and Sunshine,
Tracy

Why hide your Truth?

"You can bend it and twist it…You can misuse and abuse it…But even God cannot change the Truth." – Michael Levy

"Love takes off masks that we fear we cannot live without and know we cannot live within." – James Arthur Baldwin

"Unless your heart, your soul, and your whole being are behind every decision you make, the words from your mouth will be empty, and each action will be meaningless. Truth and confidence are the roots of happiness." – Unknown

You cannot forget about awareness…awareness will add to your happiness as well.

How often do you put on a false mask to be something for someone else? We all wear masks. I have quite a few that I became aware of and some of them are not that pretty. Why do we wear masks anyway? Perhaps, it's to hide behind so that we are not rejected as our true authentic self? Maybe…you have your reasons and I have mine but what if we all shed all those masks and just became true to ourselves? What do you think would happen? I have become aware of my masks and now I choose to wear them or not. Most of the time I do not and I am acting as me, my true self. I have taught my daughter that LOVE is the answer to everything. If we all loved with unconditional love, just think about what kind of world we would create…aaahh, total bliss!

If you can look in the mirror at the end of the day and know that you upheld your own integrity, your own truth, you may be able to live in peace, perhaps. You may be able to hide from others behind masks and lies but your Divine always knows if you are living in Truth.

Think about it…

Love and Sunshine,
Tracy

Celebrate differences

"Souls don't have races or sexes or religions. They are beyond artificial divisions." – Brian Weiss

"Beliefs separate. Loving thoughts unite." – Paul Ferrini

How often do we separate ourselves into different categories? We often evaluate ourselves as "less than" others and sometimes we put ourselves in the "better than" category. Question: Why do we have to put anyone anywhere when we are all made of the same energy? Everything you do not like about yourself plus all that you love about yourself is in everyone. Our beliefs are just stories that we create to make ourselves right or justify our actions. If we all came from unconditional love, there would be no dividing lines. What's that quote? "Together we stand, Divided we fall." There's so much truth in that statement for me. I know it may sound all "Kumbaya" but if you really think about it, if there were no boundaries wouldn't we all live in a place of love? Do not get me wrong…I'm not saying do not keep your individuality. Life would be boring if we were all the same. Even in your partnerships and relationships, if you do not keep your autonomy you may give up your happiness in a belief that someone else makes you whole. If you are not "whole" before you enter a relationship, if you are not happy within yourself, how will you be able to add happiness to the relationship?

Love is the answer to everything, self love above all else. If we all loved ourselves unconditionally the only thing that we could permeate is love.

Think about it…

Love and Sunshine,
Tracy

Love is the answer

"Life in abundance comes only through great love." – *Elbert Hubbard*

"If you begin the day with love in your heart, peace in your nerves, and truth in your mind, you not only benefit by their presence but also bring them to others, to your family and friends, and to all those whose destiny draws across your path that day." – *Anonymous*

OK, it being Valentine's Day, how could I not speak about love? How many times have I said love is the answer to anything and everything? If we all loved one another with unconditional love how could we not live in our own true happiness?

Honestly, if you started each day knowing that you first love yourself, how could you not encounter love where ever you go?

Think about it…

Love and Sunshine,
Tracy

Power

"There are two kinds of men who never amount to much: those who cannot do what they are told, and those who can do nothing else." – Cyrus H. Curtis

"Compassion, caring, teaching, loving, and sharing your gifts, talents, and abilities are the gateways to power." – Jamie Sams

I may have said this before but it wasn't too long ago that I created a different meaning for the word power. I used to think that power meant being better than someone else because I could do something that someone else could not. It was one of my mentors and teachers who told me that power is just the ability to "do" something. It changed my perception around a lot of things. I did not at times want to excel because I thought I might "look" better than someone else and they might "think" that I think the same…geesh, what a soap opera I created for myself. Honestly, if I have the power to do something that someone else isn't willing to do then it's nothing personal. I just choose to use my power in a different way.

Now, giving your power away is a different story. I know I've talked about this a lot so it should be a familiar territory. When you give up your control of your own life you are giving up your ability to be living in your own happiness. If you are allowing someone else to be in control of "making" you happy you may be putting yourself in a place of not living your own life. Stand in your own POWER! Stand in your ability to do whatever it is that you want to do. When you take full responsibility for your own life, your own actions, you may be surprised at how easy your life may become to live!

Power does not make you better than or greater than anyone else. As I said above, power just gives you the ability to do something, nothing more. I believe we all have a purpose and it is that purpose that needs to be shared with the world—whether it is that you are the best waiter/waitress or the best brain surgeon. The world needs your talents and it is through the sharing of your purpose that you gain your power to create!

Think about it…

Love and Sunshine,
Tracy

Knowledge to the power of happiness equals wisdom

"Knowing others is intelligence; knowing yourself is true wisdom. Mastering others is strength; mastering yourself is true power." – Tao Te Ching

"Never mistake knowledge for wisdom. One helps you make a living; the other helps you make a life." – Sandra Carey

How true is the second statement? How often have we put others' intelligence above the wisdom it takes to live in the moment and be happy? Some of the smartest people out there are living the most unhappy lives. Knowledge does not equal happiness. If you take your knowledge and apply it to your happiness, that will gain you wisdom.

Smarts is one thing. Knowing when and where to use your power, now, *that* is true wisdom.

Think about it...

Love and Sunshine,
Tracy

Be true to yourself

"In the final analysis, we count for something only because of the essential we embody, and if we do not embody that, life is wasted." – C. G. Jung

"A true knowledge of ourselves is knowledge of our power." – Mark Rutherford

"Be more concerned with your character than your reputation, because your character is what you really are, while your reputation is merely what others think you are." – John Wooden

Be who you are. Have the courage to accept yourself as you really are, not as someone else thinks you should be. Pretending to be someone you are not for the sake of gaining acceptance from someone else will just create more upset in your life. When you do things that are not in alignment with your core you may not be happy with yourself and may end up confused. You may be confused because you won't know who to please, or how – especially yourself.

Respect of self comes from being true to yourself by BEing who you are at your core. When you respect yourself, others will respect you. People may sense that you are strong and capable of standing up for yourself and your beliefs.

When you are true to yourself, you allow your individuality and uniqueness to shine through. You can still be open to the opinions of others but do not conform to their stereotypes or their expectations of you. BEing true to yourself does not mean that you are being inconsiderate or disrespectful to others. If someone has an issue with you on that level, then it is their issue and not yours…nothing personal. They can either accept you or deny you. Do not let others define who you are or make decisions for you that you should be making for yourself.

Be true to the very best that is in you and remember you are perfect in every moment. If you live your life consistent with your highest values and aspirations, you may realize that you are a totally different person.

Think about it…

Love and Sunshine,
Tracy

Forge the way

"To be a star, you must shine your own light, follow your own path, and don't worry about the darkness, for that is when the stars shine brightest" – *Napoleon Hill*

"Resolve to pay any price or make any sacrifice to get into the top ten percent of your field. That payoff is incredible!" – *Brian Tracy*

I think we've all put ourselves at an imaginary fork in the road thinking that the only way to go is right or left. But what about forging your own way? Why do we limit ourselves to only two choices? Do we not live in a world with unlimited possibilities? I am reminded about a physical scene that I encountered last fall. I was attending one of my training courses in the foothills of the Rocky Mountains. When we left, the lane was long and at the end there seemed to be only two ways to go: right or left. As we were driving down the lane I realized that if I went straight I'd be forging my own path and not a path pre-created by someone else's view of where I should go. I wanted to go straight towards the sun not away from it. It looked so peaceful in the hills. It dawned on me in that moment that even though I thought I was at a fork in the road in my own life, I still had more options.

Brian also makes a good point. Even though his statement is geared towards your career life, why can't you apply his message to anything you want to create in your life? If you want to be the best friend, the best partner or the best lover why not resolve to pay any price or make any sacrifice to create that in your life? Do these things for yourself and not "for" anyone else. Do them without expectation. Do them because it makes you happy to do them. If you create an upset for yourself because you didn't get the result you wanted, then maybe you need to look at your motives behind your actions. Was it for you or for someone else?

So the next time you create a fork in the road for yourself, why not forge your own path instead? You may enjoy the unpredictable excitement of off-road travel rather than the smooth boringness of the pre-cut pre-laid path.

Think about it…

Love and Sunshine,
Tracy

What if...?

"The universe is full of magical things patiently waiting for our wits to grow sharper." – Eden Phillpotts

"The greatest discovery of my generation is that a human being can alter his life by altering his attitudes." – William James

"Sometimes I've believed as many as six impossible things before breakfast." – Lewis Carrol

You could grow old playing the "what if…" game without ever leaving your home or experiencing anything in your life. You could live your whole life in fear and experience not one single thing you played out in your head…but why would you want to do that? What are you getting out of your life by creating so much upset for yourself? Is it really worth wasting your time to play crap over and over in your head? What payoff are you getting? Do you get to be the victim and have the notion that if you appear to be wounded then someone else may come along and save you? How's that working for you so far in creating happiness in your own life? Get out of your story! Stand up and say STOP!!! Reading it is not good enough, I really want you to physically stand up, oh come on now, you can do this, stand up already, and at the top of your lungs yell STOP!!! Enough already, you are too beautiful to not live in your own happiness. Why would you want someone else to make decisions for you and your life, anyway? You will never know what is going to happen five minutes from now, ever…so stop the tapes in your head and start living in this moment. Create your own happiness in this moment through acceptance. I've never said you had to like what is happening; just accept it. It is what it is, nothing more. When you accept what is happening in your life there is never anything to worry about anymore and "What if . . ." loses all its power over you.

Think about it…

Love and Sunshine,
Tracy

Here

"It is not by your actions that you will be saved, but by your being." –
Meister Eckhart

"People ask what must they become to be loving. The answer is nothing. It is a
process of letting go of what you thought you had become and allowing your true
nature to float to the surface naturally." – Stephen Levine

The first quote kind of sounds contradictory to what I've said in the past, but if you look at it more deeply it really is saying the same thing. It may be interpreted in a manner like this: Instead of acting happy, just BE happy.

Really get into the moment you are experiencing. Right now I am enjoying the smell and taste of a freshly brewed coffee, the sun is shining and the snow is sparkling. I can hear my daughter singing and playing. I am not thinking about anything in the past or anything into the future. My feet are a bit cold because I haven't put socks on yet. My hands are warm because my laptop is warm. There is nothing to worry about in this moment. I am happy…smiling…typing away. I have no concerns in this moment. Nothing is threatening me so I have nothing to fear. I am truly BEing happy.

I have let go of what others think I should be and I am who I am and I LOVE me! I am in this moment a beautiful, caring, smart, intelligent, loving, sexy, sensual woman who is unstoppable in manifesting what she desires in all aspects of her life because I choose to be happy in this moment.

Think about it…

Love and Sunshine,
Tracy

Never give up

"In order to get from what was to what will be, you must go through what is." – Anonymous

"For a righteous man falls seven times, and rises again." – Proverbs 24:16, Bible

Lol…I totally have the theme to *Rocky* running through my head…I love *Rocky!*

A story comes to mind about a man who bought a gold mine with dreams of riches and grandeur. For years he spent digging and digging with no results. He finally gave up and sold the mine and the next person who bought the mine found the largest gold deposit in the area, just six inches from where the first man stopped digging.

What do you want to create in your life that is of value to you? How do you want to spend your time? Is it worth getting knocked down 999 times in order to get what you want on the 1000th time? Do you not miss every shot you do not take? Same goes for every question you do not ask; the answer is always no. The only way you will ever fail anything is if you give up on achieving the result you want. Just keep in mind, if you are looking to attain something…what is your motive behind that want? No one will ever fulfill anything "for" you—that satisfaction or fulfillment must come from your own BEing for it to be in true alignment with your soul's desire to create true happiness in your life.

What are you working towards in your own life? Does the end result create a strong enough desire in you to always remember the above story and prevent you from stopping six inches from *your* gold?

Think about it…

Love and Sunshine,
Tracy

Fears of money

"We are all powerless as children, and money looms so powerfully…we don't grow up to claim our financial power until we look money directly in the eye, face our fears, and claim that power back." – Suze Orman

One thing that comes to mind I learned from a course I took awhile ago: Love people and use money, not the other way around. Money does not make anyone happy. Money will give you the ability to buy things and pay your bills but it does not offer you happiness. Some of the richest people in the world are still unhappy. Why would you want to live life in a constant state of never having enough? How will that ever create happiness in your life? I consider myself a Money Magnet. Whenever I have needed a certain amount of money to do something that was/is in alignment with my soul's path, the money manifested exactly when I needed it to, without fear. I believe I will create it and 100 percent of the time I have created exactly what I've needed. Now do not get the wrong impression here – I do not sit and wait for a bag of money to fall from the sky. I put my ideas into action and through my action and daily belief that the money will be there when I need it, it has always been there. I am always grateful for all the money I have now and I know in my future I will be met with abundance in PEACE, LOVE, HAPPINESS and MONEY!

Be grateful for what you have in this moment and more will come to you – it's the law.

Think about it…

Love and Sunshine,
Tracy

February 23rd

Dare!

"If you only do what you know you can do – you never do very much." –
Tom Krause

"Watch your thoughts, for they become words. Watch your words, for they become
actions. Watch your actions, for they become habits. Watch your habits, for they
become character. Watch your character, for it becomes your destiny." – Unknown

"It is not the critic who counts; not the man who points out how the strong
man stumbles, or where the doer of deeds could have done them better. The credit
belongs to the man who is actually in the arena, whose face is marred by dust
and sweat and blood, who strives valiantly; who errs and comes short again and
again; because there is not effort without error and shortcomings; but who does
actually strive to do the deed; who knows the great enthusiasm, the great devo-
tion, who spends himself in a worthy cause, who at the best knows in the end
the triumph of high achievement and who at the worst, if he fails, at least he fails
while daring greatly. So that his place shall never be with those cold and timid
souls who know neither victory nor defeat." – Theodore Roosevelt

Hmmm…I think Mr. Roosevelt says it all.

Think about it…

Love and Sunshine,
Tracy

Tracy Friesen

Attitude

"The longer I live, the more I realize the impact of attitude on life. Attitude, to me, is more important than facts. It is more important than the past, the education, the money, than circumstances, than failure, than successes, than what other people think or say or do. It is more important than appearance, giftedness or skill. It will make or break a company…a church…a home. The remarkable thing is we have a choice everyday regarding the attitude we will embrace for that day. We cannot change our past…we cannot change the fact that people will act in a certain way. We cannot change the inevitable. The only thing we can do is play on the one string we have, and that is our attitude. I am convinced that life is 10% what happens to me and 90% how I react to it. And so it is with you…we are in charge of our Attitudes." – Charles R. Swindoll

Live your life with a positive attitude and you will live your life full of happiness. Charles has a great message. Our attitudes provide us with a guide to how our life will play out. If you have a not-so-positive attitude towards the things and events that are happening in your life then how can you be surprised if your life is full of suffering and grief? You can make anything work in your life if you have the, for a lack of a better word, right attitude behind it. Maybe right isn't the word but at least a positive attitude.

I have people tell me all the time that I am always so happy and it seems nothing gets me down. Well that's not entirely true; I am only human you know. I may get into my story at times but for the most part I am able to look to the good in everything that happens to me. Eventually I find out why things happened the way they had to happen. I put out there for myself peace, love, happiness, honor, and respect and that is what I am met with when I get where ever it is that I end up.

Life is what you make it. You and only you are responsible for your happiness. Today is a new day and you can BE whoever you want to be. Yesterday doesn't matter and neither does tomorrow. Right now in this moment is what matters. I invite you to look at your attitude today. What are you willing to create in your life that matters?

Think about it…

Love and Sunshine,
Tracy

The secret is to create happy memories

"Nobody can go back and start a new beginning, but anyone can start today and make a new ending." – Maria Robinson

"The most important things in life aren't things." – Anthony J. D'Angelo

How often do we get caught in a wish to change the past? With futile efforts and lost time we try over and over to do something that cannot be done…silly humans! The past is the past, is the past, is the past…NOW, in this moment, is where everything happens. You can BE whatever or whomever you want in this moment. It doesn't matter who you were five minutes ago, unless perhaps you have to clean something up in this moment for who you were last moment. That's just keeping your integrity. I'm not saying this gives you free reign to be a jerk but if that happens, cleaning up your mess is the best way to getting back to being happy.

To me every moment is the beginning of a new chapter…a new segment in my life. I look for the good in everything that happens to me and whatever comes up for me in the moment, that's what comes up for me. Anthony says it all: The most important things in life are not things at all. Again this brings up *Into the Wild*. Have you seen it yet? Life is nothing unless you create memories to share. A new friend of mine recently asked me, "Tracy, if you spend all your time on healing something how are you creating any space for new memories? Leave the past in the past and create a new bond through doing things that make you happy in this moment." Smart lady…wish I had thought of that. She sure made me think of things in a different way. I love being opened to new thoughts. The most important thing to me is creating loving memories so that when I think about them they make me smile. When I revisit them they bring about a sense of fun, happiness, joy, laughter, love, etc.

"This is my wish for you: Comfort on difficult days, smiles when sadness intrudes, rainbows to follow the clouds, laughter to kiss your lips, sunsets to warm your heart, hugs when spirits sag, beauty for your eyes to see, friendships to brighten your being, faith so that you can believe, confidence for when you doubt, courage to know yourself, patience to accept the truth, Love to complete your life."

Life is not a destination; it's a journey. Who are you going to be today or in this moment that will create happiness now, so when the future arrives you are met with just more happiness for yourself?

Think about it…

Love and Sunshine,
Tracy

What is your body saying?

"Many people treat their bodies as if they were rented from Hertz—something they are using to get around in but nothing they genuinely care about understanding." – Chungliang Al Huang

"Your body is the ground and metaphor of your life, the expression of your existence. It is your Bible, your encyclopedia, your life story. Everything that happens to you is stored and reflected in your body. In the marriage of flesh and spirit divorce is impossible." – Gabrielle Roth

"What is always speaking silently is the body." – Norman Brown

Our bodies are telling our story. You may think that you are hiding your deepest, darkest secrets but your body is an outward reflection of what is going with you on the inside. When we experience pain it is our body's way of letting us know that something has gotten out of hand and it needs to be addressed or dealt with to some degree. Whether the pain is emotional, mental, physical or spiritual, it is a sign from our body that we have created a block somewhere that is preventing us from moving forward on our path.

If you are not honoring your body then perhaps you are not honoring your soul's desire to be who you truly ought to be. If you are not honoring your soul's desire, how are you ever surprised if you experience discomfort, pain or even dis–ease? When you can become aware of why you created the upset in your body, you will be able to lovingly release it and remove the block that stands in your way to getting what you want and get you back on your path to your happiness.

I invite you today to start listening to your body and honoring what it is telling you. You may be surprised that it really does know what's best for you.

Think about it...

Love and Sunshine,
Tracy

February 27th

Why meditate?

"Meditation brings wisdom; lack of meditation leaves ignorance. Know well what leads you forward and what holds you back, and choose the path that leads to wisdom." – Buddha

"Only in quiet waters things mirror themselves undistorted. Only in a quiet mind is adequate perception of the world." – Hans Margolius

Do you know how our monkey brain can take over at times and we have that sense that we cannot control our own minds? Well, who do you think trained that monkey to go at warp speed anyway?

I myself, in my past, would often feel a victim to my own mind taking off where I did not want it to go. It wasn't until I took a yoga class and learned to quiet my mind that I felt a sense of being in control of my own thoughts. I realized that I have complete control over what I allow to come and go in my mind. What a freeing feeling it was to be able to think of nothing. In the beginning I was able to allow thoughts to enter but I thanked them and let them leave…soon I was able to just BE in the moment with nothing in my mind. Ever since that experience I am able to think of nothing often. I trained my monkey to take a hike and I have been able, at trying times, to bring myself back to balance all on my own. What a liberating experience!

I have read that meditating for at least five minutes a day can be good for your health. Meditating doesn't mean sitting cross-legged with your fingers in the OK sign, humming the word "Ohmmmmm" over and over. Although that is one form of meditation, it isn't the only form. You can meditate in any moment doing any task. I do not suggest doing it while you are driving though…lol! (Although I am sure all of us have had those experiences of driving somewhere and not remembering how we got to where we were going. That too is a form of meditation, maybe not a safe one but it is a mediation in itself.) You can take any moment and free your mind of all thoughts…while washing dishes…taking a shower…sitting quiet in the sun…whatever it is that you are doing, you can turn that moment into a moment of meditation.

Tracy Friesen

Thinking of nothing may be the key to bringing yourself back to this present moment. If nothing is clouding your mind then you may be able to enjoy whatever is happening for you in this moment…like feeling the warmth of the sun hitting your back or smelling the aroma of the fresh cut flowers sitting on the table in front of you. You can enjoy these things without thinking about them or anything else and just BE happy in the moment.

I invite you to take five minutes out of your day today and tell your monkey brain to hit the road and just think of nothing. If thoughts enter your mind—like oh I have clothes in the dryer—just thank the thought and do not let it linger. Ask it to leave and go back to focusing on your breathing and just think of nothing. You may be surprised at how much wisdom is gained through contemplating nothing.

Think about it…er…no, wait…do *not* think about it…

Love and Sunshine,
Tracy

Levels of consciousness

"The greatest discovery of my generation is that man can alter his life simply by altering his attitude of mind." – William James

"Utilizing your conscious mind to direct the subconscious mind to enter into communication and harmony with the universal mind is the secret of personal power." – Delfin Knowledge System

I personally do not believe we have a subconscious mind. To me, that would mean that I am not in control of something that belongs to me. I think I have said this before…I believe we have a habitual mind. We ingrain a belief so much that it becomes a habit, not something we do without knowing. If we change our habits, we may be able to then change our habitual mind and possibly create a new state of BEing. The definition of insanity is doing the same thing over and over and expecting a different result. So why not through your awareness do something different to get a different result in your life? If something isn't working for you, you can always make the choice to do and BE something different. It is through our attitudes that we create the results of our BEing. It is through acceptance of our experiences in our lives that we may influence our habitual mind so that we can be happy in any moment.

Think about it…

Love and Sunshine,
Tracy

Where are you coming from?

"Do all things with love." – Og Mandino

If you are not doing things from love in your heart how are you ever surprised that people do not react the way you want them to? How are you surprised that you never get what you want and are left with the feeling that no one loves or cares about *you*? If you got rid of all your judgements and expectations and if everything you did came from LOVE how could you not be happy?

Think about it…

Love and Sunshine,
Tracy

March 1st

You know the way

*"Woe to the man whose heart has not learned while young to hope, to love…
and to put its trust in life." – Joseph Conrad*

*"I trust so much in the power of the heart and the soul; I know that the answer
to what we need to do next is in our own hearts. All we have to do is listen, then
take that one step further and trust what we hear. We will be taught what we
need to learn." – Melody Beattie*

*"I never know what the next lesson is going to be, because we're not supposed to
know; we're supposed to trust ourselves to discover it." – Melody Beattie*

Discovery of your path through living in the moment is an amazing
thing! We may get caught in having to know what to do next when really
all that there is to do is be accepting in this moment. There is no tomorrow, only right now. If you live for tomorrow it will never come. What's
there for you right now? Your true heart will guide you…everything
does happen for a reason.

Think about it…

Love and Sunshine,
Tracy

Face your truth

"If you look for truth, you may find comfort in the end; if you look for comfort you will not get either comfort or truth, only soft soap and wishful thinking to begin, and in the end, despair." – C.S. Lewis

"You can't undo anything you've already done, but you can face up to it. You can tell the truth. You can seek forgiveness. And then let God do the rest."
– Unknown

Y ou may think that facing up to your truth is a hard thing to do and it may take courage, but in reality it is such an easy and freeing experience. The sooner you claim responsibility for your actions the sooner you can start to live your life and BE happy. If something comes up for you the best time to deal with it is in the moment; otherwise you may take yourself down a downward spiral that may not be necessary—or fun, for that matter. Why do we do that to ourselves? For me it is fear of the reaction from the other person involved. Over time I have learned to let go of the personal impact of the opinion of others. It doesn't matter what another thinks of me…it only matters what I think of me. If you play by everyone else's rules then you might as well take yourself out of your own life. What does it matter what anyone else thinks of you, really? Are they the ones who are making your decisions for you? If you think yes, you have been missing the point. You and only you make the final decision to do anything…end of story.

Do the hardest thing on earth for you. Act for yourself. Stand in your own power. Face the truth. You may be surprised at the reaction you get.

Think about it…

Love and Sunshine,
Tracy

March 3rd

Tomorrow's Dream

"Of all the things that matter, that really and truly matter, working more efficiently and getting more done is not among them." – Unknown

"Yesterday is but today's memory, tomorrow is today's dream." – Kahlil Gibran

"You block your dream when you allow your fear to grow bigger than your faith." – Mary Manin

Something that was told to me a few years ago just stuck in my mind and my heart and it just feels appropriate in this moment: Fear knocked on the door…Faith answered…and no one was there.

The second quote reminds me of a poem I wrote back in '95:

> Tomorrow's Dream
>
> Walking yesterday
> Tomorrow came
> Seeing Today
> Left me dreaming
>
> Old smells
> Bring back
> Unwanted memories
>
> Yesterday can destroy
> Tomorrow's dream

Reading that makes me smile because I am in such a different place today. I have the wisdom from my knowledge to know that I am in complete control of my life and how it will unfold in this moment. The only thing that remains the same from back then and now is that dwelling on the past can prevent you from getting what you want. You can, if you want, remain in misery for the entirety of your life—if that works for you. Perhaps the victim role is yours to wear: "Oh, woe is me…everyone is against me…my life is sooo hard…boohoo, I never get what I want… blah blah blah…" How does that sound when you read it? Read it again. I'll wait...Does it bring up feelings of anger? Then maybe this is something that doesn't work for you and you are just afraid to let your barrier down and just be you? Hey, if being a victim works for you, wear that role proudly but do it with awareness! Which means you can be the victim but you can no longer complain about anything that happens to you. If it doesn't work for you, you are the only person who can create something different in your life.

I am looking at what can I create in this moment to be happy. I create the life I want through my own actions...through the things that truly matter to me, by creating moments that are full of caring, caressing, touching, sharing, bonding, joyous, passionate, loving and yes even erotic experiences. It's experiences that matter most to me, like loving interactions with those I hold most dear. It is in creating memories that are in alignment with what matters most to you that you can share your true happiness and just BE happy.

Think about it...

Love and Sunshine,
Tracy

March 4th

On sadness

"Our sadness is an energy we discharge in order to heal…Sadness is painful. We try to avoid it. Actually discharging sadness releases the energy involved in our emotional pain. To hold it in is to freeze the pain within us. The therapeutic slogan is that grieving is the 'healing feeling.'"– John Bradshaw

"To weep is to make less the depth of grief." – William Shakespeare

"There is no despair so absolute as that which comes with the first moments of our first great sorrow, when we have not yet known what it is to have suffered and be healed, to have despaired and recovered hope." – George Eliot

"Seek not happiness too greedily, and be not fearful of unhappiness." – Lao-tzu

"When the heart grieves over what it has lost, the spirit rejoices over what it has left." – Sufi

W hy is it that we run away from the feelings that are the ones that bring us the most happiness in the end? Oh trust me, I am right there with you on this one. I have been through my own tragedies in my life, some small and some not so small at all…far too many if you ask me. I have been caught in "Why me…again…ugh." The emotional pain that I have felt has been unbearable at times and I have thought that I would never recover from it. Experiences that range from ending friendships, to dealing with my Dad's suicide, to dealing with the ending of my marriage. As you already know, I now live by the philosophy that everything happens for a reason and I have found most of the reasons for most of the tragedies that have occurred in my life thus far and have gained wisdom from my experiences. Some I am still learning from and so I am honoring what has happened, and I know that my future is just filled with more wisdom. Everything is OK in the end. If it's not OK, then it's not the end.

One thing that I have learned is that if you pray for strength your Divine will give you experiences that you must create strength to get through. Instead of praying for strength, BE strong. This goes for any character trait you may have prayed for—courage, patience, forgiveness, etc. Words are powerful as they create powerful thoughts and powerful thoughts create powerful actions. That is why it's so important to be aware of what you are creating in your mind as it *will* come out in your reality.

Tracy Friesen

Sadness is necessary for you to experience in order to release the pain that you have created. Pain is our body's way of telling us that something needs to be lovingly released because it isn't working for us to move forward on our path…and "forward" is just a word I am using. Sometimes remaining exactly where you are is exactly where you need to be.

Think about it…

Love and Sunshine,
Tracy

Make time to play

"If we fail to nourish our souls, they wither, and without soul, life ceases to have meaning…The creative process shrivels in the absence of continual dialogue with the soul. And creativity is what makes life worth living." – Marion Woodman

How fitting to find this quote today of all days…my husband and I played hooky and took my daughter out of school today and we went for a family day of skiing and oh so much fun! This totally reminded me that if you do not take time out for play you may just wither away. If you spend all your time just trying to get more done, you may be missing the point of life. Get out of your "have to's" and tap into your creative mind and play for a change.

Life is meant to be enjoyed, not resented. When is the last time you did something just for fun? If you cannot remember, maybe that's a sign that it's time to turn on those creative juices and create some playtime for yourself.

When we ignite our childlike wonder you never know what may become available to us.

Think about it…

Love and Sunshine,
Tracy

Feel your emotions

"The key is to not resist or rebel against emotions or to try to get around them by devising all sorts of tricks; but to accept them directly, as they are." – Takahisa Kora

"Instead of resisting any emotion, the best way to dispel it is to enter it fully, embrace it and see through your resistance." – Deepak Chopra

"We have to become more conscious of our feeling-world. By learning to identify the emotional baggage and manage our feeling-world reactions, we can view life based on current information instead of being held captive by our past." – Doc Childre

"Our feelings are our most genuine paths to knowledge." – Audre Lorde

Whenever we carry our past into our future we remove our possibility of choice. If you release your past and leave it where it belongs you can then create whatever you want in your present. Here's an example: You meet someone. You end up feeling hurt by them ending the relationship and you say "I'm never going to let that happen again." You just put your past into the future so that anytime another someone comes along, you go back to your past experience to make your decisions for you. Even though you may not remember the statement you made when you were sixteen, you create events and experiences to prove that you were right and you sabotage every current relationship and end them before you get "hurt" again. Make sense?

Honor your feelings—all of them. You are feeling them for a reason. Feel them with awareness. Instead of using "I think" statements make "I feel" statements. It is through our feelings that we may be led onto our perfect path to happiness. You may need to "feel" something in order to grow and learn. If you don't, you may never find your happiness.

Think about it…

Love and Sunshine,
Tracy

Self-actualization

"Every human action, whether it has become positive or negative, must depend on motivation." – Dalai Lama

"The real richness is in be-ness. People can take all that you have, all that you collected. People can stop your labor, or an accident can stop you. When you are, you never lose what you are." – Torkom Saraydarian

No one can take me away from me. This is something that I have repeated to myself when I've been afraid or working on getting out of a funk. BEing you is something that you will never lose so why not BE the person who creates the most happiness? Things and stuff do not bring you happiness nor will they ever "make" you happy. You and only you will ever BE happy. Inanimate objects, even though they are made of energy, will not love you back or give you anything. You make the choice to feel the way you do about anything. You are the one who chooses your reactions to other people's actions. No one else is responsible for your feelings—only you. No one causes you to feel any way. You feel the way you do because you choose to feel that way—end of story.

What motivates you more: your negative or lower vibrational emotions or your positive higher vibrational emotions? Did you know it only takes 68 seconds to change your feeling to a higher vibration? You don't believe me? Try it. If you are in a lower vibration like anger, frustration, impatience, and/or annoyance, think about something that brings you happiness, hold that thought for 68 seconds…and see what happens.

If want more happiness in your life why not accept your moment and just BE happy? Like attracts like. If you are BEing happy you may just attract happier people to you.

Think about it…

Love and Sunshine,
Tracy

Accept change

"We cannot live the afternoon of life according to the program of life's morning; for what in the morning was true will in evening become a lie." – C.G. Jung

"Can it then be that what we call the self is fluid and elastic? It evolves, strikes a different balance with every new breath." – Wayne Muller

"We're never the same; notice how you're called to write something entirely different about a topic you responded to weeks or months ago." – Patrice Vecchione

How true is the last quote? Do you not believe me? Why not test it out for yourself? Take an experience that created an extreme emotional shift for you and journal about it or just jot down some main feelings that you are experiencing in the moment. Then let some time go by…and journal about the same experience. Most likely you'll have a different story the second time around.

The first quote, to me, is telling us that we cannot live now by bringing our past into our present because we are different people with different information from one moment to the next. So doing the same thing over and over expecting a different result is just plain crazy, in my opinion.

What I have learned is that the only constant thing IS change. It doesn't matter who you were five minutes ago; all that matters is who you are in this moment. Again, this doesn't give you free reign to go out and be a jerk to everyone around you…or does it? You are the only one who can and will have true integrity with your own actions. If you are angry then be angry with awareness. Do not experience it as an excuse or a reason of "You made me…". You chose your anger just like you will choose your happiness. It's the same thing about feeling guilty. You choose to feel guilt because you feel that you did wrong, not because someone else "made you".

With every new breath that we breathe we can BE a different person. It is and always has been your choice as to who you want to BE in any given moment.

Think about it…

Love and Sunshine,
Tracy

We can't escape

"Most of our obstacles would melt away if, instead of cowering before them, we should make up our minds to walk boldly through them."– Orison Swett Marden

"It is the trouble that never comes that causes the loss of sleep." – Chas. Austin Bates

"We learn wisdom from failure much more than success. We often discover what we will do, by finding out what we will not do." – Samuel Smiles

"Never let the fear of striking out get in your way." – George Herman "Babe" Ruth

Be like the stream when confronted with an obstacle of life. Persevere and you will eventually get through. If you let your fear run the story of your life you may end up at the end wondering why nothing ever happened in your life. What are you willing to do to have the life you want? I know I want to create, from moment to moment, a life full of love, passion and exciting adventures lavished with romance and public displays of affection! I will not settle for anything less than I deserve. Even in the quiet moments where silence is comfortable, my life will be full of love and sensuality. There will be no doubt or insecurity, just a knowingness that I am LOVABLE and I am ENOUGH. Sharing love is something that is important to me. If I let fear get in the way then I am hindering my own happiness. It does take courage to stand in your own power – but why should you be uncomfortable in someone else's ignorance? Make your requests. All someone can do is one of three things: accept, deny or counter-offer. It's up to you to accept the answer whatever it may be.

Why think about things that may never happen? The only way you will ever fail is if you stop trying to create the result you want in your life.

Think about it…

Love and Sunshine,
Tracy

March 10th

Acceptance = Happiness

"Happiness is not achieved by the conscious pursuit of happiness; it is generally the by-product of other activities." – Aldous Huxley

"Happiness is not a matter of events, it depends upon the tides of the mind." – Alice Meynell

"Happiness is where we find it, but rarely where we seek it." – J. Petit Senn

How many times have we put all our eggs in the one basket of "when this happens I'll be happy"? If you find yourself in that statement, maybe you haven't been listening. Happiness occurs in the moment of your acceptance of what is happening in your life. If you are constantly seeking happiness you may never find it, because when all the stars have aligned in your plan, new criteria are brought forward and you then change your agenda to suit the new information and begin with a new "I'll be happy when…" Happiness is not a destination; it is a way of constantly BE-ing. If something comes up for you in this moment to challenge your happiness, do whatever it takes to deal with it, move on back into acceptance and you will find your happiness again. This may require you to go outside your comfort zone and do something that you normally would not, but if it's the only thing that will help you reach your state of BEing happy is it not worth the risk of just doing it?

Your happiness is just awaiting your acceptance.

Think about it…

Love and Sunshine,
Tracy

Tracy Friesen

Give yourself praise

"If you wish to know the mind of a man, listen to his words." – *Chinese Proverb*

"Handle them carefully, for words have more power than atom bombs." – *Pearl Strachan Hurd*

"The wise weigh their words on a scale with gold." – *Bible*

W hy is it that we allow decisions we made when we were five years old to create tapes in our head that run our life? Words are powerful! Especially those we say to ourselves. We are so hard on ourselves, me included. I am my worst critic. We need to forgive ourselves and know that we did the best we could with the information we had at that moment in time. If you need to clean something up, do so. If you need to ask for forgiveness, do so. Be willing to accept the answers you are receiving and there is nothing more that you can do.

You are the most important person as you are the only one who controls your thoughts, your feelings, your decisions, your actions, your integrity and your BEing. Why not honor yourself and praise yourself for the good that you have done? Your path is your path and everything happens for a reason. Knowing in your heart that you are ENOUGH and you are WORTH it may be all that you need to get you to your goal of just BEing happy.

Think about it!

Love and Sunshine,
Tracy

March 12th

In return

"If I am not for myself, who will be? And if I am for myself alone, then what am I? And if not now, when?" – Rabbi Hillel, Pirke Avot 1:14

"Happiness is not having what you want, but wanting what you have." – Anonymous

"Unless we think of others and do something for them, we miss one of the greatest sources of happiness." – Ray Lyman Wilbur

The richest person in the world is not the one who holds the most money. The rich person is the person who is happy with what they have and what they do in this moment. Have you checked in lately with who you are BEing in this moment? It doesn't matter what anyone says or does because you can choose to BE whoever you want to be, no matter what…it's up to you! Nobody can take you away from you. If someone else is being a certain way, you do not have to like what they are doing or how they are being, just accept that they are being that way. You, in return, can BE whoever you want to be! If someone's BEing doesn't work for you it doesn't work for you and that is one hundred percent OK. You can choose to exist around it or choose to not exist around it. When you find yourself saying "I do not like it when…" this is your cue to look at what you are not accepting in the moment. The hardest thing for me to accept is when someone denies my request…I'm working on it, though.

I like Ray's quote about doing things for others. This brings into our reality someone else's happiness. If you know that someone likes a certain thing and you do that for them, you create happiness for them to share back with you…another side of BEing happy. Today do something that brings happiness to someone else. You never know what you can create in a moment of shared happiness.

Think about it…

Love and Sunshine,
Tracy

Be, do and have

"Often people attempt to live their lives backwards: they try to have more things, or more money, in order to do more of what they want so they will be happier. The way it actually works is the reverse. You must first be who you really are, then do what you love to do, in order to have what you want." –
Margaret Young

"Who does not thank for little will not thank for much."– Estonian proverb

If you are not happy with what you have now, what makes you think you'll be happy when you get what you think you want? Margaret has a good point. It is your BEing that creates your doing which then leads to your having. The more you are grateful for what you have in this moment, the more will be created for you to be grateful for in the next moment.

Think about it…

Love and Sunshine,
Tracy

Being honest

"It is discouraging how many people are shocked by honesty and how few by deceit." – Anonymous

"Our lives improve only when we take chances—and the first and most difficult risk we can take is to be honest with ourselves." – Walter Anderson

"Integrity is telling myself the truth. And honesty is telling the truth to other people." – Anonymous

Take the first quote one step farther. It's like people expect others to lie so, when it happens you can be right in your own mind that everyone is against you and you get to continue to play the victim. On the other hand, when you hear the truth you may not like what you hear because it's not what you want. Then you do not accept it and you may get into your victim role anyway. You create a vicious circle in your mind that just perpetuates your own negative belief about yourself...why? Honesty really is the best policy because then there is nothing to wonder about. I, myself, prefer the truth over any story on any given day. If I have all the true information, then I am able to make the best educated decision using my knowledge and wisdom to help me.

Honesty may scare people because they are more concerned about what other people may think about them if they tell their truth. Who cares what other people think? Wouldn't you rather be honest with someone to uphold your own integrity than to not be able to look at yourself with honor and respect at the end of each day? It is your choice...always.

Take the chance of being honest with those around you. You never know what might be created for yourself when you can stand in the power of your own integrity.

Think about it...

Love and Sunshine,
Tracy

There is always light in the dark

"Holding onto anger is like grasping onto a hot coal with the intent of throwing it at someone else. You are the one who gets burned." – Gautama Buddha

"Concern should drive us into action, not depression." – Karen Horney

"I tell you the truth, if you have faith as small as a mustard seed, you can say to this mountain, "Move from here to there" and it will move. Nothing will be impossible to you." – Matthew 17:20

"When you believe in things that you don't understand then you suffer." – Stevie Wonder

If you think that you are at the bottom then perhaps this is a good thing because the only place to look is up. There's nothing bad about darkness because it holds all the answers. Blackness contains all that is light. If you are willing to open your eyes you will see that there in the light of the dark my hand is outstretched waiting for you to take hold…

Think about it…

Love and Sunshine,
Tracy

Apply what you know

"Knowledge of any kind…brings about a change in awareness from where it is possible to create new realities." – *Deepak Chopra*

"More important than finding the teacher is finding and following the truth of the teaching…" – *Sogyal Rinpoche*

"There can be no knowledge without emotion. We may be aware of a truth, yet until we have felt its force, it is not ours. To the cognition of the brain must be added the experience of the soul." – *Arnold Bennett*

Only being aware of the truth is like understanding it at a mental, logical level. You understand what the words mean individually and strung together but it's not until you "feel" them that you may gain a deeper understanding of what is there for you. That has been my issue in the past—to "think" my feelings and not feel them. This past year has been a roller coaster of emotions for me as I allowed myself to actually feel what I was going through instead of being stuck in my story of thoughts. My logical self kept trying to take over, but every day I allowed myself to feel a little more. In the end I gained such a deeper understanding of who I am and I was able to find the reasons to why certain things had to happen the way that they did. You see, everything is OK in the end!

It's through your feeling that you gain the wisdom of your knowledge.

Think about it…

Love and Sunshine,
Tracy

Conscious communication

"If we want to be compassionate we must be conscious of the words we use. We must both speak and listen from the heart." – Marshall B. Rosenberg

"When we focus on clarifying what is being observed, felt, and needed rather than on diagnosing and judging, we discover the depth of our own compassion."
– Marshall B. Rosenberg

When was the last time you were actually listening to the other person during a conversation? Or were you just going through the motions: "yeah…uh-huh…mmhmm…" nodding your head along the way? Or were you so busy trying to figure out what *you* wanted to say that you really didn't listen to what the other person was saying at all? I know you think you know what they were talking, about but do you really?

Just because someone brings up a topic that you have some experience with doesn't mean it is the time to share it…unless the other person asks for your specific input about your experiences. Or if you really *have* to share your experience, the most polite thing to do is to ask permission to share. For example, say, "That brings up an experience for me…" or "That reminds me of something—would you like to hear it?" Using this technique you are not taking away from someone else's experience or feelings. If you interject what you want to say when someone is talking, even if it's a question about what has been said, you are disregarding that person as unimportant and you are making yourself the center of attention, as though you are the most important thing. How does that ever work for conscious communication? If you think that you are contributing to the conversation by doing this, I'm sorry to say but you are the emotional vampire that people want to avoid…harsh, I know, but it's true.

The best way to communicate with someone is to fully listen when they are speaking, and when they are done to reiterate in your own words what you think they just said for clarification. If there is a something that you didn't get, then the other person will let you know…trust me. Do not be concerned, you will always have a chance to share what is relevant for you. A great communicator will always listen more and talk less.

Think about it…

Love and Sunshine,
Tracy

Keep moving forward

"Let me tell you something you already know. The world ain't all sunshine and rainbows. It's a very mean and nasty place and I don't care how tough you are it will beat you to your knees and keep you there permanently if you let it. You, me, or nobody is gonna hit as hard as life. But it ain't about how hard ya hit. It's about how hard you can get hit and keep moving forward. How much you can take and keep moving forward. That's how winning is done! Now if you know what you're worth then go out and get what you're worth. But ya gotta be willing to take the hits, and not pointing fingers saying you ain't where you wanna be because of him, or her, or anybody! Cowards do that and that ain't you! You're better than that!" – Rocky Balboa

Oooh man, I LOVE Rocky! OK here comes the song…again…lol. I know you are singing it too…let it out…let it inspire you! WHOOO!! That was good…

Rocky Balboa has got to be one of my all-time favorite movies! It just hits home like no other. If you haven't seen it I highly recommend it. *Rocky III* is another good one to get you all fired up and inspired. This is going to be an AWESOME day! It's the eye of the Tiger. How can I top Rocky? He says it all: "What did I say to the kid…It's about how hard you can get hit and keep moving forward. How much you can take and keep moving forward?"

Think about it…

Love and Sunshine,
Tracy

March 19th

No judgment

"Do not judge, and you will never be mistaken." – Jean Jacques Rousseau

Hmmm…let's ponder this one a moment.

Have you ever noticed which eye you use the most to look at things and people, especially yourself? I have learned that your right eye is connected to your judgment and your left eye is connected to your unconditional love. When you look from your right eye you are looking at things and people from your judgment. As soon as you look from your judgment, you are making someone wrong because judgment leads you to your reasons and excuses and is not accepting of someone's BEing… this includes yourself too, you know!

I invite you today to only look from your left eye, from your unconditional love. You may find this a hard thing to do because you've created a habitual pattern to look from your judgment. Even if you have to cover your right eye with your hand or something—do it! Do whatever it takes to do something different. You never know what you can create for yourself by only looking from your unconditional love.

Think about it…

Love and Sunshine,
Tracy

Think first

"If you have built castles in the air, your work need not be lost; that is where they should be. Now put the foundations under them." – Henry David Thoreau

"It is our choices...that show what we truly are, far more than our abilities." – J. K. Rowling

"Although not every choice you make is about directions, all choices will influence where you end up." – Unknown

"Again and again, the impossible problem is solved when we see that the problem is only a tough decision waiting to be made." – Robert H. Schuller

You are where you are because you "decided" to be where you are... and perhaps it's the perfect place to be? It's through our choices that we shape our world around us. We first have to think it, and then we make a decision to make it a reality. You are the only person responsible for where you are and who you are in your life at this moment—end of story. If you think your life is tough then make it simple. Stop blaming other people for where and who you are in your own life. As soon as you go into blaming someone else for anything, you are not taking responsibility for your own life. You and only you make the final decision to do anything, period. Ask yourself the hard questions. Find out why you do things. Your answers are there...if you are willing to listen. The key is to be open to what's available to you. The good, the bad and the ugly are all ways to gain knowledge in order for you to grow or just be OK with who and where you are in this moment. Nothing is impossible if you are able to think it first.

Think about it...

Love and Sunshine,
Tracy

Outwit the storm

"To accomplish great things, we must not only act, but also dream; not only plan, but also believe." – Anatole France

"Great changes may not happen right away, but with effort even the difficult may become easy." – Bill Blackman

"What counts is not necessarily the size of the dog in the fight—it's the size of the fight in the dog." – Dwight D. Eisenhower

"It is not because things are difficult that we do not dare, it is because we do not dare that they are difficult." – Seneca

Dream your dream and dare to make it real. If you believe…you can create any future. See the good in everything. Trust in your intuition to get through the darkness and fears surrounding your dreams and goals. You do know when the time is right for you and when that time comes instead of giving up on what you want to create in your life and giving into your fears, put in the effort and outwit the storm. What are you willing to do to see the beautiful colors of the dawn on the other side?

Think about it…

Love and Sunshine,
Tracy

What truly matters

"Change does not necessarily assure progress, but progress implacably requires change. Education is essential to change, for education creates both new wants and the ability to satisfy them." – Henry Steele Commager

"Life can only be understood backwards; but it must be lived forwards." – Soren Kierkegaard

"True progress quietly and persistently moves along without notice." – St. Francis of Assisi

If you are doing things so that someone notices you, then maybe you should not be surprised when you do not get the results that you were hoping to get. As soon as you make a decision to BE for someone else you are not being true to yourself, and you give up all your power as well as the responsibility for your own life. If your BEing in this moment creates a result that is in alignment with your path, then and only then are you being true to yourself.

BE because you want to BE, not "because of" someone else. If you continue to do things "because of" then you are allowing your reasons and excuses to hold you in place. In the end you are OK with this because you just made yourself "right."

Be aware of your past by learning from it, but keep it out of your future. Your future is always OPEN. Even if something worked for you in the past it still doesn't belong in your future as a set way of BEing. Your possibilities are endless...progress is inevitable through change. Gather knowledge to create your wisdom to remain PRESENT, because this moment is the only thing that truly matters.

Think about it...

Love and Sunshine,
Tracy

Do it anyway

"*People are unreasonable, illogical and self-centered. Love them anyway. If you do good, people will accuse you of selfish, ulterior motives. Do good anyway. If you are successful, you will win false friends and true enemies. Succeed anyway. The good you do today will be forgotten tomorrow. Do good anyway. Honesty and frankness make you vulnerable. Be honest and frank anyway. The biggest person with the biggest ideas can be shot down by the smallest person with the smallest mind. Think big anyway. What you spend years building may be destroyed overnight. Build anyway. People really need help but may attack if you help them. Help people anyway. Give the world the best you have and you might get kicked in the teeth. Give the world the best you've got anyway.*" – Dr. Kent M. Keith*

If you really want something in your life, what is it going to take or what do you need in order for you to put in the effective effort to do whatever it takes to make it happen? Sometimes people choose to live in fear of a certain result…maybe because they may think they will not be able to handle the result they fear may happen. That's a great story you are telling yourself. If you fear that you cannot handle it, then maybe it's not something you really want? If it is something you really want then why not take a chance with your effort?

I live by this philosophy: "The only thing that stands between a person and what they want from life is often merely the will to try." If you do not put actions behind your talk, how can you ever be surprised that you do not have the result you are after? If you never put the effort in to get what you want you may forever wonder "what if?" What's holding you back from taking that next step? If you never ask, the answer is always no. Being vulnerable is a gift. It's in our vulnerability that we become who we truly are. Wouldn't you rather know than not know and wonder? Also, if you do have something in your life that you want, wouldn't you rather keep doing things to continue to have that in your life, instead of just assuming it's always going to be there?

I wear my heart on my sleeve and I often get burned but you know what? I do it anyway! I will NEVER stop telling and showing people how much they mean to me through my actions and words, no matter what. Do not get me wrong—I am not a glutton for punishment...lol. If I put out a request and the request is denied, I will accept it and move on but in the end I will *always* know that I did whatever I needed to do to get the result I wanted. That's all that matters to me.

One of the greatest paradoxes of our physical senses is that our eyes actually show us what we believe, not what we see.

Think about it...

Love and Sunshine,
Tracy

Wealth is in your heart

"It is the heart that makes a man rich. He is rich according to what he is, not according to what he has." – Henry Ward Beecher

"Wealth is but dung, useful only when spread about." – Chinese Proverb

"Wealth belongs to the person who enjoys it and not to the one who keeps it." – Afghan Proverb

If you are continuously stuck in your chatter of "I do not have enough," how are you ever able to create space to have any more? One thing that I have learned over time is that in order for you to have more, you must first release what's there that isn't working for you in order to make "room" for more, capiche? This goes for more of anything you want in your life.

If you are not happy with or grateful for what you have at this moment, no more will ever come to you because you'll always be in a state of want and not in a state of BEing happy. Love people and use money. If it's the other way around then you'll be chasing something that can *never* make you happy! A good friend of mine said this to me yesterday: "People who have money spend their life trying to hide…They are unhappy in their lives but they all started as people who thought 'I will be happy if I have lots of money' Crazy world!"

The only thing I would change about the first quote is it's WHO you are that creates happiness in your life, not "what" you are…the "whats" in your life are just roles that you play along the way. It is in the "who" (or what *kind* of "what" you are) that you create your BEing and you choose that every day! I used to think that I was impatient and angry because my mother was impatient and angry and I had no choice over the matter because it was locked in…lol. It sounds even sillier when I type it out. I know I am a patient, loving, caring, compassionate, empathetic, joyous, passionate, beautiful, sensual woman…why? Because I CHOOSE to be, that's why!

In your search for more wealth in your life, first maybe open your eyes and really look at what you have already around you. What's really important

Tracy Friesen

to you? Is it your brand new 45-inch TV that makes you happy or is it the people around you who love you back that create the feelings you want in your life?

Think about it...

Love and Sunshine,
Tracy

Refuse to be a victim

> *"We focus on the negatives, losing ourselves in the problem. We point to our unhappy circumstances to rationalize our negative feelings. This is the easy way out. It takes, after all, very little effort to feel victimized."* – Elizabeth Kubler-Ross

> *"A man may fall many times but he won't be a failure until he says someone pushed him."* – Elmer G. Letterman

> *"The most potent weapon in the hands of the oppressor is the mind of the oppressed."* – Steven Biko

Steven has a good point, as the victim you are an easy target. As you let your negative thoughts take over, it's easy to trigger you into your own negative tapes that you believe about yourself. You made these decisions about yourself when you were five and you did not have the wisdom to question your assumptions, and these tapes have been playing ever since. Would you let your five-year-old make important life decisions for you? Really? Well, that's what you are doing on a daily basis when you play the victim. Forgive yourself. Reassure the "little you" inside you that now you have the knowledge and wisdom to take care of him or her, and that nothing will ever harm them ever again.

A good friend of mine said in her "Thoughts Become Things" message yesterday: "When I am not feeling well, I have thoughts like 'poor me.' Then it really doesn't matter what anyone says to me that day, I think people are mean, I am the victim of my circumstances and throughout the day with these thoughts and by my language being snappy or upset, I begin to feel worse and usually by the end of the day I am completely exhausted." You see how easy it for us to fall into the trap of our own victimizations?

I love what Elmer has to say in his quote. As soon as we blame another for our situations we fall into the roll of victim…and how's that working for you? Lol…I love Dr. Phil! When you start living the role of "poor me" you immediately give up your own power and the responsibility of your own life. Why do you think it works for so many people to play the victim? It's so easy to point fingers elsewhere when, honestly, the ONLY place to look is in the mirror.

Think about it...

Love and Sunshine,
Tracy

March 26th

Remembering Nigel

"The only way to deal with loss—as a horribly unwelcome guest that you know will show up eventually. And so you deny it and reject it and ignore it and laugh in its face. You toss it out into the street and push it away and fight it off, and only it has landed square in your lap, only then do you deal with it." – Michael Johnsson

"When you are sorrowful look again in your heart, and you shall see that in truth you are weeping for that which has been your delight." – Kahlil Gibran

"The Last Battle: If it should be that I grow frail and weak, And pain should keep me from my sleep, Then will you do what must be done, For this, the last battle, can't be won. You will be sad I understand, But don't let grief then stay your hand, For on this day, more than the rest, Your love and friendship must stand the test. We have had so many happy years, You wouldn't want me to suffer so. When the time comes, please, let me go. Take me to where to my needs they'll tend, Only, stay with me till the end And hold me firm and speak to me, Until my eyes no longer see. I know in time you will agree, It is a kindness you do to me. Although my tail its last has waved, From pain and suffering I have been saved. Don't grieve that it must be you, Who has to decide this thing to do; We've been so close, we two, these years, Don't let your heart hold any tears." – Unknown

I am a bit at a loss for words today. Today I had to do something I have never had to do before. Although thoughts of doubt ran across my mind I know that I did the right thing. Releasing the physical form of a loved one is a difficult thing to do and what I know is that Nigel's spirit lives on with us and within us every day.

Today I am remembering my friend who has been with me longer than I can remember…please raise your glass with me as I honor him with LOVE and Sunshine, to Nigel!

With loving regards,
Tracy

Tracy Friesen

Ask your body for advice

"The body has its own way of knowing, a knowing that has little to do with logic, and much to do with truth, little to do with control, and much to do with acceptance, little to do with division and analysis, and much to do with union."
— Marilyn Sewell

"When you are saying that you are happy and you are not, there will be a disturbance in your breathing. Your breathing cannot be natural. It is impossible." — Osho

"Our inner guidance comes to us through our feelings and body wisdom first— not through intellectual understanding…The intellect works best in service to our intuition, our inner guidance, soul, God or higher power—whichever term we choose for the spiritual energy that animates life." — Christiane Northrup

Now it all makes sense…why our intuition gets stronger as we accept our emotions and what our own bodies are telling us. If we stay stuck in having to understand things at an intellectual level we may never fully stand in our own power of the wisdom of our intuition. Wow…for me this is HUGE. There is no wonder for me now why I blocked myself for so long. I didn't like being vulnerable in my emotions. What I get now is that even though I am vulnerable in my emotions I will not die because of them, and I am BEing true to myself by honoring what's there for me. My body has been giving me signs all along and now that I live in the present I am able to breathe deeper and see clearly what's available to me. When I connect with my own body I am able to just BE who I am without fear and without concern of what anyone else thinks.

Be still…open your mind to the possibility that you already have all your answers available to you. Be open to hearing what your own body is telling you. Your inner guidance or higher power will not lead you astray. Do not be fooled by your ego wanting to take over. If what you hear is self-serving, most likely it is your ego talking and not the gentle voice of your inner guidance. Your inner guidance will ALWAYS come from unconditional love. Learn to tell the difference. If you are able to shut your ego off and live from your inner guidance, what will you be able to create for yourself?

Think about it…

Love and Sunshine,
Tracy

Imagine your ideal future

"Your imagination is your preview to life's coming attractions." – Albert Einstein

"Change is created by those whose imaginations are bigger than their circumstances" – Unknown

"My life is my message." – Mahatma Ghandi

When is the last time you picked up a crayon and just let your imagination flow? When is the last time you allowed yourself to get swept away in your daydreams? Honestly, when is the last time you even used your ability to create…anything?

What message are you leaving with those whom you meet on a daily basis? One philosophy I live by is, "Go big or go home." What's the point of doing anything if you are not going to put in the effective effort to create what you want in your life? If you just sit back and expect things to go the way you want them to go without using your creative mind to make it happen, how could you ever be surprised if you end up not having what it is that you want?

Why are you putting conditions and reasons before your dreams? Why not let your imagination have no boundaries? Why not create every possibility to get what you want? Why not live the life you want through the creativity of your imagination? You never know what you'll end up with unless you can first create it in your imagination.

Think about it…

Love and Sunshine,
Tracy

What is love?

"When mystics use the word love, they use it very carefully—in the deeply spiritual sense, where to love is to know; to love is to act. If you really love, from the depths of your Consciousness, that love gives you a native wisdom. You perceive the needs of others intuitively and clearly, with detachment from any personal desires; and you know how to act creatively to meet those needs, dexterously surmounting any obstacle that comes in the way. Such is the immense, driving power of love." – Eknath Easwaran

"Therefore, when I say that I love, it is not I who love, but in reality Love who acts through me. Love is not so much something I do as something that I am. Love is not a doing but a state of being—a relatedness, a connectedness to another mortal, an identification with her or him that simply flows within me and through me, independent of my intentions or my efforts." – Robert A. Johnson

"When you are aware that you are the force that is Life, anything is possible. Miracles happen all the time, because those miracles are performed by the heart. The heart is in direct communion with the human soul, and when the heart speaks, even with the resistance of the head, something inside you changes; your heart opens another heart, and true love is possible." – Don Miguel Ruiz

Do you think we have lost the meaning of what it is to love? People get so caught up in what they want that they forget that in order to create true love they must do things unconditionally—do things for another because they are moved to do those things, not out of expectation.

Think about your partner right now...can you think of something that he or she would really enjoy receiving? What is it? Is it a hug from behind, a kiss on their neck and a whispered how beautiful they are to you in their ear? Is it recognizing and acknowledging them for what they do for you? Is it surprising them with their favorite flower? Or is it just simply saying to them that you are honored that they choose to be with you and that you are grateful for them being a part of your life?

The happiness that is created from one selfless act will permeate through everyone and everything...a sense of calm safety may be created. That special warmth that is shared between two people gives you that sense that no matter what, everything is OK. Do not believe me? Try it! See what is created for you by doing a selfless act. If you cannot remember what it is that your partner likes...ASK! Start asking questions. Get curious about them and what they hold important. Their tastes may have changed. You never know unless you ask. They may have discovered something new that makes them smile, do you know what that is? No? Then ask, silly!

I invite you to explore the possibilities of doing one selfless act for your partner every day. Open your heart to their heart. Make a commitment to yourself that before you lay down to rest at the end of your day that you will LOVE your partner the way *they* want to be loved without any personal attachment or condition. You never know what will be created for you by being unconditionally in love with your partner.

Think about it...

Love and Sunshine,
Tracy

Attitude is more important than facts

"There is nothing either good or bad, but thinking makes it so." – William Shakespeare

"No one can make you feel inferior without your consent." – Eleanor Roosevelt

Our attitude says it all. It is within our attitude that we create our experiences. Your attitude is ALWAYS your choice. If you have a poor attitude, how would you ever expect to have extraordinary things happen to you?

Think about it…

Love and Sunshine,
Tracy

See that light within

"People are like stained-glass windows. They sparkle and shine when the sun is out, but when the darkness sets in their true beauty is revealed only if there is a light from within." – Elisabeth Kubler-Ross

"The moment we begin to fear the opinions of others and hesitate to tell the truth that is in us, and from motives of policy are silent when we should speak, the divine floods of light and life no longer flow into our souls." – Elizabeth Cady Stanton

"Moral cowardice that keeps us from speaking our minds is as dangerous to this country as irresponsible talk. The right way is not always the popular and easy way. Standing for right when it is unpopular is a true test of moral character." – Margaret Chase Smith

Dare to be different...dare to stand out...dare to be the leader that you are! Who are you BEing when you are faced with a situation that morally doesn't jive with you? Do you stand up and speak your truth or do you cower under someone else's belief in fear of their opinion? The very second you choose to not BE who you are, you give up your power. Life stops flowing into you and through you. You become stagnant. It is not an easy thing to stand for what works for you in your life, but it truly is a simple thing.

When the darkness settles around you, go to faith, not fear. Go inside and see the true beauty that exists in you...in every one of us. See that light. Start to expand and grow it until it overtakes the darkness. If you always see yourself shining from within as a beautiful creature of your Divine, how would you ever feel that you are alone in this world?

Think about it...

Love and Sunshine,
Tracy

April 1st

Be aware of your thinking

"There is a thought in your mind right now. The longer you hold on to it, the more you dwell upon it, the more life you give to that thought. Give it enough life, and it will become real. So make sure the thought is indeed a great one." – *Ralph Marston*

"Man is made or unmade by himself. In the armory of thought he forges the weapons by which he destroys himself. He also fashions the tools with which he builds for himself heavenly mansions of joy and strength and peace." – *James Allen*

I love how Mr. Allen portrays his message. I am a gamer. I am a geek at heart! For years now, I've been playing RPGs (role-playing games) as a way to deal with stress or at times escape my own life. What I love about this genre of game is that you are always seeking to better your character—making it stronger in its strength, quicker in its dexterity, smarter in its intelligence, more knowledgeable in its wisdom, healthier so it can withstand more hits, or adding more luck so it can land more damage more often. How you build your character all depends on what your goal is for the game. There comes, with playing, great thinking and strategy on how to create the best character possible. How do you create the best? You quest, of course!

I see a similarity in real life. We are all playing in a quest-based society. We establish goals and we set out on our quests and missions to complete those goals on a daily basis. How we think about ourselves on these quests is where we determine whether or not we are going to be successful or unsuccessful in completing them. If you think you are not quick enough to get by the obstacles and mobs (monsters) along your way, you will lose and most likely get wiped out and you may experience a sense of loss in time and energy…hmmm…sound familiar? It sure does to me. If you know that you have created your character to the best of your ability, you will be successful in getting the rare treasure from the end boss mob… same goes in life.

Sometimes along the way you may need help, so you call upon your Guild members to give you a hand. Everyone has their purpose and their own special skill; when combined in your Perfect Party there is nothing that you and your team cannot accomplish or take down! Hmmm... sounds like something I tell my daughter all the time. If you do not know the answer or how to do something, what do you do? You ask for help! There is always someone you know who knows the answer to your question or how to complete whatever it is that you are working on.

Look around you...are the people who you interact with on a daily basis there to help you complete your quests in life? Your thinking has brought you those people in your life. If it's not working for you then maybe it's time for you to teleport to your local NPC (non-playing character) and get yourself a Re-Stat Stone so you can start to rebuild your "toon"— and the first place to start is within your thoughts.

Think about it...

Love and Sunshine,
Tracy

April 2nd

The art of listening

"To love for the sake of being loved is human, but to love for the sake of loving is angelic."– Alphonse de Lamartine

"When hearts listen, angels sing." – Unknown

"Tell me and I forget; show me and I remember; involve me and I understand."
– Anonymous

When is the last time that you actually "listened"? Or have you been caught in just thinking about what you want to say next and found yourself just waiting for an opportunity to unleash your thoughts without even hearing what the other person is saying? How's that been working for you? Do you often find that you are misunderstood and that no one gets you? Are you surprised? What about treating people the way you would like to be treated? If you want to be heard, do you not think that learning the art of listening would be a great place to start? I sure do. I think that is why we were given two ears and only one mouth. We should be listening twice as much as we are talking. Why not, the next time you are with someone, try to not say anything from your own thoughts and just mirror back in your own words what the person has said to you? Not only will that person know that they have been heard but you will improve your own listening skills in the process. This is a great way to remove assumptions as you will able hear what that person has to say and they will be able to clarify if you have misunderstood what they may have meant.

What do you think you would be able to create in your life by developing your art of listening?

Think about it…

Love and Sunshine,
Tracy

Get in control of your anger

"Anger makes you smaller, while forgiveness forces you to grow beyond what you were." -- Cherie Carter-Scott

"The wind of anger blows out the lamp of intelligence." – Anonymous

"Anger helps strengthen out a problem like a fan helps straighten out a pile of papers." – Susan Mancotte

"When you feel "dog tired" at night, it may be because you growled all day." – Anonymous

"A fool gives full vent to his anger, but a wise man keeps himself under control." – Proverbs 29:11

Have you ever felt out of control when you were angry? Did you accomplish anything when you were in your rage? When you finally calmed down did you feel a sense of sadness, perhaps? Although anger is an emotion we all need to feel at times, and it's 100 percent OK to be angry, it's your choice of action when you are in that state that creates your reality in the next moment. If what you are doing with your anger is not achieving your desired result, you may want to consider being someone different in your anger. Maybe if you are patient for a moment in your anger, you may not have to regret any words or actions? Pausing… becoming aware of your own body signals that are telling you over and over, hey this doesn't work for me. You may be able to be in control of a previously out-of-control situation. Sometimes the best thing to do is to be silent…say nothing…do nothing. If you allow another to trigger you into your own choices of negative unreasonableness, you are giving up your power and you and only you are responsible for your results and consequences. Instead of growling like an angry dog, next time why not purrrr like an adorable kitten? You might be surprised at how your anger will dissipate into a calmness that may lead you into your JOY.

Think about it…

Love and Sunshine,
Tracy

Question your intention

"Men are more accountable for their motives, than for anything else..." –
Archibald Alexander

"A good intention clothes itself with power." – *Ralph Waldo Emerson*

This reminds me of a parable I heard a few years back: Carrots, Eggs
or Coffee

A young woman went to her grandmother and told her about her life and
how things were so hard for her. She did not know how she was going to
make it and wanted to give up. She was tired of fighting and struggling. It
seemed as one problem was solved, a new one would pop up.

Her grandmother took her to the kitchen. She filled three pots with
water and placed each on a high fire, and soon the pots came to boil. In
the first pot she placed carrots, in the second she placed eggs, and in the
last she placed ground coffee beans. She let them sit and boil without
saying a word. In about twenty minutes she turned off the burners. She
fished the carrots out and placed them in a bowl. She pulled the eggs out
and placed them in a bowl. Then she ladled out the coffee and placed it
in a bowl.

Turning to her granddaughter, she said, "Tell me what you see."

"Carrots, eggs, and coffee," she replied. Her grandmother brought her
closer and asked her to feel the carrots. She did and noted that they were
soft. The grandmother then asked the granddaughter to take an egg and
break it. After pulling off the shell, she observed the hard-boiled egg.
Finally, the grandmother asked the granddaughter to sip the coffee. The
granddaughter smiled as she tasted its rich aroma, then asked,

"What does it mean, Grandmother?"

Her grandmother explained that each of these objects had faced the
same adversity: boiling water. Each reacted differently. The carrot went
in strong, hard, and unrelenting. However, after being subjected to the
boiling water, it softened and became weak. The egg had been fragile. Its
thin outer shell had protected its liquid interior, but after sitting through

the boiling water, its inside became hardened. The ground coffee beans were unique, however. After they were in the boiling water, they had changed the water.

"Which are you?" she asked her granddaughter.

What is your intention when you face your adversity? How will you use your power to get through to the other side? Will you be like the carrot and give up your power and become weak, be like the egg and stand still and become hard against life from the inside out, or will you be like the coffee and adapt your power to permeate with positivity the people and your environment around you? Your success and your happiness are ALWAYS your choice! It now makes sense to me that wherever I go I can always smell the rich aroma of a freshly brewed cup of coffee.

Think about it…

Love and Sunshine,
Tracy

Really be there for another

"Listening is a magnetic and strange thing, a creative force. You can see that when you think how the friends that really listen to us are the ones we move toward, and we want to sit in their radius as though it did us good, like ultraviolet rays." – Brenda Ueland

"So when you are listening to somebody, completely, attentively, then you are listening not only to the words, but also to the feeling of what is being conveyed, to the whole of it, not part of it." – Jiddu Krishnamurti

"The first duty of love is to listen." – Paul Tillich

Have you been working on developing your art of listening? No? Hmmm…are you surprised that you are getting the same results in your life? Really? Listening is an important key to being unconditionally in love with someone. Hearing what they say and being able to mirror back to them their feelings is a way for you to understand the one you love. It doesn't mean that you have to agree or even like what they are saying, but if you are able to accept that person for who they are in that moment you will BE truly loving without your own agenda behind your BEingness. You will just BE loving to your partner, make sense?

If you quiet your mind to your own thoughts of only getting what you want and open yourself and your heart and truly listen to your partner, what do you think could be created for yourself in the end?

Think about it…

Love and Sunshine,
Tracy

Life is a mirror

"Everything that irritates us about others can lead us to an understanding of ourselves." – C. G. Jung

"We discover in ourselves what others hide from us and we recognize in others what we hide from ourselves." – Vauvenargues

If you've been listening you may have heard me say this before. When you go into "I don't like it when…" the first place to look is in the mirror. It is easier to point fingers away from you and say it's because of "x" that "y" happened to me. In reality, you are the only person making decisions for yourself and your life. If you do not like someone's behaviour, before attacking them, first look within and ask yourself, "Why does this bother me so much?" If you truly want to take on your life and live the most extraordinary life possible you will be willing to see that what you do not like about that other person is really what you do not like about yourself.

Think about it…

Love and Sunshine,
Tracy

April 7th

By Fear or by Faith

"Once a little girl and her father were crossing a bridge. The father was kind of scared so he asked his little daughter, 'Sweetheart, please hold my hand so that you don't fall into the river.'

The little girl said, 'No, Dad. You hold my hand.'

'What's the difference?' asked the puzzled father.

'There's a big difference,' replied the little girl. 'If I hold your hand and something happens to me, chances are that I may let your hand go. But if you hold my hand, I know for sure that no matter what happens, you will never let my hand go." – Unknown

This parable brings up a whole bunch of things for me. How are you approaching the people you love and care about in your life? Are you like the father, offering yourself in fear and really putting it all on the other person to do all the work? Or are you like the daughter, able to ask for what you need in complete faith that no matter what happens, you are "safe" in your request?

How you look at things in your life determines how your success, your prosperity, your abundance, your joy, your passion, your happiness, and your love will happen in your life. Will it be surrounded by fear or by faith? It's your choice.

Think about it…

My request to you…Will you hold my hand?

Love and Sunshine,
Tracy

Go one more round

*"To try is to risk failure. But risk must be taken because the greatest hazard of
life is to risk nothing. The person who risks nothing does nothing, has nothing,
is nothing. He may avoid suffering and sorrow, but he simply cannot learn, feel,
change, grow, live, and love." – Leo Buscaglia*

*"A life spent in making mistakes is not only more honorable, but more useful
than a life spent doing nothing." – George Bernard Shaw*

"Only those who risk going too far can know how far they can go." – Unknown

Are you happy with your life? Have you let your "have to's" get you
down and in the way of your true happiness? When did you stop dreaming and striving for what you really want in your life? If you stop risking
you may avoid sorrow, but you will not ever experience the happiest part
of your life. Do you want to go through life stuck in a rut of routine and
complacency? How's that working for you now? There's always a way
to get what you want in your life—ALWAYS! It all depends on what
you are willing to do to get it. If it means simplifying your life, then do
it! If it means that for a short period of time you go without luxuries,
then do it! If it means that you may have to put faith before fear, then
DOOOO EEET!!!

What do you have to lose? There's no such thing as security. It's a story
you've made up in your head. If you give up your meaning to the word
try, which for most people is a reason or excuse to be able to say, "It's OK
I failed, at least I tried…" HA! Such a cop out! Be like Yoda: "Do or do
not, there is no try." Another good excuse is "I'm too busy." HA! Bulllll-
loan-neeeee! Just another excuse for you to remain exactly where you
are, complaining that your life is boring and you'll never get what you
want. Be willing to be open to what's available to you and for you. Take
on your life with FULL awareness!

What have I said before? The only way you fail is if you stop working
towards what you want to create in your life. So what if you make a
thousand mistakes? Get up, dust yourself off and go for one thousand
and one! Do not stop six inches from *your* gold! Be like Rocky: "Going

one more round when you don't think you can, that's what makes all the difference in your life!"

Think about it...

Love and Sunshine,
Tracy

Love is the answer

"Love doesn't make the world go round. Love is what makes the ride worth-while." – Franklin P. Jones

"If you love someone you would be willing to give up everything for them, but if they loved you back they'd never ask you to." – Anonymous

"The time we have to share our love is brief, it lasts only a lifetime." – Anonymous

"Love is patient, love is kind. It does not envy, it does not boast, it is not proud. It is not rude, it is not self-seeking. It is not easily angered, it keeps no record of wrongs. Love does not delight in evil, but rejoices with the truth. It always protects, always trusts, always hopes, always perseveres. Love never fails."– I Corinthians 13:4-8 (I love this passage! It was read at my wedding.)

Love is in the air…why am I thinking of Bambi and Thumper and being all twitterpated? Is it because it's spring? Or that the ducks are back in the yard, both male and female together? Who doesn't want to think about the joys of being in love? When you are in love you can feel ten feet tall and bulletproof…no, wait…or is that when you are drunk…lol. It's all the same if you ask me. Drunk on gin or drunk on love, you have the courage to take on anything. (But I highly suggest that you stick to love!)

Love is a choice that you make from moment to moment. You may feel inspired by love and guided to create a choice full of wisdom, to be able to BE the best person you are and create the good life you always dreamed of living. When in love, you love the other person, not for what or who they are, but for who *you* are when you are with them…always remember that.

I love thinking about love, sharing love and being in love. Everything seems possible and there is nothing that stands in your way. Love brings hope and excitement to your life. Being in love brings you things to look forward to: unexpected surprises, stolen kisses, whispered secrets, knowing looks, passion to follow…wink, wink. Where there is love there is no competition, no conflict, no resentment, no fear—just love. It's how I have taught my daughter; I'll ask her, "What is the answer to every-thing?" "Love!" she'll say.

I will leave you with this to think about:

"Love is a symbol of eternity. It wipes out all sense of time, destroying all memory of a beginning and all fear of an end." – Unknown.

Love and Sunshine,
Tracy

Valuing the moment

"...the only time you ever have in which to learn anything or see anything or feel anything, or express any feeling or emotion, or respond to an event, or grow, or heal, is this moment, because this is the only moment any of us ever gets. You're only here now; you're only alive in this moment." – Jon Kabat-Zinn

"Very few of us know how much we can put into life if we use it properly, wisely, and economically. Let us economize our time—lifetimes ebb away before we wake up, and that is why we do not realize the value of the immortal time God has given us." – Paramahansa Yogananda

Stop. Look around you...what is happening in this moment? Are you being threatened by anyone or anything? Open your eyes—the sooner you get out of your story the sooner you can start living your life, happy. The feelings that you attach to any event in your life is the meaning or the story you have attached to that particular event. Let me repeat that... The feelings that you attach to any event in your life is the meaning or the story you have attached to that particular event. Did it really happen that way? Or have you attached so many adjectives and adverbs around your words that you don't even know what really happened anymore? If you are willing to take on your life and live it happily, you'll be willing to look at how you affect your own life with your own stories.

Here are two great examples of how I know you are living from your story and not taking on your life. One would be dealing with the end of a relationship and the other would be dealing with betrayal. We have all been there so we can all relate...trust me.

Let's look at betrayal first. What are some of the phrases that come up for you when thinking about an event in your life in which you feel that you were betrayed by another? "They stabbed me in the back" is probably the most common phrase used when dealing with betrayal. OK... really? Did someone actually come up to you and stab you with a sharp object in your back? Really? No, I didn't think so...You want to be sooo dramatic describing the betrayal to another so that they will feel for you and allow you to remain as a victim. Oh poor me...look what happened to me...blah blah blah. What is betrayal? The truth of the matter is that betrayal has nothing to do with the other person. Did you hear me? I said betrayal has NOTHING to do with the other person. Yeah, you heard me right. Betrayal concerns trust…the more you trusted the other person, the greater distress you may feel when that trust has been compromised. What you may not be willing to see is that you are more upset with yourself for allowing yourself to trust that other person…and the only person who is responsible for the decision to trust that person is you. You are really just upset with yourself. You may not be able to accept this, so you may point fingers elsewhere to remove the responsibility from yourself and on to another, so that you can remain the overdramatic victim. How's that working for you for bringing happiness to your life?

OK, now let's look at what story we create around when a relationship ends. What's one of the most common phrases we use: "My heart is broken." Hmmm…really? Check in on yourself right now. Do you have a pulse? Are you still alive? If you are reading this then I guess you are OK and your heart is working perfectly fine. Even using phrases like "losing love" or "lost love" is a story. If you lost the love where is it? You cannot lose a feeling; you just choose to feel it or choose not to feel it…it is always a choice. Here's another statement often heard: "It hurts so much I'm barely breathing." Hmmm…if that is the case, you need to go see your doctor because if you are barely breathing then there IS something seriously wrong with the physical you.

What if the other person has chosen to be with someone else? Ooh, then we have stabbing in the back, a broken heart and barely breathing… lol. GET OUT OF YOUR STORY! What has happened? Someone has made a decision to no longer be involved in your life…end of story.

Here's an exercise that I love to share with people. 1) On a piece of paper draw a large circle on the left-hand side of the page that takes up almost half the paper. At the top of this circle you will write "What happened?" then describe the situation. 2) Then draw another circle on the right-hand side of the page, just as large as the left one so that the circles are almost touching but not quite. At the top of this circle you will write "This is what I made it mean," then describe everything that you made the events that happened mean, and be as descriptive as you can. 3) Now draw a small tiny circle between the two circles, joining them both together. This circle is called "This is the truth." For every meaning that you wrote down in the circle on the right, ask yourself, "Is this the truth?"

Here is an example of how it may look: 1) In the "What happened" circle you could write: My partner/spouse didn't get me anything for Valentine's Day. 2) In the "This is what I made it mean" circle you could write: They didn't get me anything because they do not love me. They didn't get me anything because I am not worth it. They didn't get me anything because I am unlovable. They didn't get me anything because they do not care about me. They didn't get me anything because they are seeing someone else. They didn't get me anything because they are not attracted to me. They didn't get me anything because they think I'm ugly. They didn't get me anything because they think I'm fat. OK, I think you get the picture…and I am sure you can come up with a whole bunch more. Trust me, I've been there. The truth is coming up next and this is where you will either take on your life and get responsible for it or you will continue to hide behind playing the victim and remain unhappy in your life—the choice is yours. 3) So, for every meaning you wrote, you ask yourself "Is this the truth?" Is it the truth that they didn't get me anything because they do not love me? The answer is no, it is not the truth. They didn't get me anything because they didn't get me anything, end of story. Is it the truth that they didn't get me anything because I am not worth it? The answer is no, it is not the truth. They didn't get me anything because they didn't get me anything, end of story. Is it the truth that they didn't get me anything because I am unlovable? The answer is no, it is not the truth. They didn't get me anything because they didn't get me anything, end of story. Is it the truth that they didn't get me anything because they do not care about me? The answer is no, it is not the truth. They didn't get me anything because they didn't get me anything, end of story. Is it the truth that they didn't get me anything because they are seeing someone else? The answer is no, it is not the truth. They didn't get me anything because they didn't get me anything, end of story. Is it the truth that they didn't get me anything because they are not attracted to me? The answer is no, it is not the truth. They didn't get me anything because they didn't get me anything, end of story. Is it the truth that they didn't get me anything because they think I'm ugly? The answer is no, it is not the truth. They didn't get me anything because they didn't get me anything, end of story. Is it the truth that they didn't get me anything because they think I'm fat? The answer is no, it is not the truth. They didn't get me anything because they didn't get me anything, end of story.

OK…you see how that works? Now apply it to whatever event it is that you are upset about and see what happens. If you need any help with it you can always contact me and I can help step you through it. I love you and I want to help support you taking on your life and getting responsible for it so that you can live the most extraordinary life possible! By doing the above exercise you will see how you have let your stories run your life. You may be able to understand that whatever meaning you have attached to that particular event is not the truth.

Choose to be direct with what has happened in your life and get straight with the facts, not the story. The more direct you are with what you experience, the easier it is to accept the situation (whether you like what happened or not) and just get back to being happy in this moment.

This is my request to you, for one day when talking to other people do not use any adjectives, adverbs, similes or metaphors to describe anything that has happened to you. You never know what you can create for yourself when you are able to be straight and speak directly.

Think about it…

Love and Sunshine,
Tracy

It is OK to make mistakes

"Accomplishment of purpose is better than making a profit." – Nigerian Proverb

"Better to do something imperfectly than to do nothing flawlessly." – Robert Schuller

"Aim for success, not perfection. Never give up your right to be wrong, because then you will lose the ability to learn new things and move forward with your life. Remember that fear always lurks behind perfectionism. Confronting your fears and allowing yourself the right to be human can, paradoxically, make yourself a happier and more productive person." – Dr. David M. Burns

It is 100 percent OK to make mistakes. This is what I tell my daughter all the time. If we didn't make mistakes then we would never learn or grow. If you are upset because you are striving to be perfect all the time maybe you just need to realize that you are already perfect as you are.

Think about it…

Love and Sunshine,
Tracy

Let go of the past

"Your journey has molded you for your greater good, and it was exactly what it needed to be. Don't think that you've lost time. There is no short-cutting to life. It took each and every situation you have encountered to bring you to the now. And now is right on time." – Asha Tyson

"The next message you need is right where you are." – Ram Dass

"Getting over a painful experience is much like crossing monkey bars. You have to let go at some point in order to move forward." – Unknown

"There's no need to miss someone from your past. There's a reason they didn't make it to your future." – Unknown

How many of us hold onto our past so desperately that we lose who we are in the process? We attach ourselves so definitely to who we were, that we may forget to BE who we are. Living from your past removes any chance of the possibility of ever living free or happy. Why? Because you have already set in motion a repetition of the experiences from your past by having decided what is going to happen. You will never choose to be anything different or experience anything new. You may then feel that you are helpless and have no choice, but realistically you already made your choice.

Events happen and people come and go in our lives. Not letting go of what we attach to the events and people in our past may create blocks that prevent us from moving on in our lives. I come from the philosophy that everything happens for a reason, especially when it comes to people entering and leaving our lives. People enter our lives to teach us something about ourselves. If they are no longer in our lives, then they have fulfilled their part and it's up to you to figure out what it was that you were to learn from that experience. It may be that you or that person has changed to the extent that it's necessary to let go of the relationship or friendship so that each of you can fulfill your life path. Maybe that other person was there to teach you something about how treat others in your life? You will know the reason when you know the reason.

If you continually put your past into your future, you will never open up the possibility of experiencing anything new in your life and you may remain bored, unfulfilled and unhappy. Accept your past—I never said you had to like it, just accept it—because you cannot change what has happened. Accepting your past is the key to leaving it in your past so that you can BE whomever you want in this moment and not be a predetermined you.

Think about it…

Love and Sunshine,
Tracy

Be like the bird

"Hope is like a bird that senses the dawn and carefully starts to sing while it is still dark." – Anonymous

"We all have big changes in our lives that are more or less a second chance." – Harrison Ford

"What seems to us as bitter trials are often blessings in disguise" – Oscar Wilde

No matter what happens in our lives there is always a reason to be learned. How do you look at the big changes in your life? Do you cloud them with fear or do you open yourself up to greater possibilities of hope? If you haven't found your reason yet it's OK. It's just like Garth Brooks said "Some of God's greatest gifts are unanswered prayers." Be like the bird and sing your song of faith in the darkness and know that your light is always there.

You can always start over in your life and choose to be whoever you want to be. Be the romantic sensual lover, be the caring consoling parent, be the trusting friend, be the hand to hold everything together. Just choose to BE the person you want to be, end of story! Second chances happen all the time…are you willing to be open to yours?

Think about it…

Love and Sunshine,
Tracy

Change your attitude change your life

"The greatest discovery of my generation is that man can alter his life simply by altering his attitude of mind." – William James

What have you put up today to block yourself from moving forward? Did you know that it only exists in your mind? Your attitude about your life will determine how happy you will be. No matter what is happening in your life at any given moment, you can change it. Adjust your attitude and your life will adjust accordingly. It is that simple.

If you want to remain in your story and not take responsibility for your life and continue to quote sad love songs as your existence, then there is no one to blame but you for what you are experiencing in your life. You are the only one in control of your thoughts, feelings and emotions. It has nothing to do with another person, ever. The sooner you realize that your feelings are not "because of" another person and you are feeling them only because you choose to feel them, the sooner you will be able to leave your story behind and start living happily in this moment.

Think about it…

Love and Sunshine,
Tracy

April 15th

Life really is simple

"It is only when we realize that life is taking us nowhere that it begins to have meaning." – P.D. Ouspensky

"All major mystical traditions have recognized that there is a paradox at the heart of the journey of return to Origin…Put simply, this is that we are already what we seek, and that what we are looking for on the Path with such an intensity of striving and passion and discipline is already within and around us at all moments. The journey and all its different ordeals are all emanations of the One Spirit that is manifesting everything in all dimensions; every rung of the ladder we climb toward final awareness is made of the divine stuff of awareness itself; Divine Consciousness is at once creating and manifesting all things and acting in and as all things in various states of self-disguise throughout all the different levels and dimensions of the universe." – Andrew Harvey

"Look at you, you madman, Screaming you are thirsty And are dying in a desert when all around you there is nothing but water!" – Kabir

"After changes upon changes, we are more or less the same." – Paul Simon

How many of us walk around with blinders on so we cannot see that what we are searching for is right in front of us or already within us? Life really is simple. Once you realize that it is up to you and only you to create or choose your own happiness, you may see that the imperfect you is really the perfect you.

Think about it…

Love and Sunshine,
Tracy

Tracy Friesen

Consciously create your own experiences

"If you're proactive, you don't have to wait for circumstances or other people to create perspective expanding experiences. You can consciously create your own."
– Stephen Covey

Nothing is lost upon a man who is bent upon growth; nothing wasted on one who is always preparing for…life by keeping eyes, mind and heart open to nature, men, books, experience…What he gathers serves him at unexpected moments in unforeseen ways." – Hamilton Wright Mabie

"Nurture great thoughts, for you will never go higher than your thoughts." – Benjamin Disraeli

If you are just sitting around waiting for something to happen in your life, how are you ever surprised that nothing is happening in your life? Or if you are just waiting for someone else to do something to make a difference your life, how is *that* working for you to bring about happiness for yourself? I bet you are sitting there steaming in your story that no one cares about you or no one loves you because they are not "doing" some-thing for you…geesh…really? The only way to get what you want is to be proactive and actually DO something. Your life is yours to command. Why would you ever want to put your happiness in the control of someone else? Do you really think that person is actually thinking about you? HA! If you do, then you are more ingrained in your story than you care to believe. A person, including yourself, is only ever concerned with what makes them happy. This might be hard to grasp but no one really thinks of another when they are concerned about their own happiness. You may feel happy around another but it is still you who feels happy, not "because of" another. So how can you just sit there and wish and hope for someone else to change *your* life?

Think about it…

Love and Sunshine,
Tracy

The power of silence

"Growth takes place in a person by working at a deep inner level in a sustained atmosphere of silence." – Dr. Ira Progoff

"Only when one is connected to one's own core is one connected to others… And, for me, the core, the inner spring, can best be refound through solitude." – Anne Morrow Lindbergh

"In the sweet territory of silence we touch the mystery. It's the place of reflection and contemplation, and it's the place where we can connect with the deep knowing, to the deep wisdom way." – Angeles Arrien

Have you ever felt like you were drowning from the sound of your own voice? Maybe it is a sign that you need to stop talking and start listening? It's time to start listening to those around you and especially listening to yourself. Once you hear what you have to say maybe the next step to attaining your happiness is to find the time to silence your mind. Then connect to your inner knowing and just BE.

Why is it that we are so afraid to be alone? I find that it is in our own comfort of being alone that we can truly be who we are. If you are not comfortable being by yourself, how can you ever be comfortable being around other people? Even though I know I was built to be with someone, it wasn't until I was able to love myself completely and be totally alone and comfortable with that solitude that I was able to allow someone else to be who they are. Then, through that acceptance, I was able to remain me and share a connection with someone.

If you are able to be by yourself you may then be able to stop taking things personally from other people, because no matter what they say it's never about you anyway. If you are sitting there thinking the world is going to end because you are not with someone, the first place to look is in the mirror because you are never alone. In order to ever truly be with someone you must be able to be OK with being by yourself and love yourself completely. If you are not OK with being by yourself or you do not love yourself completely, you will never be true to yourself and will always BE for someone else and we all know this does not work. Don't believe me? Really? How's it working for you now?

My request for you today is to take some time to be by yourself. Do whatever it is that you love to do, as long as it's only for you. Write down the things you love to do and especially things you love to do but do not do anymore. Make a commitment to doing these things for yourself on a weekly basis or better yet a daily basis. Get to know yourself again…love yourself! You are an amazing creature of your Divine all by yourself, not "because of" someone else.

Think about it…

Love and Sunshine,
Tracy

Tolerate the indifferences

"Your neighbor's vision is as true for him as your own vision is true for you."
– Miguel de Unamuno

"In the practice of tolerance, one's enemy is the best teacher." – *Dalai Lama*

Everyone has their own perception of every event that happens in their life. Two people who experience the same thing will perceive the event in a different way. A good friend of mine had this to share with me the other day: "The truth is that no two people have ever met. You are who I believe you to be. I believe my thoughts about you, so that is who you are. It's a perception that lives in my head alone…just a different way of lookin' at things eh?" So if two people really haven't met then you really do not "know" anyone. You have your own perception of who they are but do not know who they really are. If you think someone is a certain way, they really are not because it's just what *you* create about them in your own head.

This is where what the Dalai Lama says about tolerance may come into play. If you are tolerant of those things you do not like in others, you may be able to allow them to just be who they are. What you do not like about them is actually what you do not like about yourself and has absolutely nothing to do with the other person. If you believe something about someone (including yourself), it is only in your mind that it exists.

Think about it…

Love and Sunshine,
Tracy

Be like the duck

"Fear less, hope more, eat less, chew more, whine less, breathe more, talk less, say more, hate less, love more, and good things will be yours." – Swedish Proverb

"Life is like a game of cards. The hand that is dealt you represents determinism; the way you play it is free will." – Jawaharal Nehru

"Most of the shadows of this life are caused by our standing in our own sunshine." – Ralph Waldo Emerson

How long are you going to stand in your own way? Your fear only exists in your own head. All your "what ifs" may never happen so why dwell on them? Wouldn't you rather just be happy in this moment with whatever is happening? Through your acceptance of your life you will gain your happiness. Remember, I never said you had to like it—just accept it. If you also develop tolerance you may then become like the duck and everything will then just roll off your back. There's no need to hang onto anything anyway, and you can just keep swimming along…happily…quack.

Think about it…

Love and Sunshine,
Tracy

Love life and yourself

"Being deeply loved by someone gives you strength while loving someone deeply gives you courage." – Lao Tzu

"It matters not Who you love, Where you love, Why you love, When you love, Or how you love, It matters only that you love." – John Lennon

"Why not go out on a limb? Isn't that where the fruit is?" – Frank Scully

W hy is it that we hold back in loving when we do not feel loved back? In my opinion, that may be the perfect time to be more loving towards another. Also, with the things that we really want in our lives, why is it that we sit and wait for things to happen when what we should really be doing is anything and everything to make it happen? If you didn't get what you wanted, can you really say that you did everything you possibly could to get it? If yes, well then kudos to you! If not, how can you be surprised at the result you got? As Frank says, why not go out on a limb for what you want? If you do not ever make the request the answer is ALWAYS no, so why not give yourself a head start with a 50-50 chance rather than one hundred percent no?

Think about it…

Love and Sunshine,
Tracy

Are you taking your love for granted?

*"To really know someone is to have loved and hated him in turn." –
Marcel Jouhandeau*

*"Find a guy who calls you beautiful instead of hot, who calls you back when
you hang up on him, who will lie under the stars and listen to your heartbeat,
or will stay awake just to watch you sleep…wait for the boy who kisses your
forehead, who wants to show you off to the world when you are in sweats, who
holds your hand in front of his friends, who thinks you're just as pretty without
makeup on. One who is constantly reminding you of how much he cares and
how lucky he is to have YOU…The one who turns to his friends and says,
that's her…" – Unknown*

*"Love is as much of an object as an obsession, everybody wants it, everybody
seeks it, but few ever achieve it, those who do will cherish it, be lost in it, and
among all, never…never forget it." – Curtis Judalet*

I look at love like taking care of a favorite plant. This may sound silly but
it's true. If you are taking care of a plant and you have great hopes of it
blossoming into its beautiful bouquet of sweet-smelling flowers, but then
do nothing to help it along, will it ever get a chance to bloom? If you
leave the plant in the corner and give it no water but just have an expectation that it will grow and bloom will it ever happen? Love is the same
way…if you do not nurture the love and give it what it needs to grow
will it ever blossom into its beauty? If you think about what you need in
order for you to feel love and it is created for you, how does that affect
you on a daily basis? I bet you are happy and joyous and feel like you can
take on anything that comes your way. I am assuming that the love you
are feeling comes from an interaction with another person. Just like the
plant ready to bloom, wouldn't you want to nurture the love to keep it
healthy so that it will continuously bloom day after day? Do you know
what your partner needs in order to feel love? With your actions are you
leaving them with the same feeling of strength and joy? Everyone is different in what they need in order to feel their own love. Are you a taker
and take all you can get without ever considering about giving back? Or
are you a giver and you give and give until you feel spent? Love really is
a balance of the two. Give and take does play a significant role in a loving
partnership. Some might call it compromise but as long as both partners

are getting what they need to feel their own love isn't it better than one going without? If it makes no difference to you to do certain things that your partner likes so that they feel love within themselves, why wouldn't you just do it to create a happy memory for both of you?

If you do not know what your partner likes then ask! You may have been in a relationship for a long time and have some preset notions of your partner. Honestly, things change more than you care to acknowledge and I bet your partner has different things that make them happy now than when you first met. I bet their favorite color has changed; maybe they have a new favorite flower, a new favorite song, or a new favorite food. Do you know for sure? No? Then ask the questions! Make it a fun game to get to know your partner again. Even if the answers are the same at least you know. You may not think it's important, but maybe your partner thinks differently. Curiosity creates a sense of mystery and you can create a whole new adventure for yourself and your partner...and adventures can lead to a whole new level of togetherness, passion and love.

Think about it...

Love and Sunshine,
Tracy

April 22nd

On freedom

"Our ultimate freedom is the right and power to decide how anybody or any-thing outside ourselves will affect us." – Stephen Covey

"Freedom is what you do with what's been done to you." – Jean-Paul Sartre

"One cannot make a slave of a free person, for a free person is free even in a prison." – Plato

These statements bring up a couple of things for me—*BraveHeart* for one: "FFFFRRRRREEEEDDDDOOOOMMMM!!!!" I love, love, love that movie! The other is something I used to say to myself when I would get scared in the dark. Trust me, it wasn't that long ago that I found myself repeating this mantra: "Nobody can take me away from me!"

When I read the above quotes I get this overwhelming sense of my own power. I love this feeling of strength, courage and balance. Maybe I just understood the words more deeply today, which means I actually felt the feeling attached to them instead of just intellectually knowing what the words mean when all strung together. Can you feel a sense of your own POWER after reading the above quotes? I'm getting goosebumps reading Stephen's quote! If you are not feeling it, here's something that I invite you to do: Stand up...yes, I am asking you to move so come on. Stand up and repeat this statement out loud: "My ultimate freedom is the right and power to decide how anybody or anything outside myself will affect me!" Oooh, say it again! "My ultimate freedom is the right and power to decide how anybody or anything outside myself will affect me!" Now one more time, say it like you mean it! "My ultimate freedom is the right and power to decide how anybody or anything outside myself will affect me!" WHOOOO! How do you feel now? I bet you are more focused, you are standing taller and maybe even feeling a bit sexier, eh? Lol...If you had trouble saying those words out loud then it's your own self getting in the way of you claiming this statement as a part of you. The reason I asked you to say it three times is because three is the number of manifestation.

Affirmations are a great way to reset your thinking patterns. I invite you to copy out the quote, "My ultimate freedom is the right and power to decide how anybody or anything outside myself will affect me!" and keep it somewhere where you can, throughout your day, and as many times as you can, take out the paper and read it out loud three times. Let's see how we can all reset our thinking into standing in our own power of our true happiness!

"My ultimate freedom is the right and power to decide how anybody or anything outside myself will affect me!"

Think about it...

Love and Sunshine,
Tracy

Get committed

"You gain strength, courage, and confidence by every experience in which you really stop to look fear in the face. You must do the thing which you think you cannot do." – Eleanor Roosevelt

"Courage is not the absence of fear, but rather the judgment that something else is more important than fear." – Ambrose Redmoon

"Your current safe boundaries were once unknown frontiers." – Anonymous

"A coward gets scared and quits. A hero gets scared, but still goes on." – Anonymous

"Twenty years from now you will be more disappointed by the things you didn't do than by the ones you did do. So throw off the bowlines. Sail away from the safe harbor. Catch the trade winds in your sails. Explore. Dream. Discover." – Mark Twain

I'm inspired by one of my BESTEST friends; she had this to say today: "No matter how afraid of leaping I may be at times, it's never about me or my feelings. It's about commitment. Get passionate about what lights you up! Take it on like a fire roaring out of control! Get uncomfortable! Fail and get back up again! Live your life with NO woulda shoulda coulda's!" I nuff you MTG!

If you say something is important to you and you really want it, what are you willing to do to get it or achieve it? If you sit back and do nothing you may want to re-evaluate if it is really something you want and is it really that important? Or what are you afraid of if you actually step out of your comfort zone and go for what you want? Wouldn't you rather do whatever you possibly can and fail than ALWAYS wonder what if?

Think about it…

Love and Sunshine,
Tracy

April 24th

Act or React

"Angry desperation is the reaction of the artificial self to whatever threatens its shaky pretense." – Vernon Howard

"You can have a life of stimulation or you can have a life of inspiration." – Vernon Howard

I was sooo impacted by the second quote that, for a moment, it stopped me in my tracks. It made me think that for my whole life I have been creating a life of stimulation. In other words, I have been creating drama whereever I went so that I could react to it. I could then be right in my belief that I am unlovable, I never get what I want or that I am not worth it. Wowzers…What a light bulb moment I am having. Now, that I think about it, how uncreative I have been all this time just to be what I thought was "in control". I know I owe MTG a HUGE apology. I understand it now. If I didn't create some kind of upset in my mind about what was happening in my life I was feeling "off". I felt that I had no worth. I created all that negativity to feel useful. Crazy, I know…Reacting to this comment…Reacting that comment…Reacting to no comment…For what? So that I get to say I am so upset because this person isn't doing what I want them to do or this person isn't saying what I want them to say? When you take the blinders off it all becomes so clear. Reacting to a situation puts the other person in control—ALWAYS!

To inspire people you need to ACT not react, you need to come from nothing going on in your mind or no preset way of being and just BE yourself. It doesn't matter what someone thinks about you or what they think about anything for that matter. Although, just acknowledging someone else's point of view is all you need to do but that's another topic altogether so we'll just leave it at that for the time being.

If you are wondering why you have so much drama around you all the time, the first place to look is whether or not you are reacting to your situation. Are you taking away from it and coming from a point of defence and giving the other person control of the situation or are you coming from nothing going on in your mind and acting on what you know to be what and who you are to create a happy outcome? To me it's simple. No matter how much you think reacting to someone's words or

Tracy Friesen

actions, defending your point of view or protecting your belief is keeping you in control of the situation think again. As soon as you react, defend or protect you are giving up your power and control of any situation and you become the pawn.

Think about it…

Love and Sunshine,
Tracy

April 25th

Being bored is an excuse

"In order to live happily and free, you may have to sacrifice boredom. It is not always an easy sacrifice." – Richard Bach

"Boredom is the feeling that everything is a waste of time; serenity, that nothing is." – Thomas S. Szasz

"The cure for boredom is curiosity. There is no cure for curiosity." – Ellen Parr

If you are stuck in a rut believing life is boring, how would you ever open yourself to experience any excitement or joy? In your boredom you get to be right that life sucks and that everything you do is a waste of time...yippee! How's that working for you, other than you get to say to yourself that you are right? Me, I'd rather be happy than right on any given day. If you are bored then stop being boring! It *is* that simple. Get curious about your life and start asking yourself the questions that may trigger you into a different belief. If you find it difficult to find joy in your life, why not start with just being grateful that you are alive and then go from there? No matter what is happening in your life there is ALWAYS something to be grateful for.

Think about it...

Love and Sunshine,
Tracy

The past in the present

"If you accept a limiting belief, then it will become a truth for you." –
Louise Hay

"There are no limitations to the self except those you believe in." – Seth

I know I have touched on this before but maybe we just need a
reminder, myself included. If you keep putting your past into your future
you will not be able to create anything new for yourself in the present,
because you have already made the decision to have things work out the
way you already believe they will work out. You will end up creating the
same result over and over again and again. Here is an example: If you had
an experience in your past when you did not like the feelings you were
feeling and you, at that time, knowing or not, made a decision to not feel
those feelings again, you have created a preset way of being because you
believe something about yourself and the way things are going to play
out. Let's say you had a crush on someone when you were sixteen and
you created feelings of love for that person. Then something happened
and they decided to not be in a relationship with you and you took it
personally. You created feelings of hurt and abandonment and said to
yourself, "I am never going to let that happen to me again." Then as you
grew older, you would sabotage every relationship that you got involved
in and end the relationship before the other person would be able to hurt
you. Sound familiar? What you have done is to put your past into your
future, closing down the ability to create any new results for yourself.
The belief you created, that "the other person will leave me and hurt
me so I better do it first so that I will not feel those feelings again," has
limited you into not experiencing your life to the fullest. What you may
not realize is that you are allowing the mentality of a sixteen-year-old
to make decisions for you every day. Do you not think that as you have
aged you have gained more knowledge and wisdom to possibly make a
different decision?

Trust me, I get this because I let a four-year-old little Tracy make decisions for me for years and for years. I was just sitting there in my life year
after year complaining and wondering why things were not the way I
wanted them to be. It wasn't until a few years ago that I realized, thanks

to a communications course I was in, that I made a decision at four years old that if my own mother didn't love me then how would anybody else ever love me? How silly is that? Everyone is different and they are certainly not my mother. I know that I am a strong, confident, loving, caring, smart, intelligent, beautiful, sexy, sensual woman who is unstoppable in creating the unlimited passion, joy and abundance in my life that go way beyond what I desire!

How long are you willing to limit yourself by putting your past into your future?

Think about it…

Love and Sunshine,
Tracy

Fake it until you make it

"When one door of happiness closes, another opens; but often we look so long at the closed door that we do not see the one which has opened for us." – Helen Keller

"Most people would rather be certain they're miserable, than risk being happy." – Robert Anthony

" 'Well,' said Pooh, 'what I like best,' and then he had to stop and think. Because although Eating Honey was a very good thing to do, there was a moment just before you began to eat it which was better than when you were, but he didn't know what it was called." – A.A. Milne

Oooh, I just love Pooh! He really does have a lot of interesting ways to look at life and he makes a really good point here. Pooh is showing us that it is in our thoughts that we first create our happiness and sometimes our thoughts are better than the actual experience.

You can create anything in your mind that doesn't exist and it can be as powerful as you want it to be. You can create fear, sadness, pain or even love. What do you think you are missing in your life if you are creating things that do not exist? One thing that I do know about us humans is that no matter what, we each need to be right in our own minds about anything that we are thinking or believing or else we would go crazy.

This reminds me of how I look at our minds. In them live what I call a Thinker and a Prover. The Thinker thinks and the Prover proves. The Prover proves what the Thinker thinks. So no matter what you are thinking, your Prover will prove you to be right every single time! If you are thinking your life is boring and it sucks or maybe that you are unlovable and never get what you want, guess what you are going to prove to yourself at every given moment? If you think you are "stuck" in something—remember words are powerful—are you really stuck? Can you move and get around? Yes? So really? Are you "stuck"? If you think you have no choice about a way of being, are you ever going to stop being that way if your Prover is constantly proving you to be right? One thing that I have learned over the years is that if you want to BE a certain way, and you have been being something else for a long time, a great way to start the new BEingness is to just "fake it until you make it"! It all starts as a thought, anyway. If you just repeat the words "I am HAPPY!" over and over even if you do not feel it, eventually your Prover will prove to you that you are happy! Do not believe me? Why not give it a whirl and see what you are able to create for yourself by faking who you think you want to be?

Think about it...

Love and Sunshine,
Tracy

Honor yourself

"If everyone really knew how much they were loved, not only from 'above,' but by everyone now in their life, there'd be little hearts drawn on everything from wheelbarrows to skyscrapers to jumbo jets.

And I so look forward to that day.

Big heart." – the Universe

"I think that when we look for love courageously, it reveals itself, and we wind up attracting even more love. If one person really wants us, everyone does. But if we're alone, we become even more alone. Life is strange." – Paulo Coelho

"If you aren't good at loving yourself, you will have a difficult time loving anyone, since you'll resent the time and energy you give another person that you aren't even giving to yourself." – Barbara De Angelis

What have you done today that is just for you and only you to show yourself love? Have you put all your "have to's" in front of your own personal joy? If you are sitting there saying to yourself "I have no personal life…" maybe it's because you have not made the time to do the things you enjoy. Everyone has fifteen minutes in their day to do something for themselves—no excuses, no reasons. You do, period—end of story. Even if it is just taking a relaxing bath, you may have to schedule it in but… just dooo eeet!

We all need time for play and if you've forgotten what it is that you enjoy, maybe that is a great place to start. Take the first scheduled fifteen minutes and ask yourself, "What is it that I really enjoy doing and haven't allowed myself to do?" Then write down your answers. If you have a "to do" list put all your "enjoy doing" things at the top and all your "have to's" below them. When you write them down they become more real and accountable. Also, if they are at the top, we as humans will deem them more important and you will train yourself to put yourself first in the process.

Honor yourself and others will follow suit. When you are in a place of loving yourself there is no room for doubt or sacrifice or aloneness, just more LOVE!

Think about it...

Love and Sunshine,
Tracy

Stretch yourself

"In each of us are places where we have never gone. Only by pressing the limits do you ever find them." – Dr. Joyce Brothers

"If you limit your choices only to what seems possible or reasonable, you disconnect yourself from what you truly want, and all that is left is compromise."
– Robert Fritz

"Our imagination is the only limit to what we can hope to have in the future."
– Charles F. Kettering

"A belief is not an idea held by the mind, it is an idea that holds the mind."
– Elly Roselle

Have you ever noticed that when you venture outside your comfort zone to do something you may have feared to do before, that the next time you do that very same thing it no longer feels uncomfortable? Hmmm, interesting, let me get this straight: so by venturing outside your comfort zone you actually have "grown"? Wow, for someone who says that nothing ever changes how does it feel to know that you have just moved your boundaries and stretched your limitations and in the process you have changed?

Do not let your beliefs hold you back. Open yourself to be available to all possibilities not just the ones that seem doable. If you really want something in your life, how far outside your comfort zone are you willing to go to get it?

Think about it…

Love and Sunshine,
Tracy

Honor your feelings, not your story

"People, like nails, lose their effectiveness when they lose direction and begin to bend." – Walter Savage Landor

"The most beautiful discovery true friends make is that they can grow separately without growing apart." – Elisabeth Foley

"The best way of forgetting how you think you feel is to concentrate on what you know you know." – Mary Stewart

This is what I know…your story isn't important. No matter how much detail you put into it, it just doesn't matter. What matters is the feeling that you create because of your story. You can ramble on and on about what happened to you, but in the end the only thing that you are left with is your feeling—not the story. If you are not getting this, here is an example: Let's say you had an interaction with someone and the results didn't turn out how you wanted them to turn out and you decide to share this with a friend over coffee. You start describing every detail of what was said, the actions that were taken and all the events that took place. It may go something like this: "You'll never guess what happened to me! So-and-so has ripped my heart out and I'm falling to pieces because of it…I'm in sooo much pain I can barely breathe…why are they treating me this way…we shared soooo much; I thought that it would be forever and now they just left me like a pile of garbage by the side of the road… they said that they would be there for me through anything and now, what? They are gone…they are such a liar…you know they said this and this and this…and that and that and that…and I said this and this and this…all I do is sit and listen to sad love songs all day and I can barely move…oh woe is me…look what happened to me…poor me…and then I forgot about this and that and the whatever…geesh, I never get what I want…how did this happen…how can they leave me all alone like this to struggle in surviving…my life sucks…blah blah blah…" and you go on like this for hours.

OK, I think you get the picture. All of the above just doesn't matter because you could have summed it all up in one short sentence, owning it completely by saying, "I FEEL rejected, betrayed, angry and lonely." End of story. The details do not matter EVER! If someone asks you why you feel a certain way, it doesn't matter because it changes all the time. What does Jim Rohn say? "Effective communication is 20 percent what you know and 80 percent how you feel about what you know." If you can get this you will start to communicate at a different level that is so powerful that by consequence you will change your thinking and create a new way of BEing. Understanding that it is always about the feeling and what you are going to do about that feeling, and not the story, will have you developing your listening skills as well. You will start to look through everyone's story and start to really hear how they feel about things. And that is all that matters to them anyhow...how they are left feeling about things.

This is my request to you: Instead of going into your story with all the details of the events of your life, identify your feeling about it and what you are going to do either to improve it or to continue to create that feeling day after day, and just share that with someone. You never know what you will be able to create for yourself if you just own your FEELINGs instead of your story.

Think about it...

Love and Sunshine,
Tracy

Create a new feeling

"Self-esteem is based on feeling capable and feeling lovable." – Jack Canfield

"We all walk in the dark, and each of us must learn to turn on his or her own light." – Earl Nightingale

"To him that waits all things reveal themselves, provided that he has the courage not to deny, in the darkness, what he has seen in the light." – Coventry Patmore

"Your emotions affect every cell in your body. Mind and body, mental and physical, are intertwined." – Thomas Tutko

"Mankind are governed more by their feelings than by reason." – Samuel Adams

OK, wow…yesterday was some great information for us to learn from. The first thing I would like you to do, if you really want to take on your life and live happily, is to go back to yesterday's message and read it again and possibly reread it once more…

Welcome back. Here is a response that I received to yesterday's Message from a close and dear friend, someone who I hold close in my heart:

"Very good grasshopper!

Now let me put a spin on it. You NEVER have to even share the feeling as the feeling is not real. Hmmm you say…How can the feeling be real if it is made up from a story that you created in your head? Oh the twists :) You can get anything complete by just recognizing it's a feeling you are having and it is not real and *you can* create something totally new to feel!

I say this AND I am clear sometimes I want people to know how I feel! tehehehe…"

Aww…MTG, I nuff you!

Think about it…

Love and Sunshine,
Tracy

One step at a time

"What saves a man is to take a step. Then another step." – *Antoine De Saint-Exupery*

"You don't have to see the whole staircase, just take the first step." – *Martin Luther King, Jr.*

"The first step towards getting somewhere is to decide that you are not going to stay where you are." – *John Pierpont Morgan*

"One of the secrets of life is to make stepping stones out of stumbling blocks." – *Jack Penn*

"Most great people have attained their greatest success just one step beyond their greatest failure." – *Napoleon Hill*

If you can separate your end result into small steps, how much closer do you think you will be to attaining what you want and your happiness?

Think about it…

Love and Sunshine,
Tracy

Ego's tricks

"One of the great dangers of transformational work is that the ego attempts to sidestep deep psychological work by leaping into the transcendent too soon. This is because the ego always fancies itself much more advanced than it actually is." – Don Richard Riso and Russ Hudson

"Enlightenment is ego's ultimate disappointment." – Chögyam Trungpa

"Anytime there is a struggle between doing what is actually right and doing what seems right, then your ego is interfering with your decision." – Darren L. Johnson

"The moment you drop the search, you drop the ego also." – Osho

"Those that fight don't listen—those that listen don't fight." – Fritz Perls

How often have you been caught up in the game of making others wrong to make yourself right? Have you ever noticed that while you are doing this you may have shut down your listening skills? Hmmm…What have you sacrificed in your life to get to say, "I am right, dammit!"? Was it worth it? Really?

This is what I know…if you want to get to your happiness one of the things that you may have to do is to go beyond your ego. Release the need to control, release the need to be approved by someone and release the need to judge…because it is these things that may be preventing you from experiencing your own JOY in your life.

I know I have said this before but it still remains true for me. On any given day, I'd rather be HAPPY than right.

Think about it…

Love and Sunshine,
Tracy

No judgment

"Do not judge, and you will never be mistaken." – Jean Jacques Rousseau

"Everything that irritates us about others can lead us to an understanding of ourselves." – Carl Gustav Jung

"If you judge people, you have no time to love them." – Mother Teresa

"We judge ourselves by what we feel capable of doing, while others judge us by what we have already done." – Henry Wadsworth Longfellow

How often have you been caught in the game of judgment? Hey, we are only human, right? At least that's what I tell myself when I catch myself in a judgmental statement. I really do see that what I do not like in others *is* what I do not like about myself. What frustrates me is that people get stuck in thinking that there is only ever one way to do something... their way...always their way...lol. I'm not saying that my way is better either. What I am getting at is that there are unlimited possibilities for achieving anything. Close-minded people bug me...so I have to think where am I being close-minded in my own life? Hmmm...I guess maybe I am wanting you to see that my way of unlimited possibilities is better than pigeon-holing yourself into only one way. Wow, I guess I *am* just like everyone else, unique in my own "way."

Judging people can be an endless vicious circle of continual upset or if you release the need to judge the situation can be overflowing with love...it's your choice. If you removed all judgment of yourself and the people who surround you what kind of world would you live in then? Just consider that everyone is just as capable as you...

Think about it...

Love and Sunshine,
Tracy

Your song to sing

"If God is the DJ, then Life is the dance floor; Love is the rhythm, and You are the music." – Unknown

"Some men see things as they are and say 'why'? Others dream things that never were and say 'why not?'" – George Bernard Shaw

"Your aspirations are your possibilities." – Samuel Johnson

When reading the above I am reminded of Mark Twain's quote: "Sing like no one is listening, dance like no one is watching, love like you have never been hurt and live like it's heaven on earth."

Where have you not shown up in your own life because you were too concerned about what another person thought of you? How's that working for you to create happiness in your life? If you are the music to the Dance of your life, why are you just sitting there wishing someone else would remind you of the rhythm that is already in your heart? Is it not your song to sing? Hmmm…Interesting. Why let someone else's judgment of what they do not like in themselves prevent you from being true to yourself and your happiness? So, if it is *your* song to sing why not belt out your tune at the top of your lungs? You never know who you might inspire by the courage it takes to stand in your own power, loving yourself as you are and doing whatever it takes to make your dream come true.

Think about it…

Love and Sunshine,
Tracy

You know the way

"Woe to the man whose heart has not learned while young to hope, to love… and to put its trust in life." – Joseph Conrad

"I trust so much in the power of the heart and the soul; I know that the answer to what we need to do next is in our own hearts. All we have to do is listen, then take that one step further and trust what we hear. We will be taught what we need to learn." – Melody Beattie

"I never know what the next lesson is going to be, because we're not supposed to know; we're supposed to trust ourselves to discover it." – Melody Beattie

We all have our own answers within us, within our hearts and our minds. All we need to do is listen. Our Divine will not ever give us anything that we cannot handle, so trust in yourself and you may find that you are not only stronger but also smarter than you think you are. If you take a leap of faith and just trust that you will be safe in your next move, what do you think you will be able to create for yourself in this moment?

Think about it…

Love and Sunshine,
Tracy

May 7th

Be you not someone else's you

*"We have all been placed on this earth to discover our own path, and we will
never be happy if we live someone else's idea of life." – James Van Praagh*

*"Have you noticed how moving towards a great dream summons from life's
jungles the fiercest lions, the scariest tigers, and the grizzliest bears…who eventually turn out to be the noblest teachers, the bravest guides, and the dearest
friends?" – the Universe*

Have you been listening? Listening to the signs that are available to
you each and every day to guide you towards your perfect path? Are
you living someone else's idea of what you should be or are you being
the perfect you? Hmmm…let's check in on that. How happy are you in
this moment? Are you being you or are you pretending to be someone
else for someone else? Guilty! Not you, me…I am a happy, intelligent,
beautiful, sexy, sensual, erotic woman and I often curb who I am because
I think someone may not be able to "handle" me. How's that working
for me, you ask? Well at the moment, it's not working for me as I am
left feeling unsatisfied and unfulfilled…and who's fault is that? Mine of
course! It is my own fault because I am choosing to live someone else's
idea of who I am or who they want me to be. Who I am being is not me,
that's for sure—so why am I doing this? I am human and I want to be
accepted but at what cost? I am not being true to myself by doing this
and it creates, for me, resentment and sadness in the end. What am I afraid
of? Hmmm…an interesting place to look.

A friend of mine told me that it is my nature to accommodate others
and sacrifice my wants and likes for them because that *is* who I am.
Hmmm…really? That is another interesting place to look. Is it worth my
happiness if those actions and the feelings created for them are not recip-
rocated and I don't have the satisfaction of feeling appreciation and love
the way I like to have those things created for me? Just like everyone else,
I deserve the same experiences and feelings of love the way I want them
to be created and/or felt for myself. Not in expectation but in that loving
exchange of "wanting" to do for another. Or have people just come to
expect me to just do for them and be OK with only doing what they
want? So, who's responsible for that? Me or them? Lol…Obviously it is

Tracy Friesen

my responsibility to be me and not someone else's idea of who I am and not worry about how they respond. I do this for them out of love and I now expect nothing in return. I have wanted something from them in the past, but that was me being human. Isn't that how we started this in the first place? You see, I am just as human as anyone else!

Think about it…

Love and Sunshine,
Tracy

Has your belief got you down?

"Your chances of success in any undertaking can always be measured by your belief in yourself." – Robert Collier

"Nobody can make you feel inferior without your consent." – Eleanor Roosevelt

"It's not who you are that holds you back, it's who you think you're not." – Anonymous

Where has your belief taken you lately? Well, for me, yesterday it took me into a downward spiral of thinking that what I do is not important and I am not worth the effort. I continued my downward path until I was able to really look at what I was creating for myself and go to those scary places of taking responsibility for my own thoughts. What I discovered along the way is that I was also upset with myself and my own lack of integrity. Here's a look into my world and the coaching I received over what I was "in" (copied exactly from a Skype conversation):

Tracy: Boy, I'm "in it" today

MTG: Yeah, you are and you are choosing to make them totally wrong. You are never going to get the response to these most basic questions that you want answered until you stop making them wrong and then talk about it.

MTG: I am soo happy that you are clear you are in it!

MTG: Do you know how many people walk this earth making others wrong and never stop to notice they are in it?

Tracy: I didn't think I was making them wrong?

MTG: Well, you are in it. In your head, asking all these questions, like why don't they hear you…

MTG: you are in it.

MTG: you are in the "I am not being heard" conversation.

MTG: It is really great you see it!

Tracy: OK…I get that.

MTG: Here is the ugly truth about it all and I call it ugly cuz I didn't want to face it either…

MTG: So because you are someone who always puts others needs before your own, just like I was, people unconsciously know they can walk all over you.

MTG: It is not that they do it intentionally

MTG: but it is like you said, you make a request to do something and they say yes I will do it tomorrow, but then you don't call them on it immediately, the day it is due to be done.

MTG: you wait to see how long it will take and you let your righteousness fester and you don't take responsibility for it not getting done and you get mad at the person who didn't do it. In actual fact, it is your integrity that is out too for not having said anything on the day it was due to be done and creating a world for why it is important that it got done or counter-offered for a new date.

Tracy: Hmmm...interesting.

Tracy: Blah blah blah I'm done with it!

MTG: I know! It totally sucked to me when I got this! LOL!

MTG: Like really got it! LMAO!

Tracy: I get it MTG.

MTG: So then let me ask you—.

Tracy: Yes?

MTG: Going forward, can you have fun, make requests, follow up on the days they are due? Keep having fun, not make people wrong, enjoy who you are with for who they are even when they make you feel all nutty sometimes?

Tracy: I wish it was that they just made me feel nutty...I could take that...lol.

Tracy: But yes, I can...

So when you feel that you are the only one that gets "in it"...trust me, we are all human and from time to time we all could use a bit of coaching and releasing!

Your belief in yourself is what brings you to every outcome or result that you experience in your life...So whatever you are thinking about yourself you will create it to be true, and wouldn't you rather just experience joy and happiness in your life?

Think about it...

Love and Sunshine,
Tracy

May 9th

Believe you are a creator

"Every moment of your life is infinitely creative and the universe is endlessly bountiful. Just put forth a clear enough request, and everything your heart desires must come to you." – Shakti Gawain

"By believing passionately in something that still does not exist, we create it. The non-existent is whatever we have not sufficiently desired." – Nikos Kazantzakis

When we believe we can…we will…that's the beauty and the strength of our own minds. Whatever we are holding as truth in our minds we will be it or create it. Life is not hard, vicious or cruel. If you think differently then it exists only in your own mind. You are the only one creating that world around you, so how are you ever surprised at the results you get if you are thinking in such lower vibrations? Life is simple, abundant and kind and everyone I meet is in some way there to help me along my path to staying in my happiness.

A new friend of mine said to me the other day…"I would love to spend one day in your mind." When I asked her why, she said, "You are always so happy and bubbly and I think it would be fun!" Thanks Deborah! It's awesome for me to feel that I leave the people around me with a sense of joy and laughter. It shows me that when I am creating happiness by my thoughts that I am being effective with creating a world of love, joy and laughter around me. So even if I get to being a little human from time to time, I recognize that it's my thoughts that are dragging me down and that I have the ability to choose a different thought to bring me back to my happiness. It's sad for me to think that there may be people out there who will live their whole life not knowing that it is and always has been their choice to be happy.

Think about it…

Love and Sunshine,
Tracy

The power of acceptance

"There comes a time when you have to stand up and shout:

This is me damn it! I look the way I look, think the way I think, feel the way I feel, love the way I love! I am a whole complex package. Take me...or leave me. Accept me—or walk away! Do not try to make me feel like less of a person, just because I don't fit your idea of who I should be and don't try to change me to fit your mold. If I need to change, I alone will make that decision. When you are strong enough to love yourself 100%, good and bad—you will be amazed at the opportunities that life presents you." – Stacey Charter

"Being happy doesn't mean that everything is perfect. It means that you've decided to look beyond the imperfections." – Unknown

"Sometimes what seems like surrender isn't surrender at all. It's about what's going on in our hearts. About seeing clearly the way life is and accepting it and being true to it, whatever the pain, because the pain of not being true to it is far, far greater." – Nicholas Evans

Learning to accept what is happening in the moment may be the key to being at peace with yourself and others. If you are in love with yourself you may not concern yourself with another's idea of who you "should" be because you will just BE who you are and accept yourself completely... and in the process maybe accept them for who they are too. Remember I have always said that you do not have to "like" what is happening just accept it as is...and if "it" is not where you want it to be, then you have the ability to change it through your own power of CHOICE!

Think about it...

Love and Sunshine,
Tracy

Worry is a wasted emotion

"Who of you by worrying can add a single hour to his life?" – Matthew 6:27

"Worry never robs tomorrow of its sorrow, it only saps today of its joy." – Leo Buscaglia

"If you can't sleep, then get up and do something instead of lying there worry-ing. It's the worry that gets you, not the lack of sleep." – Dale Carnegie

"There is a great difference between worry and concern. A worried person sees a problem, and a concerned person solves a problem." – Harold Stephens

How much of your life are you willing to give up in the daunting task of worrying about things that may never happen? FEAR can cage us into not taking responsibility for our own lives…and what is fear again? False Evidence Appearing Real. Our fears only exist in our own mind and you are powerful enough to overcome that which does not exist. If you are playing the "what if" game, what have you been missing as opportunities fly by you moment to moment? Most people at the end of their lives do not regret the things they have done, but regret the things that they were too afraid to do. We have so many examples of this and yet there you are still worrying about whatever it is you are worrying about and not living your life to its fullest. How is that working for you?

I have people tell me all the time that they admire my strength—that I am able to take things on without fear—but what I tell them is that I am scared but yet I do it anyway. Why? I would rather attempt to do some-thing and fail than always wonder what if, that's why. At least that way I can release the thought because I have an answer for it and I never have to think it again. It's when I do not have the information that I need that I may get caught in a broken record of wondering. I got tired of laying in bed night after night with endless scenes playing through my head of things that might not even happen. I was losing sleep and getting angrier and more frustrated at myself day after day for not making a decision. All my relationships were suffering as I was not happy. I would get sucked into the idea that I had to make the "right" decision but what I realized along the way is that no matter what decision I make, it is always the right decision for me in that moment. I also learned that it is sometimes easier to ask for forgiveness than it is to ask for permission.

In my opinion, I believe that worry is a wasted emotion because you can sit and worry your whole life away and never BE. When all that you may have to do is just accept what is and be happy in this moment of your life with whatever it is that you are experiencing. At least it's real!

Think about it...

Love and Sunshine,
Tracy

Denial or excited acceptance?

"The most common way people give up their power is by thinking they don't have any." – Alice Walker

"Man stands in his own shadow and wonders why it's dark." – Zen saying

Where have you been giving up your power in your life? I can guarantee you that it first exists in your mind and then by nurturing these thoughts you create the physical experiences in your outward life so that your Prover can prove to you that you are right! How does it feel to know that you are responsible for every experience in your life? Ooh, ouch, eh? When you get this and I really mean "GET IT," there are two things that may possibly happen: 1) You get scared that it really is your life to manage. Then you get mad and go into denial that you really are responsible for your life. Then you may go into avoidance and frantically start pointing fingers everywhere but at yourself so that you do not have to face yourself in the mirror and acknowledge that you may have to clean some things up in your life. 2) You get that powerful "A-ha" moment and you may sit in quiet contemplation, first to create a new plan for yourself and your newfound joy that you *are* responsible for your life and no one is controlling you and/or your feelings. You may be bursting with a sense of excitement, the anticipation that your life IS and WILL BE the way you want it to be, always. Oh sure, you may have to clean some stuff up but that's the exciting part about sharing your newfound happiness in yourself…and from this moment on you know beyond a shadow of a doubt that your ultimate freedom is the right and power to decide how anybody or anything outside yourself will affect you! Whoo hoo!!

Which are you going to choose?

Think about it….

Love and Sunshine,
Tracy

Appreciation

"You can never get to peace and inner security without first acknowledging all of the good things in your life. If you're forever wanting and longing for more without first appreciating things the way they are, you'll stay in discord." – Doc Childre and Howard Martin

"Generally, appreciation means some blend of thankfulness, admiration, approval, and gratitude. In the financial world, something that appreciates grows in value. With the power tool of appreciation, you get the benefit of both perspectives: as you learn to be consistently thankful and approving, your life will grow in value." – Doc Childre and Howard Martin

Have you been appreciating the good things in your life or have you been taking for granted that they will just be there for you? If you are not grateful for what you have in this moment, if you don't show your gratitude by means of acknowledgment and recognition through your actions, how could you ever be surprised if it seems to you that you have nothing? Even the littlest of things need your grateful attention. If you are thinking you have nothing to be grateful for, then why not start by taking a deep breath…oh come on, appease me and just dooo eeet…take a deep breath and be grateful that you are alive in this moment and you have the ability to create whatever life you want by the power of your CHOICE!

Think about it…

Love and Sunshine,
Tracy

Pump up the Volume

"The inability to open up to hope is what blocks trust, and blocked trust is the reason for blighted dreams." – *Elizabeth Gilbert*

"You can't shake hands with a clenched fist." – *Indira Gandhi*

"No matter how deep a study you make, what you really have to rely on is your own intuition and when it comes down to it, you really don't know what's going to happen until you do it." – *Konosuke Matsushita*

How many times have you wanted to do something, but just sat there and let the opportunity pass you by? How long are you going to take your own self for granted in being able to do what you want? Do not get stuck in needing to know how to do something; just trust yourself that you will know what to do in the moment you need to do it. Think about how you are able to maneuver around in your place when it's dark and no lights are on. Are you able to get to the bathroom when you need to? Did you have to stop and think about "how" you were going to get there? Or did you just do it without thinking because you were trusting yourself that you knew what to do and where to go and it was no big deal? Life really is the same way. You *do* know what to do in every moment. If you think not, maybe you've just turned down the volume on your inner voice. Next time you think you are challenged with "What do I do now?" stop for a brief moment. Go in and turn up the volume to your little voice and listen. Trust what you hear and then do it. You really do know what to do.

Think about it…

Love and Sunshine,
Tracy

Do not think away your feelings

"When emotions are managed by the heart, they heighten your awareness of the world around you and add sparkle to life. The result is new intelligence and a new view of life." – Doc Childre and Howard Martin

Have you noticed that you haven't been honoring your emotions? Why? Maybe because they are the ones that you fear will overtake you? Or they may appear to be too painful or uncomfortable to actually delve into? What I have learned from my own experiences is that I had been caught in "thinking" my emotions and not actually "feeling" them. It wasn't until I allowed myself to go to the scary place of experiencing the feelings—instead of intellectually knowing what they were—that I realized I had never opened up my heart to the wondrous sparkle of what life is all about. It was by honoring my feelings, and allowing myself to experience them without making it mean anything, that I was able to release the attachment I had to the notion that my feelings were created by someone else. I figured out that I am responsible for my life and my own happiness. Isn't it about time you gained some new intelligence and a new view of your life by actually "feeling" your own feelings?

Think about it...

Love and Sunshine,
Tracy

The key to creativity

"Imagination is more important than knowledge. Knowledge is limited. Imagination encircles the world." – Albert Einstein

"Just as our eyes need light in order to see, our minds need ideas in order to conceive." – Napoleon Hill

"Anyone can look for fashion in a boutique or history in a museum. The creative explorer looks for history in a hardware store and fashion in an airport." – Robert Wieder

Our imagination creates for us what is possible in our lives. Not in the sense that it may one day happen, but in the sense that we can have whatever "it" is in the present moment! The more you let your creative juices flow and create the world you want for yourself, the more possible it will be for you to experience it now. Your world has to come from somewhere and it is first created in your mind. If you really get that you create your life by your thoughts first, why not use all the vibrant colors of the rainbow to paint your world the way you want it? Why keep the same old faded pictures from your past and wonder why your world looks so drab? It's time to get creative!

Think about it…

Love and Sunshine,
Tracy

Life should be enjoyable

"Life should be enjoyable; too often we think it's about achievement. The truth is that making life enjoyable is an achievement in itself." – Unknown

"Changing what you have comes from changing who you are. And changing who you are comes from changing what you think." – the Universe

"Many things in life will catch your eye, few will catch your heart. Pursue those!" – Unknown

There are many things in our life that catch our eye and distract us enough to think that it is what we really want in our lives. It is up to you to check in and listen to how you hold that thought in your heart. If you hear nothing from within your heart, then maybe it's not what is in alignment with your path. Sometimes these things can distract us all our lives, and then at the end of it all we may wonder why our lives were not the way we wanted them to be. If at this moment you think you have what you want, but yet there is still something missing, maybe it's because what you are "thinking" you want isn't what is best for you to create joy—joy that transcends your whole being and leaves you and all those who interact with you with peace, love and happiness. It's just somewhere to look for yourself, that's all.

If you are only looking to achieving something in your life, you may leave out the most important part which is finding enjoyment in what you do. If you let society and/or others decide for you that "you should do this" or "you should do that," how are you ever surprised that you do not love what you do? There is always a way to get whereever you want to go in your life and get everything you want out of your life as well. You can have the life you want and it's through your thoughts that you will get there first!

Think about it….

Love and Sunshine,
Tracy

May 18th

Where's your limit?

"Move out of your comfort zone. You can only grow if you are willing to feel awkward and uncomfortable when you try something new." – Brian Tracy

"It is not because things are difficult that we do not dare, it is because we do not dare that they are difficult." – Seneca

"One can choose to go back toward safety or forward toward growth. Growth must be chosen again and again; fear must be overcome again and again." – Abraham Maslow

We all have a comfort zone where everything feels safe and familiar, and we tend to not want to venture out beyond it. If we allowed ourselves to stay there we would not challenge ourselves, experience personal growth, or even learn new and exciting things. In other words we would be dying instead of living. Do you want to live the rest of your life in a stagnant mess of constantly complaining about the same things over and over, wondering why no one ever listens to you and why you are not happy? Really? Wow, you really *are* ingrained in your story far too deep! Remember it is just a story you are telling yourself; the more you venture out of your comfort zone the more you may expand who you are. The more you expand who you are the more related you may become to those around you and you actually may create the joy that you are so desperately looking for in your life.

Have the faith to know that you can handle any situation. No matter what happens, the next time you attempt the same thing you will not feel as awkward or uncomfortable, you have my word. Trust me. Dare to go beyond your complacency! You never know what you can create in your life when you have the courage to feel the fear and do it anyway!

Fear knocked on the door, FAITH answered and no one was there.

Think about it…

Love and Sunshine,
Tracy

Tracy Friesen

What it means to be poor

"How you see the world. How you deal with it. That determines your real wealth." – God *(from the Joan of Arcadia TV series)*

One day, the father of a very wealthy family took his son on a trip to the country with the express purpose of showing him how poor people live. They spent a couple of days and nights on the farm of what would be considered a very poor family. On their return from their trip, the father asked his son, "How was the trip?"

"It was great, Dad."

"Did you see how poor people live?" the father asked.

"Oh yeah," said the son.

"So, tell me, what did you learn from the trip?" asked the father

The son answered: "I saw that we have one dog and they have four. We have a pool that reaches to the middle of our garden and they have a creek that has no end. We have imported lanterns in our garden and they have the stars at night. Our patio reaches to the front yard and they have the whole horizon. We have a small piece of land to live on and they have fields that go beyond our sight. We have servants who serve us, but they serve others. We buy our food, but they grow theirs."

The boy's father was speechless. Then his son added…

"Thanks Dad, for showing me how poor we are."

I received this message from Chris Cade from Inscribe Your Life. I was moved by it and thought that it would be a perfect message for all to hear. It really does show you that it is your thoughts about how you live that create your abundance and joy. It reminds me of all the love and support I have from my friends and heart family, who have shown me how abundant my life is and I am grateful for every experience. I am so HAPPY in this moment and I love you all! You are all ROCK awesome! Thank you for being you!

What do you think you can create in your life if you change your perspective of "what is"?

Think about it...

Love and Sunshine,
Tracy

Is your ego involved?

"There is no room for God in him who is full of himself." – Hasidic saying

"Do not feed your ego and your problems, with your attention…Slowly, surely, the ego will lose weight, until one fine day it will be nothing but a thin ghost of its former self. You will be able to see right through it, to the divine presence that shines in each of us." – Eknath Easwaran

"Why aren't you happy? It's because ninety-nine percent of everything you do, and think, and say, is for yourself—and there isn't one." – Wu Wei Wu

Have you ever noticed that when you do something or give something in a selfless way how alive you feel? When you are able to come from unconditional love instead of coming from "what's in it for me," you create giving without expectation of getting anything in return. If you in your head are thinking, "What can I get out of this?" then you are coming from your ego trying to control the situation. If you in your heart are feeling love and joy about the situation, then you are coming from unconditional love. Think about coming from ego. How do you think people are left by your presence of always wondering what's in it for you?…OK, now think about coming from your heart. How do you think people are left by your presence of unconditional love and leaving them with no expectations? Hmmm…interesting isn't it?

What do you think this world would look like if everyone removed their own expectations and always gave from their heart?

Think about it…

Love and Sunshine,
Tracy

Words are powerful

"If you wish to know the mind of a man, listen to his words." – *Chinese Proverb*

"Handle them carefully, for words have more power than atom bombs." – *Pearl Strachan Hurd*

"The wise weigh their words on a scale with gold." – *Bible*

Words are powerful…we create our world with our words. It is through our words that we create the images in our minds that are transformed into our actions and then into our outward experiences.

Do this with me. Say the words:"I do not want to be alone." What images are created in your mind? For me, I see myself sitting alone in a room. I am feeling sad and abandoned. Do you have your own image? OK, great. Now say these words: "I am surrounded by people who love and care about me." What image comes into your mind? For me, I see myself in a room with all my loved ones around me. I am feeling happy and LOVED and I am smiling. Do you see how in both statements you want to create the same thing in your life? Which one for you is more effective to create exactly what you want? Words are powerful. It is always best to be mindful in how you talk to yourself— how you create the images in your mind that will create the life you want.

Whatever it is that you are looking to create in your life, first check in on how you are talking to yourself about what you want to create. If you are not getting what you want maybe it is as simple as reforming the words you are using. If you want to take on your life and see what is possible for you, I invite you to write out those things you want to create in your life. Then go through each one and see what image comes into your mind from the words you wrote down. If the image in your mind does not match what you want, then choose different words to evoke the exact image you are looking to create. Once you have the exact image you want in your life, use the statements that you just created as mantras or affirmations every day. How do you think you would feel if you actually had that image in real life? FEEL IT! BELIEVE IT! CREATE IT!!

Tracy Friesen

You are stronger than you think you are. You can have the life you want by simply choosing the words to create the appropriate images for you to have what is DIVINELY right for you.

Think about it!

Love and Sunshine,
Tracy

May 22nd

Daily forgiveness

"As long as you don't forgive, who and whatever it is will occupy rent-free space in your mind." – Isabelle Holland

"Whatever we have done, we can always make amends for it without ever looking back in guilt or sorrow." – Eknath Easwaran

"The weak can never forgive. Forgiveness is the attribute of the strong." – Mahatma Gandhi

Alexander Pope once said, "To err is human; to forgive, Divine." Forgiveness…what comes up for you when you say that word? Forgiveness…If you are stuck in a statement of "I can never forgive them after what they did to me," do you realize that you are giving up your power to them every time you think about them or what happened? In this you are choosing to believe that you have no choice in the matter and that you can continue to remain the victim. How's that working for you to move forward and create what you want in your life?

Forgiveness does not mean forgetting. Forgiveness allows you to create peace in your heart and mind. There is nothing you can do to change the past. What happened, happened. It is just one moment in time. It is you that recreates the wounded feelings over and over again. Why are you punishing yourself day after day, thinking about those same feelings that bring your vibration down? You will not be able to let those feelings go until you make the choice to forgive. Do not forgive for *their* sake; forgive for *your* sake! Forgive yourself above all else! Not forgiving allows you to remain in the struggle. Do you want to be right or do you want to be happy? Forgiving brings you hope and removes your sense of anxiety and depression. You are the only one who continues to attach the same feeling to your memory of that past event and you create those feelings for yourself in this present moment.

Here is an excerpt taken from a site I was reading about forgiveness and what it is for:

"Forgiveness is a journey. You may never forget AND you can choose to forgive. You can forgive and tomorrow you may feel the pain all over again. As life goes on and you choose to remember and feel the pain, then is the time to once again remember that you have already forgiven. Mentally forgive again if necessary, then move forward. When we allow it, time can dull the vividness of the memory of the hurt; the memory will eventually fade.

Always remember that you are human. Sometimes people do and say hurtful things. It is important to focus on what you have done to learn from the experience.

. . .

Begin again! It is truly impossible to start new and to make clear, healthy, life giving choices until we have let go of past hurts, confusion and resentments. Old wounds have a drawing power and pull our attention to them over and over, taking energy and hope from us, preventing us from starting again. Old wounds raise fearful spectres of the same thing happening again in the future. For this reason it is so important to spend time understanding the true nature of forgiveness, and what it really entails.

To forgive means to "give up," to let go. It also means to restore oneself to basic goodness and health. When we forgive, we are willing to give up resentment, revenge and obsession. We are willing to restore faith not only in ourselves, but in life itself. The inability or unwillingness to do this causes harm in the one who is holding onto the anger."

> *"If you are at war with others you cannot be at peace with yourself. You CAN let go…and forgive! It takes no strength to let go…only courage. Life either expands or contracts in direct proportion to your courage to forgive. Your choice to forgive or not to forgive either moves you closer to what you desire or further away from it. There is no middle ground. Change is constant."* — Larry James

My sentiments exactly Larry!

> *"Forgiveness allows us to let go of the pain in the memory and if we let go of the pain in the memory we can have the memory but it does not control us. When memory controls us we are then the puppets of the past."* – Alexandra Asseily.

Think about it!

Love and Sunshine,
Tracy

May 23rd

Feeling trapped? Slow down!

"If you're having difficulty coming up with new ideas, then slow down. For me, slowing down has been a tremendous source of creativity. It has allowed me to open up—to know that there's life under the earth and that I have to let it come through me in a new way. Creativity exists in the present moment. You can't find it anywhere else." – Natalie Goldberg

"It's important to be heroic, ambitious, productive, efficient, creative, and progressive, but these qualities don't necessarily nurture soul. The soul has different concerns, of equal value: downtime for reflection, conversation, and reverie; beauty that is captivating and pleasuring; relatedness to the environs and to people; and any animal's rhythm of rest and activity." – Thomas Moore

Have you ever been caught up in "I'm too busy" or "There's never enough time to do what I want"? Did you know that busy is a choice? We all have the same amount of time in each day so why do some people who have just as many things to do as you seem to get more done or have time left over to do what they really want to do? Like spend time with their families, friends, lovers...hmmm...Yeah, why is that? Time is an illusion. It is made up by man. If you keep thinking you will not have enough time...what do you think you will create in your life? I approach life believing "I have more than enough time to get things done and more" and sure enough I accomplish my have to's and still have more than enough time to spend with those that I hold dear to my heart. Am I different from you? No. Sometimes people use busy as an excuse not to take responsibility for their own lives and they let time control them. This may then perpetuate the "I'll be happy when..." spiral. Let me ask you this: If you were able to slow down go within—breathe—and find out what is really important to you, do you not think that you would live your life in a different way? What would you be able to create in your life if you looked at your "have to's" in a different way or even got rid of them altogether?

Life is about creating! Creating your joy, your tranquility, your passion, your happiness and your creativity requires focus or clear thinking. If you are cluttering your mind with "I have to do this" and "I have to do that" before you can do anything else, are you really surprised that you may

Tracy Friesen

feel ripped off at the end of the day that you did not get to do what you wanted to do? Everyone has fifteen minutes in the day to do something completely for themselves. Schedule it in, if you have to...lol. If you do not, how will you ever create the time for yourself?

What do you think you would be able to create in your life if you allowed yourself to slow down and create the time you need?

Think about it...

Love and Sunshine,
Tracy

May 24th

Forgive the hurts

"Forgiveness will never fail to free you." – Jerrold Mundis

"Forgiveness does not change the past, but it does enlarge the future." – Paul Boese

I think that's why people do not forgive so easily: It's because they think that it makes the wrong OK. But this is entirely untrue. Nothing can change the past. The only thing you can change about the past is how you feel about it, but that is still something you do in this moment. It is an amazing freeing exercise that you can do at any time. Maybe during a time of silent reflection you can think about something that has happened in the past, but instead of reliving the event as you normally would, be a third party and be there with compassion and understanding. You can then easily forgive yourself because you can see the decisions you made were made with the best of your ability with the knowledge you had at that time. You can easily see that if that same event were to present itself today that you would definitely do something different. By forgiving yourself in the past you are able to free yourself from the guilt and/or rage or any other emotion that you have attached to that particular event that you may still be creating in the present. Forgiveness...isn't it worth a shot? You never know what you would be able to create for yourself today in this moment if you were not shackled to your past.

Think about it...

Love and Sunshine,
Tracy

See the dawn

"The road of life twists and turns and no two directions are ever the same. Yet our lessons come from the journey, not the destination." – Don Williams, Jr.

"Too often we are so preoccupied with the destination, we forget the journey." – Unknown

If the road of life didn't have the twists and turns unique to everyone of us, life would be boring and we would never learn anything new. It's what life throws at us that makes us who we are…well, it's not the obstacle itself that makes us who we are but what we do about that particular bump in the road that makes us the person we are today. Focusing only on your destination will just cloud your life with want and lack and everything will seem bleak and miserable because you do not have what you want. Everything is darkest before the dawn so in order to get through your darkest hour you must remember that life exists in the journey.

Think about it…

Love and Sunshine,
Tracy

Direct your habitual mind

"The power to move the world is in the subconscious mind." – William James

"If a man devotes himself to the instructions of his own unconscious, it can bestow this gift [of renewal], so that suddenly life, which has been stale and dull, turns into a rich unending inner adventure, full of creative possibilities." – Marie-Louise von Franz

For me, what comes up in the above statements is to look at our habits. It may seem overwhelming to think we need to change our subconscious because isn't our subconscious something that we are suppose to be unaware of? How do you think you would impact your own life and the lives of all those that you interact with, if you went within and looked objectively at your experiences so you could recognize the patterns in your life? You know, the pattern that takes you around the vicious circle of getting the same result time and time again? So instead of throwing up our hands and being resigned that this is as good as it will ever get, you recognized the pattern and stopped it before you even started.

I've said this before, awareness is the key. If you become aware of the patterns you have created for yourself then you can remove the helpless feeling of not having a choice in the matter. Through awareness what is recognized is that you really do have a choice. The next time a certain event comes into your existence you can, through your awareness, choose to do the same thing as last time—and most likely get the same result—or you can choose to do something different. There's no right and no wrong; just what works for you in that moment. Through your awareness you take the responsibility of your own life without giving up your power to someone else. Remember it is and always has been your CHOICE to feel and act the way you do.

Think about it…

Love and Sunshine,
Tracy

Stop chasing your happiness

"Live like there is no tomorrow, and live tomorrow like there was no yesterday."
– Lindsay Matheus

"Not everything that is faced can be changed. But nothing can be changed until it is faced." – James Baldwin

"There is a difference between interest and commitment. When you're interested in something, you do it only when it's convenient. When you're committed to something, you accept no excuses, only results." – Ken Blanchard

If you are not willing to face what it is that you fear, how are you ever surprised at the results you get in your life? If you are not willing to go within and find what matters to you, find what truly makes your heart sing, how are you ever surprised that you may feel like you are chasing your happiness? "I'll be happy when…" Fill in the blank. Do you not see by doing this you are only perpetuating the same existence over and over? If you continue this pattern or theme in your life there will always be something else that you want to attain or achieve before you will ever be happy. Why not just BE happy with where you are and what you have in this moment?

Stop right now! Think of at least one thing that you can be grateful for in this moment. If it comes to you quickly then think of another and another and another. There is no end to this. If you are having troubles finding one thing to be grateful for, why not just be grateful that you are alive in this moment? Or be grateful that you have the ability to choose to not think about anything that you are grateful for…that's surely something to be grateful for! Aha…tricked you, yes? No!

Stop chasing your happiness in your life. If you become aware of what truly matters to you, you may just realize that you already have it in your life and then there is nothing more for you to do except BE HAPPY!

Think about it!

Love and Sunshine,
Tracy

May 28th

Ready, set, ACTION!

"…words are words, explanations are explanations, promises are promises, but only performance is reality." – Harold Geneen

"Adventure is not outside man; it is within." – David Grayson

"Knowing is not enough; we must apply. Willing is not enough; we must do."
– Johann Wolfgang Von Goethe

What's coming up for me right now is a song that really makes me think. It is B.o.B. feat. Eminem & Hayley Williams—Airplanes (Pt. 2). There are a few different ways you could look at this song. You may just focus in on the chorus and think you could really use a wish right now and continue on your downward spiral of why you do not have what you want in your life. Or you could really listen to the lyrics and hear what they are saying. Even though B.o.B. and Eminem have success in their life right now, it wasn't always the case. What do they have that you do not? Nothing! What they did have is a wish, a desired outcome, for their life. And what did they do to create that desired outcome? They took ACTION! They did not let anything or anyone get in their way of creating their dream. If they did not take action on creating their dream they would still be sitting there just like you, waiting on a wish. *Ouch!*

Think it! Dream it! Believe it! Do it!

Think about it…

Love and Sunshine,
Tracy

Experience stillness

"My greatest wealth is the deep stillness in which I strive and grow and win what the world cannot take from me with fire or sword." – Johann Wolfgang Von Goethe

"For peace of mind, we need to resign as general manager of the universe." – Larry Eisenberg

Have you ever found yourself in a jack of all trades, master of none situation? If you are trying to control everything that happens to you and your environment, do you not find yourself exhausted at the end of the day, the middle of your day or even the second you realize you are awake? Finding stillness in your day may be the key to helping you find the serenity to tell the difference between what you can change and what you may not be able to. It may be the key to helping you in accepting "what is." Letting go of your need to control everything or be in charge of everything may be what you need to do to find your peace of mind. Some things, no matter how hard you try, are not meant for you to control and the harder you try to control them the more helpless you may feel. Letting go and giving these things to your Divine, whatever that may be for you, may be what is necessary for you to find your stillness. Remember, no one can take you away from you so if you are willing to give up your need to control, what do you think you would be able to create in your life in this moment?

Think about it…

Love and Sunshine,
Tracy

Ode to Gratitude

"The day I acquired the habit of consciously pronouncing the words "thank you," I felt I had gained possession of a magic wand capable of transforming everything." – *Omraam Mikhael Aivanhov*

"If a fellow isn't thankful for what he's got, he isn't likely to be thankful for what he's going to get." – *Frank A. Clark*

"Gratitude unlocks the fullness of life. It turns what we have into enough, and more. It turns denial into acceptance, chaos to order, confusion to clarity. It can turn a meal into a feast, a house into a home, a stranger into a friend. Gratitude makes sense of our past, brings peace for today, and creates a vision for tomorrow." – *Melody Beattie*

"Silent gratitude isn't much use to anyone." – *G.B. Stern*

If you are continuously looking at the things that you do not have and living in a state of want, how are you ever going to be thankful for the things that you *do* have? Have you ever noticed that you take for granted the things that may deserve your gratitude the most? Hmmm...interesting isn't it? If you are not thankful for those things that you have in your life at this moment, what makes you think if you get what you think you are lacking that you'll be grateful for those things?

Express your gratitude for every single thing in your life! No matter how small you may think it is, the gratitude that you create will expand and come back to you tenfold! Do not believe me? Why not test out my theory? Or are you afraid that I may be correct and that you may have to look at your life in a different way and actually accept what you have and be happy about it? Hmmm.... gotcha.

Think about it...

Love and Sunshine,
Tracy

Tracy Friesen

Which will you feed today?

"One cannot think crooked and walk straight." – Anonymous

"What happens to a man is less significant than what happens within him."
– Louis L. Mann

Every man, woman and child has the same ability to create what they want out of their life. It is through your beliefs that you create your choices and through your choices you create your path. At the end of the day you are the product of all your choices put together.

If you do not like what is happening in your life you are the only one who can make a difference in it. The choice is and always has been yours to make. If you are getting the same results in your life and you already know it isn't working for you, why not make a different choice? What do you have to lose? Do you really care what other people think? I can almost guarantee you that whatever you think that particular person is thinking, you are so far off that you may get yourself worked up over something that isn't even real. Nine times out of ten, I bet that other person is thinking "geesh, I could never do that...I wish I could be like so and so (referencing *you*)." Lol...it's true.

I play a game with my lover all the time. It's called "This is what I just made up in my head." I say whatever it is that I just made up in my head about him and/or me. There are times when I am on track with what he is thinking and sometimes I am so far off, but most of the time it creates laughter that transcends everything into love instead of lower vibrational antics. We get past whatever it is that is in our way in a matter of seconds, rather than days and days as it used to be in our past. We get back to living, laughing and sharing with each other to continue to create our happiness. In that happiness we create a house so full of LOVE that you can feel it as soon as you enter the door! Ahhh, I *am* blessed! :)

Who are you willing to be today in order to create your own happiness in your own life? For some reason this reminds me of something that I heard a few years back: We each have two wolves that live in our hearts who are constantly fighting each other. One is made of love and the other is made of hate. Which wolf will win, you ask? The answer is simple: the one you feed the most.

Think about it...

Love and Sunshine,
Tracy

Where are you responsible?

"Remember, people will judge you by your actions, not your intentions. You may have a heart of gold—but so does a hard-boiled egg." – Unknown

"When you blame others, you give up your power to change." – Unknown

"It is a painful thing to look at your own trouble and know that you yourself and no one else has made it." – Sophocles

If you are going to continue to point fingers and blame others for the results in your life, how can you ever be surprised that what is happening in your life doesn't work for you? The more you blame others for the events in your life the more you are allowing yourself to remain a victim. You are giving yourself permission to not do anything different to take the responsibility for your own life. I know I made choices for my life based on the information I had at the time; now that there is new information I can see what I have caused through the actions of the stories I had going on in my head. I take full responsibility for my part in my own life. There is no sense in blaming anyone else. I am the one who made the final decision to do anything. Why would I want to perpetuate living in lack or sadness when all I have to do is choose to accept "what is"and move forward!

What do you think you would be able to create in your life if you were willing to take responsibility for your own actions or lack of actions and the results that you experienced from those choices? I know I'd rather make egg salad than live a life full of unfulfilled intentions. What about you?

Think about it…

Love and Sunshine,
Tracy

June 2nd

Truth and lies

"Truth stood on one side and Ease on the other; it has often been so." – *Theodore Parker*

"There are two ways to be fooled: One is to believe what isn't so; the other is to refuse to believe what is so." – *Soren Kierkegaard*

"A lie may take care of the present, but it has no future." – *Unknown*

If you think you are doing someone a kind act by not telling them how you really feel or if you do not tell the truth because you are trying to prevent hurt feelings...think again. You change who you are when you do not fully express yourself. On the other hand, people make choices based on the information that is given to them and if the information given to them is false then they are making life decisions based on false information without them even knowing it. Who are you to decide what information is appropriate for anyone? We base our beliefs on the information that is given to us. And through our beliefs we make our choices in life. At the end of the day you are the only person who will be able to look at yourself in the mirror and know beyond a shadow of a doubt that you lived the best day that you could with no regrets on how you treated anyone, including yourself. Live each moment with honesty. If it's not meant to be then it's not meant to be. Stop lying to yourself. Clean up your messes. Restore your integrity by understanding the impact of your actions on others and declare how you will be from this moment on. Then pick yourself up, dust yourself off and continue to move forward. You are a beautiful creature of your Divine. You are not broken and you do not need to be fixed. Believe, if only for this one reason: there is at least one person out there who loves you for who you are. I LOVE you! What do you think you would be able to create for your life if you chose to be honest about everything?

Think about it...

Love and Sunshine,
Tracy

Tracy Friesen

Creativity is your power

*"If you're not prepared to be wrong, you'll never come up with anything origi-
nal."* – Sir Ken Robinson

*"There is no doubt that creativity is the most important human resource of all.
Without creativity, there would be no progress, and we would be forever repeating the same patterns."* – Edward de Bono

*"It is better to have enough ideas for some of them to be wrong, than to be
always right by having no ideas at all."* – Edward de Bono

*"An idea is a point of departure and no more. As soon as you elaborate it, it
becomes transformed by thought."* – Pablo Picasso

We all have talents within us that are unique and are needed to make
this world flourish. Have you stifled your talent because you chose to
create a belief about what society says? A belief that you "have to" be
something you are not? If you are repeating the same patterns in your
life, have you ever thought to look to your talents to express your unique
creativity, to get yourself out of your rut? If you are not doing something
that you are passionate about then you are not living. You are just existing or dying, why? If you can find once again what brings about your
creativity, whatever that is for you, you may then find your happiness.
Have you ever noticed that when you are doing something you enjoy
that time seems to have a different effect on you? You do have the power
to create the reality that you are seeking. Do you remember what power
is? The dictionary's first definition of power is: "the ability to do or act;
capability of doing or accomplishing something." Look to your creativity,
your talent, as your power to create your happiness. How do you think
your world would look if you followed your dreams and began to express
yourself through your own creativity?

Think about it...

Love and Sunshine,
Tracy

Is your attitude worth catching?

"It's not what happens to you that determines how far you will go in life; it is how you handle what happens to you." – Zig Ziglar

"The state of your life is nothing more than a reflection of your state of mind."
– Dr. Wayne W. Dyer

I am secure in my knowing that our attitudes are the key to our success or our failure of anything we take on in our lives. Your perspective—your attitude—the way you see and feel about others and yourself determines your actions, your priorities, your values, your point of view and your outcomes in your life. It is your attitude that will determine how you interact with other people and how you interact with yourself.

A positive attitude may be what you are missing in order for you to find your own happiness. Have you ever heard the saying, "Fake it until you make it"? Even Muhammad Ali knew: "To be a great champion you must believe you are the best. If you're not, pretend you are." We limit ourselves more by our own attitudes than by any other influence that may come across our path. We may then miss out on great opportunities because of our attitudes. You are the only one in control of how you will ever feel about anything.

For me, what I know is that it is better for me to put a positive twist on everything that happens in my life because it is better to look at the positive aspects instead of dwelling on those things that I cannot change. I believe that everything happens for a reason and everything is OK in the end, so if it's not OK then it's not the end. A positive attitude may not solve your problems, but it might get to enough of the people who have a less than positive attitude to make it worth the effort and create some joy and laughter amidst all your woes.

Think about it…

Love and Sunshine,
Tracy

Tracy Friesen

The power of your smile

"One who smiles rather than rages is always the stronger" – *Japanese Proverb*

"A smile confuses an approaching frown." – *Unknown*

"A smile is the light in the window of your face that tells people you're at home." – *Unknown*

Mother Teresa says, "Let us always meet each other with smile, for the smile is the beginning of love." I could not have said it any better. A smile has no monetary value but the wealth that it brings to you and your heart and/or the heart of another is immeasurable! A smile is ageless, sexless, and raceless. It has no language barrier and above all else you can give it away for FREE with a HUGE rate of return!

Smiles are contagious—just think of how many people you can impact with giving away just one of your smiles. If you smile at someone who may be thinking that there is nothing to smile about in their own life, and your smile allows them to change their mood, they may then find a spark of love in their heart which makes them smile at the next person, which then transforms that person and so on and so forth. Wow! Look at how many people that can be touched by the love of your one smile! Doesn't it just make you want to go out and never stop smiling? I read this the other day and it is so true: "A smile is a curve that sets everything straight." A smile has no limits. It has no boundaries to how far it can reach. A smile has infinite power! If along your way you find people who may be too tired to give you a smile, why not give away one of yours? If you think about it, who needs a smile more than the person who may think they have no more to give? Today, give a stranger one of your smiles. It might be the only sunshine they see all day.

Think about it…

Love and Sunshine,
Tracy
:)

Celebrate your mistakes

"Do not be afraid of making mistakes, for there is no other way of learning how to live!" – Alfred Adler

"There are no mistakes. The events we bring upon ourselves, no matter how unpleasant, are necessary in order to learn what we need to learn; whatever steps we take, they're necessary to reach the places we've chosen to go." – Richard Bach

Why has it become that the worst thing you can do is to make a mistake? Hmmm…What is a mistake anyway? The dictionary says that a mistake is an error in action, calculation, opinion, or judgment caused by poor reasoning, carelessness, insufficient knowledge, etc. OK…so what? Making a mistake is not the end of the world or the worst thing that can ever happen. We need to make mistakes in order to grow, expand and evolve ourselves into who we are. You can, at any given moment, create a new start or be someone different than you were in the last moment. That's the power of choice. You can always have another chance, if you choose to make one for yourself. If you are able to become aware of your mistake and then restore your integrity around it by understanding your impact on others and then committing to a new way of being, then what is so bad about making a mistake? Mistakes are made and bad judgment is used, that is life. Life isn't defined by how flawless we are. It is defined by how we surpass the obstacles thrown in our path.

Think about it…

Love and Sunshine,
Tracy

Why compare when it's easier share?

"Why compare yourself with others? No one in the entire world can do a better job of being you than you." – Unknown

"Winners compare their achievements with their goals, while losers compare their achievements with those of other people" – Nido Qubein

"To wish you were someone else is to waste the person you are." – Unknown

If the focus in your mind is to compare your life to another's life, you will always find someone that you perceive to be better than you and your self-image will take a beating. No one is greater than or better than anyone else. I give this advice to others, so why am *I*, at times, still caught in comparing myself to someone else? When I go within and ask why, what comes up for me is that I am looking for someone's approval. I guess I am human after all. I read an interesting article this morning about how to gain the inner freedom to remove your puppet strings which give someone else control of how you feel about yourself and eliminate your need for someone else's approval of who you are.

Henrik Edberg says: "The thing about lessening your need for approval is that you have to give up both positive and negative approval. They are connected because when if you no longer crave positive cheers and approval from people, then you will no longer have fears of not getting that approval either.

When you really start to give it up – which might have to be done over time and with patience as your ego probably will want to snap back to seeking that sweet, sweet approval – you start to realize that neither of them are that important. They are really only as important as you decide they are. You are what you think you are and the world is what you think it is."

He also goes on to say that whenever you feel a feeling that you may not want to be feeling, like neediness for approval from someone, do not struggle with that feeling. If you resist it, it will only make that feeling stronger. If you accept the feeling as "what is" you may, in a short while, experience something wonderful: the feeling just vanishes...

When you no longer need the approval from others and stop comparing yourself to them, you may find that you will have an inner freedom to do what you want and just BE who you are without limitations. You may start to notice uplifting opportunities in your life that you may not have seen before.

What comes up for me when thinking about the above is that this last year I decided that for me to be who I am I had to end my relationship with my husband. What I get is that I was seeking his approval of who I am, and not just being who I am. When I did not get what I thought I was looking for, I made it mean that I needed to remove myself from the situation. What I know now, for sure, is that I do not need his approval of who I am, just his acceptance.

Everything does happen for a reason and now my husband and I have a more loving relationship than ever before. We talk about everything that comes up for us in the moment and we share what's important to us so that we are conscious of not creating blocks to our love. Our lives together have been simplified and through our open communication we have created a closer intimacy that never existed before, both inside and outside the bedroom. We are able to accept each other for who we are, and through that acceptance each of us is much happier than we ever were before. All this was possible for me through letting go of my need to get approval of who I am from someone else.

This reminds me of the first quote. "Why compare yourself with others? No one in the entire world can do a better job of being you than you." I LOVE me! The gifts of who I am to those around me are incomparable to anyone or anything else. I am unique and special and there is no one else on this planet who will ever come close to being me. Accept me or do not accept me, I am one of a kind! So are you!

What would you be able to create in your life if you removed your need to get approval from someone else?

Think about it…

Love and Sunshine,
Tracy

Learn to remove your concerns

"Listening is a magnetic and strange thing, a creative force. You can see that when you think how the friends that really listen to us are the ones we move toward, and we want to sit in their radius as though it did us good, like ultraviolet rays." – Brenda Ueland

"So when you are listening to somebody, completely, attentively, then you are listening not only to the words, but also to the feeling of what is being conveyed, to the whole of it, not part of it." – Jiddu Krishnamurti

"The first duty of love is to listen." – Paul Tillich

We must need a refresher on listening or else the above quotes would not have come up for me today. If you have a concern about someone—that they do not like you or that they do not respect you—and you go into a conversation with this person with these concerns in your focus, how do you think this will affect your listening to that person? Do you not think you will be judging everything that person is saying, qualifying it with "well…they do not respect me anyway"? Then the conversation goes sour. Hmmm…are you surprised? Really? How's that working for you anyway?

Here's something you can do to not only improve your listening skills but to improve your overall communication with everyone around you. I invite you to think about someone that you wish you had better communication with. Think about a partner, a family member, a friend, a lover, or a co-worker. Now write down all the concerns you may have about this particular person. Come on, I know you can do this! OK, I have someone in mind and what comes up for me is: they never listen to me, they are arrogant, they do not respect who I am, they do not understand what I do, they are self-centered, they are a one-upper (which means that they always have to out-do or be one better than what I just said, or reply to what I am saying with I do that or I have that or I did that, only better), they are conceited, they think the world revolves around them… OK, I think that's enough…lol. Now if I go into a conversation with this person with all these concerns about them in my mind, how do you think I will be listening to whatever that person is saying to me—whether it is something nice about me or even just about the weather? Do you think

I'll ever create a safe open communication with this person? Will I ever understand where that person is coming from or will either of us ever come away with a sense of "I've been heard"? With all these concerns floating around in my mind I will not ever see that person as an ally or a friend and most likely I will stop communicating with them altogether. Hmmm…whose fault is that?

All my concerns about this person only exist in my mind, and I am the only person who is responsible for keeping them alive and having an incomplete communication with them. I can choose instead to remove the concerns completely and listen to them with nothing going on in my mind and allow them to be whomever they are in that moment, creating an awesome space to communicate with that person. And the next time I speak with them I listen from nothing again…and nothing again… and nothing again…Which do you think would be the most effective in creating happiness in my life? The latter of course! Wow! No more stress of carrying around the baggage of preset ways of being with anyone… Whew! (She wipes the sweat off her brow.) That's a relief!

What do you think you would be able to create in your life if you removed your concerns about the people you communicate with and listen to everyone from no set way of being going on in your head?

Think about it…

Love and Sunshine,
Tracy

What are you willing to see?

"Everything that irritates us about others can lead us to an understanding of ourselves."– C. G. Jung

"We discover in ourselves what others hide from us and we recognize in others what we hide from ourselves." – Vauvenargues

If you have been practicing your listening skills and you are still in a place of discontent with someone, why not check in and see where you may be responsible for that dissatisfaction? Maybe what you do not like about that other person is something you are not willing to own in yourself? People really are mirrors into your self. When you are willing to take on your life and really get that you are the only one who is in charge of your happiness, you may find that life becomes a beautiful reflection of simplicity and grace. If you accept others and, especially, yourself for "what is" in every moment how will you ever have a need to be concerned about "what isn't"?

Think about it…

Love and Sunshine,
Tracy

June 10th

Responsibility brings power

"Conscious evolution begins as we take responsibility for clearing our own obstructions." – *Dan Millman*

"Blame and Excuses Are the Hallmarks of an Unsuccessful Life" – *Susan M. Heathfield*

"Accountability breeds response-ability." – *Stephen R. Covey*

Do you know what it means to be responsible? I think that we have put too many of our own meanings behind what responsible actually means, to—maybe—not be responsible?! Lol…Being responsible is to answer or be accountable for something within one's power, control, or management. To be accountable for something means you are capable of explaining or justifying something. So-oO? Where does blame fall into all of this? Have you ever noticed that all the people who are caught in living an unsuccessful life are never responsible for it and they are continuously blaming someone or something else for their circumstances? Are you one of these people? As soon as you make an excuse for anything that is happening or has happened in your life, you are admitting that you are not in control of your own actions. Really? Even if someone put a gun to your head, as scary as that may be, you are still the only one who can make a decision about what thought or action you are going to play out into your reality. No excuses! So I invite you to listen to yourself, to the voice in your head, when you speak to others and especially when you speak to yourself. When you hear yourself making up a reason or an excuse of why your life or situation is the way it is, why not make an effort to see where you yourself are responsible for it?

What would you be able to create in your life if you stopped and looked at your situation to see where you may be the cause in your own life? If you can get that it is and always has been you, through your choices, who makes up how you feel about your own life, you may begin to make choices that create a way of living that surpasses any kind of joy and happiness that you may have ever imagined yourself experiencing!

Think about it…

Love and Sunshine,
Tracy

BE genuine

"To be yourself in a world that is constantly trying to make you something else is the greatest accomplishment." – Ralph Waldo Emerson

"Be who you are and say what you feel, because those who mind don't matter and those who matter don't mind." – Dr. Seuss

If you are not being yourself then who are you? If you are constantly trying to be something you are not, are you really surprised that you are unhappy, bitter and resentful at the end of the day? The way to finding your happiness is to first accept who you are; then through your own self acceptance you may find that it doesn't matter what other people think about who you should be and you can just BE! If you continue to squash and stuff your true being you may find that you will start to experience emotional, mental, spiritual and also physical ailments. Do not get in your head about this, there is always hope. You *can* release every block that you have put in your own way to completely BE you and only you. You can accept and love who you are in every moment of your life. (Through what I do I have helped many people remove the blocks they have created and they were able to love and accept themselves, release what was no longer working for them to move forward on their path.) If someone doesn't accept you for who you are then it has nothing to do with you and everything to do with how they feel about themselves. Remember "hurting" people hurt people. Do something different, accept yourself, and then give them a hug. Love is always the answer!

You can be whomever you want in any given moment as you are constantly evolving the "who" of you that you present to the outward world. I am a beautiful, gorgeous, smart, intelligent, understanding, caring, nurturing, loving, sensual, sexy woman who is unstoppable in manifesting the abundance of peace, love and happiness as well as all the money and income that I desire to have in my life! Who are you?

Think about it!

Love and Sunshine,
Tracy

Never wonder what if

"To try is to risk failure. But risk must be taken because the greatest hazard of life is to risk nothing. The person who risks nothing does nothing, has nothing, is nothing. He may avoid suffering and sorrow, but he simply cannot learn, feel, change, grow, live, and love." – Leo Buscaglia

"A life spent in making mistakes is not only more honorable, but more useful than a life spent doing nothing." – George Bernard Shaw

"Only those who risk going too far can know how far they can go." – Unknown

Let's take Leo's statement one step farther: to "try" is actually giving yourself permission to fail. Have you ever heard yourself saying to someone or yourself , "At least I tried." But did you really? I've said this before, take Yoda's advice: "Do or do not…there is no try." There has to be risk in order for you to find out what you are capable of doing or capable of handling. If you do not risk then you will never ever *know*. I would rather risk it all and know one hundred percent sure about something than always wonder "what if?"

Think about it…

Love and Sunshine,
Tracy

June 13th

Remove your de-fence

"The good life, as I conceive it, is a happy life. I do not mean that if you are good you will be happy; I mean that if you are happy you will be good." –
Bertrand Russell

Have you ever observed a person becoming so defensive that you saw them lose all their rational thinking or even get the paranoid idea that someone was actually attacking them physically? Have you noticed also that the person often turns off their listening and acts as if there is no one talking but themselves? Just not receiving any reason you may bring before them? Have you sensed that they are stuck in an "I am right" attitude so that nothing will sway them, ever? How does it feel to be in their presence? Kinda icky, isn't it? Let's turn the tables now. Have you ever been on the defensive? How did it feel for you to be with yourself? Kinda icky, eh? How do you think others around you were feeling? Hmmm…Interesting isn't it? Let's sit with that for a bit…

When we become overly defensive it is usually created from a state of fear. We start to build walls around ourselves, thinking that it may be the only way to protect ourselves from some form of pain. That pain may be emotional, mental, or spiritual. What we may not know is that by doing so, we end up only hurting ourselves. By putting a wall around us, we not only keep out the enemies we think we have, we also resist receiving the love and care of others who are truly concerned for us. And isn't that what we are all after? Receiving love and care from others? Seems self-defeating to me!

When we become defensive, we become disconnected, even from our own powers. Instead of fighting to be right, why not open your heart to someone else's point of view and start to take down the walls that you created to protect yourself? Honestly, it's just your own point of view that you are defending and no one can ever take that away from you, so why does it matter if someone thinks different than you?

What do you think you would be able to create for yourself if you took down your armor and fences so that, when interacting with someone, you came from a place of love in your heart and nothing in your mind?

Tracy Friesen

It's just a point of view—and who says you are the only one who can have one?

Think about it…

Love and Sunshine,
Tracy

June 14th

Dream!

"The most pathetic person in the world is the person who has sight, but no vision." – Helen Keller

"Far away there in the sunshine are my highest aspirations. I may not reach them, but I can look up and see their beauty, believe in them, and follow where they lead." – Louisa May Alcott

"The only limits are, as always, those of vision." – James Broughton

Have you ever heard the Law of the Lid? It goes something like this: if you put fleas in a jar and put the lid on (yes, of course, there are air holes in the lid, silly), the fleas will start to attempt to get out of the jar and continuously hit the lid. When you finally remove the lid, the fleas will remain trapped in the jar because they have made a decision that they can only jump so far and will never attempt to jump any higher than where the lid used to be. Kind of sad, isn't it? :(

Have you put a lid on your dreams? When is the last time you stretched yourself to go beyond the limitations *you* have put on yourself? Or have you been, like the flea, caught in an "I can only go so high or only have so much" mentality so that you have forgotten how to dream? Or can you even remember what your dreams once were? Kind of sad, isn't it? :(

Your attitude about your life is the only thing that you can control, ever! You *can* have everything you have ever dreamed about and more! You first must create or recreate your dream as a belief, in your mind. Recreate that belief that you can have it or you can attain it or, even better, that you already have it! See yourself already living the life you want! Your inner vision is the only thing you will ever see as a result in your outward world! What would you create in your present life if you removed your own lid and started to dream again—and not just dream but dreamt BIG?

Think about it…

Love and Sunshine,
Tracy

Every journey begins with a single step

"Everyone who got to where they are had to begin where they were." – Richard Paul Evans

Have you ever imagined yourself to be a hamster caught in its exercise wheel—constantly spinning but getting nowhere? Have you ever stopped to think that where you are is exactly where you need to be in order for you to get where you want to go?

Think about it…

Love and Sunshine,
Tracy

June 16th

Open to possibilities

"Become a possibilitarian. No matter how dark things seem to be or actually are, raise your sights and see possibilities – always see them, for they're always there." – Dr. Norman Vincent Peale

"One of the saddest lines in the world is, 'Oh come now—be realistic.' The best parts of this world were not fashioned by those who were realistic. They were fashioned by those who dared to look hard at their wishes and gave them horses to ride." – Richard Nelson Bolles

"It's kind of fun to do the impossible." – Walt Disney

If you are in a "my life sucks" state of mind, how are you ever surprised that your life doesn't show you anything but suckiness? When you open yourself up to other possibilities—and a possibility is not a "maybe someday it will happen," it's a different choice or alternative way of living your now—you may no longer have a preset way of being and you can BE whoever you want in this moment. And the BE that you decide to BE will always be the perfect BE—no matter what!

Think about it…

Love and Sunshine,
Tracy

Are you living a life sentence?

"We cannot rise higher than our thought of ourselves." – Orison Swett Marden

"We do not believe in ourselves until someone reveals that deep inside us something is valuable, worth listening to, worthy of our trust, sacred to our touch. Once we believe in ourselves we can risk curiosity, wonder, spontaneous delight or any experience that reveals the human spirit." – e. e. Cummings

Every decision you make comes from a belief that you created about yourself many years ago. I created a "life sentence" for myself that I am unlovable and therefore I am not worth it. And every experience in my life has reflected this underlying belief. Kind of sad, isn't it?: (I created this belief from the understanding of the four-year-old little Tracy. Wow—a four-year-old has been running my life for the last thirty-five some-odd years. It really seems silly, now, doesn't it? Although I understood this intellectually and brought awareness to it by attending some educational life courses, up until about a month ago I still thought my four-year-old perspective was true. In this last course, I realized by going back through my memories of my life that I had to really look at where I was responsible for my experiences. I wanted to be right about everything that I believed, so I did (or didn't) do everything to make that statement true about myself. What it has cost me over the years has been enough to make anyone believe that very same thing about me. I even went so far as to end my marriage over it.

We all, at some point in our lives, have either done something or had something done to us that led us to create a belief about ourselves and who we are at our core. We then develop a way to continually prove it's true over and over and over again. It affects how we relate to other people and especially ourselves, to continually recreate this underlying belief about ourselves in our lives. It's just a story we created and it isn't the truth! Hey, don't make yourself wrong in this moment. Awareness is the first step into realizing that you are not a preset person and you do have a choice to be who you really are in any moment!

I invite you to have a look at your own life to see where you may have created a belief about yourself through an experience from your past that may still hold top billing in all the experiences in your life today.

The beauty about it all is that you can, at any moment, start over and live the life of your wildest dreams and more. If you believe you can, you can! If this statement brought up something negative for you, then that may be the first place to start to look about what life sentence you may have created for yourself.

Think about it...

Love and Sunshine,
Tracy

You are already complete

"The reality is that no one will ever be more complete than you already are."
— the Universe

"In about the same degree as you are helpful, you will be happy." — Karl Reiland

I'll let you in on a little secret . . . you already have everything that you will ever need to get you where you want to go so that you can have everything that you have ever wanted. Shhhh . . . we wouldn't want that to get out now would we?

Stop looking to others to complete you because you are already whole and complete all on your own. Start doing things that make you happy and I can guarantee you that you will feel a sense of completeness that you have never felt before, which will then create more happiness for you and in return you will feel more complete, which will then create more happiness for you and so on and so on . . .

Think about it...

Love and Sunshine,
Tracy

Balance = Happiness

"My soul is the bridge between spirit and body and, as such, is a uniter of opposites…Without soul at center, I would either transcend into spirit or become mired in matter." – Marion Woodman

"Walk in balance with one foot in your spiritual understanding and one foot in your physical world of accomplishment." – Lynn V. Andrews

"Pure and simple, balance is happiness." – Frederick Lenz

Hmmm…. balance. Isn't that the habit of calm behavior? And/or isn't it the power or ability to decide an outcome by throwing one's strength, influence, support, or the like, to one side or the other? Isn't it finding the equilibrium between those things that you find important in your life? If you are continuously saying "I wish I had more…" whether it be more time, more money, more friends, more love, more peace and calm, more freedom or more whatever…maybe your life just needs a bit of balance? If you are unhappy about anything, and I mean anything, that is going on in your life you are out of balance. You are out of balance because if you were in balance then there would be no need to be in "want" of anything.

Think about it…

Love and Sunshine,
Tracy

Go beyond

"If you're proactive, you don't have to wait for circumstances or other people to create perspective expanding experiences. You can consciously create your own."
— Stephen Covey

"Nurture great thoughts, for you will never go higher than your thoughts." —
Benjamin Disraeli

W hy wait for someone else to make a move in order for you to get to the happiness that you crave? Wouldn't it make more sense for you to be the creator of your own life instead of leaving it in someone else's control? Oh yeah, if someone else controlled you and/or the situation, you wouldn't have to be responsible for the things that happen in your life…yeah, how's that working for you?

Here's a gift for you from Buddha: "Do not dwell in the past, do not dream of the future, concentrate the mind on the present moment." If you were able to forget the past and not worry about the future and truly lived in this moment what could you possibly be afraid of that would be holding you back from anything? Look around you—is there actually anything there in your vicinity that is harming you or restraining you in any way? Really? If you can get that the stories you tell yourself in your head are not true and may never happen, then maybe, just maybe, you might be able to find some joy and happiness in your life. And we wouldn't want that to happen now would we?

Think about it…

Love and Sunshine,
Tracy

On your mark, get set, wait...

"Patience has its limits—take it too far and it's cowardice."– George Jackson

"Patience is waiting. Not passively waiting. That is laziness. But to keep going when the going is hard and slow—that is patience." – Unknown

"He that can have Patience, can have what he will." – Benjamin Franklin

"Patience is also a form of action." – Auguste Rodin

Have you ever wanted something so badly that you forced things to happen—and then when you didn't get what you wanted in the end you went into your stories of why you didn't get it after all? Sometimes we just need to let go of our expected results and have the patience to allow things to fall into place as they are meant to fall. If it is not meant to be yours by Divine right then forcing it will not ever make it better. Wisdom and patience go hand in hand. If you are able to keep yourself in this moment and not be focused on the next one, the patience that you create will bring you more joy and happiness than you can ever imagine.

Think about it...

Love and Sunshine,
Tracy

Transform regrets

"Do you feel sadness and disappointment for what you have failed to do? Then you have some powerful energy for moving yourself forward. Do you feel regret for the missed opportunities? That painful regret has a positive purpose. For although those past opportunities are gone, even more powerful ones have arisen to take their place. What's even better is that you now have more reason than ever to make the most of them. You can easily and naturally transform sadness into motivation. You can transform the regrets into powerful and unstoppable determination. Feel the intensity of your own energy. Realize you can point that energy in any direction you choose. Choose to point it forward, in alignment with your highest purpose and most treasured dreams. Now is the time that matters, and now you can make life great." – Ralph Marston

Why are you giving energy to something that you can never change? It only is what it is, nothing more. This doesn't mean that you still do not have an opportunity to clean up your regret, either for yourself or for someone else. Be BOLD and daring to take on your life full-on with no blinders! Life is meant to be lived NOW, not back then. Do what you have to do: forgive, apologize, let go…then get back to being here and living now instead of wasting your time with reliving a story in your head about something or someone that will never change or be different ever.

WAKE UP TO THE NOW OF YOUR LIFE!!!

I will leave you with another of Ralph's quotes: "You don't need anyone else's permission to be happy. Your life is magnificent not because someone says it is, but because you choose to see it as such."

Think about it…

Love and Sunshine,
Tracy

Use your breath to relax your body

"Breath is the link between the inner and outer worlds." – Alice Christensen

"Controlled deep breathing helps the body to transform the air we breathe into energy. The stream of energized air produced by properly executed and controlled deep breathing produces a current of inner energy which radiates throughout the entire body and can be channeled to the body areas that need it the most, on demand." – Nancy Zi

If you want to be full of strength, courage, peace, hope, assurance, gratitude, joy, balance, inspiration, creativity, patience, calmness, tranquility, grace, passion, decisiveness, confidence, determination, focus, accomplishment, excitement, happiness, love and/or energy…sometimes all you need to do is breathe.

Think about it…

Love and Sunshine,
Tracy

Calm the mind

"All man's miseries derive from not being able to sit quietly in a room alone."
– Blaise Pascal

"Meditation helps me feel the shape, the texture of my inner life. Here, in the quiet, I can begin to taste what Buddhists would call my true nature, what Jews call the still, small voice, what Christians call the holy spirit."– Wayne Muller

"When you find peace within yourself, you become the kind of person who can live at peace with others." – Peace Pilgrim

Have you let your Monkey Brain take over your life? You know, the one that doesn't let you rest for a second—that voice in your head or the constant movie that just doesn't stop? Well then...how can you be surprised that you do not feel at peace? Did you know that you are the only one feeding your monkey on a daily basis? If your monkey brain isn't working for you, you have the ability to ask it to leave or to stop. You have the ability to not hold onto the thoughts that are generated in your head.

For me, I had to create an image in my mind of tempting a monkey with a banana. Sounds silly, I know! Then when my monkey got to the edge of my mind I threw the banana far, far, far out so that it would take a long long long time for her to find her way back...lol. I have also created a tiny image of myself running around my mind pushing all the unwanted thoughts out. I made it a game. Oh there's a thought that isn't serving me...push push push to the edge then POP! It's gone...lol. I have also allowed the thought to come in and I thanked it for its lesson then said I no longer need that medicine so you can go now. There are many different techniques that you can use to quiet your mind and stop your monkey from working overtime. Find one that works for you. Taking up yoga was where I was finally able to quiet my mind and think of nothing and just be at peace within myself.

I invite you to start to take at least ten minutes every day—schedule it in if you have to—to go within and train your monkey to take a rest for a change and just BE with yourself thinking of nothing, being concerned about nothing, contemplating nothing, organizing nothing, trying to figure out nothing. Just imagine: Nothing to think about to stress you out! If you never ask your monkey to rest or to stop, how will you ever know the happiness you would be able to create for yourself by just being at peace?

Think about it!

Love and Sunshine,
Tracy

The face in the mirror

"Our inability to see beauty doesn't suggest in the slightest that beauty is not there. Rather, it suggests that we are not looking carefully enough or with broad enough perspective to see the beauty."– Rabbi Harold Kushner

"The sun shines not on us but in us. The rivers flow not past, but through us, thrilling, tingling, vibrating every fiber and cell of the substance of our bodies, making them glide and sing." – John Muir

Why is it that we have trouble seeing our own good and our own beauty? Why is it that we turn a blind eye to all that we do that is awesome and extraordinary? And when someone points it out we go, "It's no big deal." Can you say…victim? You should be celebrating when someone acknowledges you, not trying to pretend that it doesn't matter and slough it off. At every chance you get I invite you to CELEBRATE your beauty! CELEBRATE your greatness! CELEBRATE your uniqueness! CELEBRATE your magnificence! Just CELEBRATE all that is YOU!

Open your eyes! The sooner you see your own beauty the sooner people will start to see something different in you. How is it working for you to hide behind your wall day after day? The wall may keep the enemies out but it also keeps your allies at bay as well. How can any love get to you if you are constantly repelling everything that comes your way? Take down your wall. Look in the mirror and truly see your beauty through love, not judgment. I wish that for just one moment you would be able to see yourself through my eyes and really get how beautiful and complete you are. What would you be able to release and create for yourself by allowing yourself to actually see your own beauty?

Think about it…

Love and Sunshine,
Tracy

Perfect self-expression

"Follow your inner moonlight; don't hide the madness." – Allen Ginsberg

"Never be bullied into silence. Never allow yourself to be made a victim. Accept no one's definition of your life, but define yourself." – Harvey Fierstein

While at the park today with my daughter and her friend I was reading a from the collections of Florence Scovel Shinn and I came to a chapter in her first book, *The Game of Life & How To Play It*, titled "Perfect Self-Expression or The Divine Design" which lead me to a different belief about being self expressed. A bit of background about the author I think is necessary. She was a popular teacher of metaphysical spirituality. Shinn was teaching self-help back in the early days of the century, long before the current craze for self-help books took over. If you believe in the power of positive thinking, you'll enjoy Florence Scovel Shinn. She wrote *The Game of Life* back in 1925! Wow…just amazing!

Before reading this chapter I had believed that to be fully self-expressed was to be able to say and communicate what is going on in your mind without having fear of what others might think about you. Now, I have another belief altogether. Florence begins her chapter like this:

"There is for each man, perfect self-expression. There is a place which he is to fill and no one else can, something which he is to do, which no one else can do; it is his destiny!

This achievement is held, a perfect idea in Divine Mind, awaiting man's recognition. As the imagining faculty is the creative faculty, it is necessary for man to see the idea, before it can be manifest.

So man's highest demand is for the Divine Design of his life.

He may not have the faintest conception of what it is, for there is, possibly, some marvelous talent, hidden deep within him.

His demand should be: 'Infinite Spirit, open the way for the Divine Design of my life to manifest; let the genius within me now be released; let me see clearly the perfect plan.'

The perfect plan includes health, wealth, love and perfect self-expression. This is the square of life, which brings perfect happiness. When one has made this demand, he may find great changes taking place in his life, for nearly every man has wandered far from the Divine Design.

. . .

Perfect self-expression will never be labor; but of such absorbing interest that it will seem almost like play. The student knows, also, as man comes into the world financed by God, the supply needed for his perfect self-expression will be at hand."

So what I got out of reading the above is that to be fully self-expressed one must find what is perfect for them to do in this world—whether that be the perfect garbage collector, the perfect waiter, the perfect husband, the perfect mother, the perfect brain surgeon, the perfect bartender, the perfect brother, the perfect teacher or the perfect rocket scientist. Whatever it is for you to do that's what is for you to do and it doesn't matter what that is because you are the only one meant to do that very thing. Although my first belief has a lot to do with being self-expressed it surely is only one small component of it. I am always grateful for being open to expanding my knowledge and learn something new.

I invite you to get a copy of the writings of Florence Scovel Shinn and see how one woman's beliefs back in the early days of this century can help you become the Perfect Self-Expression that you were meant to be!!!

Think about it...

Love and Sunshine,
Tracy

It's time to make a different choice

"Happiness is not a reward—it is a consequence. Suffering is not a punishment—it is a result." – Robert Green Ingersoll

"Unless it's your path, it's pointless to follow. But if it is your path, then, alas, it's pointless to follow any other." – Harvey Arden

If you are not happy in your life, what are you? Are you, perhaps, trying to follow someone else's path or a path that someone else thinks you should be on? How's that working for you? We are a product of the choices that we have made thus far, and if the consequence of your choices have not brought you happiness, do you not think it's about time to make a different choice?

Think about it…

Love and Sunshine,
Tracy

Are you searching?

"We spend our time searching for security and hate it when we get it." – John Steinbeck

"The mind is always present. You just don't see it." –Bodhidharma

If we spend all our time looking and searching for something we may just miss that very thing we are seeking to fulfill our life, because we were not present to realize it is right in front of us. How many times in your life have you suddenly become aware and wondered, where did all the time go? If you were present you would not have missed a single second. If you put importance and priority to the things that you are seeking, you may one day realize that most, if not all, are irrelevant to what will bring you happiness in the end. Not sure you believe me? Then go back in your memory and really look at the things you sought that you actually achieved—only to realize that they weren't what you wanted after all. Then you began another search for something else. If you were living your life moment to moment, appreciating what you have now, being grateful for all that you have, you would never be left with the feeling that you are missing out and that you need to continue searching for something to fill your void because you would already be full.

Think about it…

Love and Sunshine,
Tracy

June 29th

Expand your limits

> *"People are defeated by easy, victorious and cheap successes more than by adversity."* – Benjamin Disraeli

> *"Success means fulfilling your own dreams, singing your own song, dancing your own dance, creating from your heart and enjoying the journey, trusting that whatever happens, it will be OK. Creating your own adventure!"* – Elana Lindquist

Just because you are creating your own adventure it doesn't mean that you have to do it alone. People come and go in our lives. They all serve a purpose—whether it is to help you stand your ground or to stand by you forever. Every single interaction is important for you to fulfill your dreams. Even that person that ticked you off so bad, you know the one, the one that you are still holding a grudge against. Yes, they too are there for a reason. Have you learned the lesson yet?

Stretch yourself…go beyond where you think your limits are. How will you ever expand yourself if you never go out into the unknown? Do not fool yourself into thinking that only going to the edge is far enough.

What would you be able to create in your life, if you did something—every day—that was outside your comfort zone?

Think about it…

Love and Sunshine,
Tracy

Slow down and enjoy

"Adopt the pace of nature, her secret is patience." – Ralph Waldo Emerson

"Racing through life is very stressful. If we stay in high gear too long, we lose our ability to shift down. And when we're stressed, we can't access happiness, appreciation, fun, compassion, generosity, awareness of beauty and other wonderful qualities. High stress also triggers negative emotions like frustration, impatience, anger and fear.

Life has so much to offer if we will slow down and truly experience it. We must always remember that we are the ones in control of the accelerator. We CAN choose to brake." – Unknown

"Slow down and enjoy life. It's not only the scenery you miss by going too fast—you also miss the sense of where you are going and why." – Eddie Cantor

Couldn't have said it any better myself. All I need to add is:

Think about it…

Love and Sunshine,
Tracy

July 1st

Do or do not

"Thinking about interior peace destroys interior peace. The patient who constantly feels his pulse is not getting any better." – Hubert van Zeller

"So many people work so hard, to achieve, attain, accumulate and cherish their fortunes. How many of us blissfully fill our days and nights being the Divine expression we are? This is the meaning of life. It is to be. As a result, all of your creations are a natural outflow from the Divine within your being. This is the joy of life." – Barbara Rose

Isn't that the truth...the more you try to attain something the farther away it seems. If you put something out of your reach it will always be just that...out of your reach! The more you are grateful for what you *do* have the more likely you are to get that which you are seeking to attain—or you'll realize you didn't want it after all. What is trying, anyway? It is just an excuse for you to be OK with failing. Perhaps we should take a lesson from Yoda: "Do or do not; there is no try." Yoda is so right in saying there is no try. You cannot "try" to do anything. Here is an example: Try to sit down. Go ahead try. You can't, can you? You either sit or you do not sit; there is no trying to sit. The same goes with everything else you "try" to do in your life.

Think about it...

Love and Sunshine,
Tracy

Making life our own

"Life is not lost by dying; life is lost minute by minute, day by dragging day, in all the thousand small uncaring ways." – Stephen Vincent Benet

"It is so easy to waste our lives: our days, our hours, our minutes…It is so easy to exist instead of live. Unless you know there is a clock ticking. So many of us changed our lives when we heard a biological clock and decided to have kids. But that sound is a murmur compared to the tolling of mortality." – Anna Quindlen

If you spend every day just rush rush rushing around, with no time to think or focus because you are overwhelmed with all that you have to do and all that is going on in your life, how are you ever surprised that you are not finding your life enjoyable? It's time to slow down. You are missing out on sooo much happiness by filling your life with stuff. Whatever you are giving your time to is what you are giving your priority to in your life. When asked you may say that your family is a priority, but all you do is rush them here and rush them there. Your priority is driving not spending quality time with your family. It's time to check in on your life and find out what you truly hold valuable. Is it the people and relationships or is it things and image that are top priority in your life? If you do not know just look at what you spend most of your time doing. Your life is your own. Don't you think it's about time you lived it that way?

Think about it…

Love and Sunshine,
Tracy

Time to blossom

"The voice of our original self is often muffled, overwhelmed, even strangled, by the voices of other people's expectations." – Julie Cameron

"For all those years you've protected the seed. Its time to become the beautiful flower." – Stephen C. Paul

What are you waiting for? Why are you still hiding from the world? Personally, I feel gypped that you continue to refuse to show and BE your true self. Why do you think it is OK to be something you are not day after day? You really think that other person knows better than you? Ha! And double HA! If it is happiness that you are after, then why do you continue to do what others want you to do instead of being the perfect you that you were meant to BE?

It really is time to come out and show the world that you are perfect just the way you are and that the world is a better place because of it! There is no longer a need to protect yourself. Remember, you will always have one person in this world that accepts you for who you are, exactly where you are and exactly who you are in this moment. So why not let your light shine? Let your petals open for the world to see and BE who you truly are! If you do not stand for you, you stand for nothing.

Think about it…

Love and Sunshine,
Tracy

Are you afraid to be different?

"Nature never repeats herself, and the possibilities of one human soul will never be found in another." – Elizabeth Cady Stanton

I see you are still sitting there in your fortress with your moat and High Guard around the edges. It is protecting you from what? Allowing the world to see who you really are? Why are you so afraid of what someone else might think or say about who you are or who you are meant to BE? Did you ever think that they themselves are sitting there wondering what you think of them? It can be a vicious circle, if you want it to be, that is.

Let go of your need to control other people's thoughts and ideas about you and just BE who you are. I can almost guarantee that you will feel such a weight lift off your spirit that just maybe, somehow, you may get to the Happiness that you are seeking. Wow—and why would we ever want to do that? Lol…

Think about it…

Love and Sunshine,
Tracy

The four D's of spiritual growth

"Strive to be so strong that nothing can disturb your peace of mind. To be too wise for worry, too tolerant for hate, and too courageous to be fearful. In short, to be happy." – Unknown

"Reflect on this pathway for meaningful growth:

DISCIPLINE—To create change in our lives, we need to consistently focus on what we want.

DETACHMENT—Practice the art of detached observation. Let go of automatic defenses and patterns.

DISCERNMENT—Seek to discern the lower from the higher. What is self-serving and what is soul-inspired? Discernment carries no judgment. There are no goods and bads. Remain as a detached witness.

DHARMA—This is an East Indian word meaning 'living your unique purpose.' How do you find meaning and fulfillment in ways that are natural to you? How do you best serve and contribute to the world?" – Unknown

"If you wish to travel far and fast, travel light. Take off all your envies, jealousies, unforgiveness, selfishness, and fears." – Glenn Clark

Have you ever felt so weighed down that you thought you couldn't take another step? Lighten your load. Stop taking things so personally that you think everyone is against you. Let go of your need to control people and your outcomes. The only thing you can ever control is your own thoughts, your own feelings, your own emotions and your own actions. Everyone has "stuff" going on in their life. Don't let "stuff" get in the way of your happiness. Let go of your judgments and your own personal agenda and just live as if you already have all that you need...because you do. Your Divine will never let you down.

Think about it...

Love and Sunshine,
Tracy

No one else

"If you want to know your past—look into your present conditions. If you want to know your future—look into your present actions." – Chinese Proverb

You are where you are because you are a product of your choices. There is no one else to blame. There is no one else to point a finger at. There is no one else but you who is responsible for how your life is at this moment. And wouldn't you rather be happy than right?

Think about it…

Love and Sunshine,
Tracy

Have you had enough yet?

"Actually, it's easier to accept others, than to change them. It's wiser to understand them, than to get angry. And most of the time, it's more fun to love 'em, than to leave 'em."

"He who knows that enough is enough will always have enough." – Lao Tzu

Do you know when enough is enough? Or are you stuck in trying to make everyone around see your point of view as THE point of view? Are you so relentless that you've even forgotten that other people are actually involved? Have you not only put blinders on but stuffed cotton in your ears as well? That's right, I forgot…no one could ever, possibly, have a different point of view from yours because you are always right! Hmmm… How's that working for you in feeling like you are being heard or even understood? How does that ever create happiness and/or joy in your life? You are only upset because you didn't get something you wanted, and now you are throwing a grown-up size temper tantrum. Get over yourself. Take responsibility for your own actions and your own life. Whether you did something, or didn't do something to create this in your life, deal with it. Accept it—and move on! If you really check in and be honest with yourself you will see that you are only mad at yourself. There really is no one else to blame—ever.

Think about it…

Love and Sunshine,
Tracy

Is your Ego playing tricks again?

"One of the great dangers of transformational work is that the ego attempts to sidestep deep psychological work by leaping into the transcendent too soon. This is because the ego always fancies itself much more advanced than it actually is." – Don Richard Riso and Russ Hudson

"Enlightenment is ego's ultimate disappointment." – Chögyam Trungpa

"There are two kinds of people in this life. Those who walk into a room and say, 'Well, here I am.' And those who walk in and say, 'Ahh, there you are.' Let us each strive to be an 'Ahh, there you are' person." – Leil Lowndes

Why do you think that enlightenment is ego's ultimate disappointment? Hmmm…Good question. What I know is that when you transform into enlightenment you no longer look to your ego for guidance, because you are no longer looking at your life in a "what's in it for me?" kind of way. When dealing with people, instead of checking every brick in your wall of protection, you are able to be free and come from the unconditional love in your heart. You realize that we are all related. We are all brothers and sisters walking this planet and NO one is better than or greater than anyone else. There is no need to compare yourself to anyone. There is no need to compare yourself to who they are or what they have done. You no longer have the need to be validated in any aspect of your life. You are able to keep your ego shut off when someone is speaking and you no longer have the need to let them know that you too have done the same thing. This is why the ego is disappointed: because it realizes that it is no longer needed.

Think about it…

Love and Sunshine,
Tracy

Energy...

"It is wonderful how much time good people spend fighting the devil. If they would only expend the same amount of energy loving their fellow men, the devil would die in his own tracks of ennui." – Helen Keller

This is what I know about energy. Energy is never created or destroyed; it just is. It is never ending. It runs through everything and everyone. There is no positive or negative and no right or wrong. It runs on whatever you feed into it. It is up to you to decide how you want to live your life and whatever you decide is what you decide. If you want to feed your life energy of self pity and continue to wallow in your view of yourself as a victim, then do it without complaint because you are choosing it. You are the only one responsible for the outcomes in your life. It is never too late to start again and you can do this as many times as you like. Remember five minutes from now will be then and you can choose to be whoever you want—now in this moment and again in this moment and this one and this one and this one…

"Too many of us are hung up on what we don't have, can't have, or won't ever have. We spend too much energy being down, when we could use that same energy—if not less of it—doing, or at least trying to do, some of the things we really want to do." – Terry McMillan

Think about it…

Love and Sunshine,
Tracy

The sushi effect

"Try a thing you haven't done three times. Once, to get over the fear of doing it. Twice, to learn how to do it. And a third time, to figure out whether you like it or not." – Virgil Garnett Thomson

Is there something that you are still afraid to do? Hmmm…Did you know that the fear of it only exists in your own thoughts? You have completely made up the whole event from start to finish without ever knowing the truth about it. Why not do something different for a change and just GO FOR IT! You will never know the truth unless you take that first step into the unknown.

Think about it…

Love and Sunshine,
Tracy

What do you value?

"We do not act rightly because we have virtue or excellence, but we rather have those because we have acted rightly." – Aristotle

"Price is what you pay. Value is what you get." – Warren Buffett

"There are so many men who can figure costs and so few who can measure values." – Unknown

"Beauty, truth, friendship, love, creation—these are the great values of life. We can't prove them, or explain them, yet they are the most stable things in our lives." – Jesse Herman Holmes

What is the most important thing that you value? Is it something that you can touch? Something that may someday breakdown or deteriorate enough that you have to replace it? Or is it something that you feel in your heart? Something that, if you choose to, you can keep new, fresh and alive every day?

Think about it...

Love and Sunshine,
Tracy

I believe...

The following was taken from an email that I received today. It was a great way to start my day and I really enjoyed reading it so I thought I would share some of its wisdom with all of you as well:

I Believe... That we don't have to change friends if We understand that friends change.

I Believe... That no matter how good a friend is, they're going to hurt you every once in a while and you must forgive them for that.

I Believe... That sometimes when I'm angry I have the right to be angry, But that doesn't give me the right to be cruel.

I Believe... That maturity has more to do with what types of experiences you've had And what you've learned from them and less to do with how many birthdays you've celebrated.

I Believe... That our background and circumstances may have influenced who we are, but, we are responsible for who we become.

I Believe... That credentials on the wall do not make you a decent human being.

I Believe... The happiest of people don't necessarily have the best of everything: They just make the most of everything they have.

Take it easy on others, especially yourself. Look at your life and be grateful for all that you have. If you look and think about what you do not have you will just create more of that "not having" and I can guarantee you that does not ever create happiness for yourself—ever! Even if you think there is nothing good in your life to be grateful for just be grateful that you have another day to be alive! Everything happens for a reason. You are here for a reason. And you are meant to live happy!

"Happy is the person who knows what to remember of the past, what to enjoy in the present, and what to plan for in the future." – Arnold H. Glasgow

Think about it...

Love and Sunshine,
Tracy

Chillin'

"Fact of the matter is, everything is a non-issue, until someone decides other-wise...And that means you can now chill." – the Universe

How are you going to spend *your* time today...creating issues or chilling out? It is, as it always has been, your choice!

Think about it...

Love and Sunshine,
Tracy

Who needs Jerry Maguire?

"The purpose of relationship is not to have another who might complete you, but to have another with whom you might share your completeness." – Neale Donald Walsch

Are you still looking to someone else to make you whole? How's that been working for you? Maybe you need to realize that you are already complete and whole just by being who you are. Give yourself some credit and know that you are doing the best you can with the knowledge that you have now in this moment.

Think about it…

Love and Sunshine,
Tracy

A focus for parents

"Parents: persons who spend half their time worrying how a child will turn out, and the rest of the time wondering when a child will turn in." – Ted Cook

Schneider says, "Their soul is in charge of their lives, and nothing that you do can greatly interfere nor greatly help. Who you are as a being and what you model is the important reality."

"The most important thing that parents can teach their children is how to get along without them." – Frank A. Clark

"There are only two lasting bequests we can hope to give our children. One of these is roots; the other, wings." – Hodding Carter

Being a parent is the easiest and the most difficult task all rolled into one. All you need to do is feed them, water them and love them without giving your own interpretation of what their life "should" be.

Think about it…

Love and Sunshine,
Tracy

Consider there is a fly on the wall...

"Improve relationships with others by assuming that they can hear everything you say about them." – Stephen R. Covey

And that means everything. Inside your head and what you say to others when they are not around. Do you think that they would still want to be around you if they heard everything you say about them? If you want happiness in your life then stop trying to control other people and judging their actions. The only thing that you *can* control is your own thoughts and your own actions.

Think about it…

Love and Sunshine,
Tracy

What's important to you?

"What most people need to learn in life is how to love people and use things, instead of using people and loving things." – Unknown

What are you giving the most importance to in your life? Is it the car you drive or is it your wonderful partner, friend, or family member sitting next to you in the passenger seat?

Think about it...

Love and Sunshine,
Tracy

Communicating without words

"The gesture is the thing truly expressive of the individual—as we think so will we act." – Martha Graham

"An avoidance of true communication is tantamount to a relinquishment of my self-being; if I withdraw from it I am betraying not only the other but myself." – Karl Jaspers

What Karl is saying is that if you do not follow through your words with actions then you are doing the same as surrendering your true BEing—as well as having a not-so-positive impact on the other person. Then you are not only out of integrity, you are also denying your "self" its happiness.

Think about it...

Love and Sunshine,
Tracy

July 19th

It's time to get creative!

"I am a child of God. I came from the womb of creation." – Tao Te Ching

"Our grand business in life is not to see what lies dimly at a distance, but to do what lies clearly at hand." – Thomas Carlyle

"Embrace fully your capacity to create, to think in unlimited ways, and to pursue everything that you have been wanting. Be flexible, open and willing to let the new come to you. This can be the most joyous, prosperous, and creative time of your life." – Sanaya Roman and Duane Packer

When is the last time you used your imagination for anything? Do you remember what it was like to create a new world on a whim just because? And just because you are older that does not mean that you are required to lose your child-like view of the world to create anything and everything you want here in the now.

What is power again? Oh yeah...the ability to *do* something. Instead of standing still, going backwards or maybe even destroying...why not use your power to create?

Think about it...

Love and Sunshine,
Tracy

Connect with the life force

"The spirit down here in man and the spirit up there in the sun, in reality are only one spirit, and there is no other one." – The Upanishads

"Everything you see has its roots in the unseen world. The forms may change, yet the essence remains the same. Every wonderful sight will vanish; every sweet word will fade, But do not be disheartened, The source they come from is eternal, growing, Branching out, giving new life and new joy. Why do you weep? The source is within you And this whole world is springing up from it." – Jelaluddin Rumi

If you look within, you will find what is in everything. We are all made of the same energy, the same spirit, the same love. We are forever changing, forever growing, forever evolving. The question is, have you found your true form or are you still in your cocoon? It doesn't matter which one it is for you. Whereever you are is the perfect place for you to be, so do not worry or fret. Every journey begins the same way: with a single step.

Think about it…

Love and Sunshine,
Tracy

The first step to forgiveness

"To get to forgiveness, we first have to work through the painful experiences that require it." – Christiane Northrup

"We must let ourselves feel all the painful destruction we want to forgive rather than swallow it in denial. If we do not face it, we cannot choose to forgive it." – Kenneth McNoll

Now, just because it says you have to feel the pain, that doesn't mean that you are required to torture yourself. It says that you must let yourself feel the painful destruction in order to know what there is to forgive but it doesn't say that you have to continue to punish yourself over and over. Awareness is the key. Truthfully, it is up to you, or I mean, it is your choice how long you decide to feel the pain in order for you to realize that you just need to forgive yourself and know that you did the best you could with the knowledge that you had in the moment. Do you really think if back then you had the knowledge you have right now in this moment, you would have made the same choice?

Think about it…

Love and Sunshine,
Tracy

Create consciously

"No man has a chance to enjoy permanent success until he begins to look in a mirror for the real cause of all his mistakes." – Napoleon Hill

"He who is false to present duty breaks a thread in the loom, and will find the flaw when he may have forgotten its cause." – Henry Ward Beecher

Read again both quotes and sit with it for a moment...

It is true. You are the only one responsible for all the mistakes that you have made in your life. No ifs, ands, buts or maybes...you, end of story. No one else is to blame—ever! SO WHAT? Get over it. Forgive yourself and move on. All it takes is awareness and the integrity to clean up any messes you may have created. Be aware and accept that you are responsible for your life. Then you may see that your life will take a turn for the better. Once again it is, as it always has been, your choice to live a happy, successful life.

If it *is* happiness and success you are after then stop—and I mean STOP— all talk of any woes or upset in your life, because all you are doing is bringing more upset instead of the happiness and success you desire. For example if you find yourself wanting to tell others about all the mishaps and crappy things that have happened to you, are you really surprised that you are not happy and successful? Stop sharing the upsetting things in your life. Start talking only about what you are grateful for and you may be pleasantly surprised that your life will suddenly and unexpectedly turn for the better and you will feel the happiness and success that you desire.

Think about it...

Love and Sunshine,
Tracy

July 23rd

Learn from experience

"Experience is not what happens to a man; it is what a man does with what happens to him." – Aldous Huxley

"Ask the experienced rather than the learned." – Arabic proverb

"Experience is that marvellous thing that enables you to recognize a mistake when you make it again." – Franklin P. Jones

Just because someone is book smart does not mean they have all the answers.

Think about it…

Love and Sunshine,
Tracy

Dance through your day

"Mix a little foolishness with your serious plans: it's lovely to be silly at the right moment." – Horace

"We look at the dance to impart the sensation of living in an affirmation of life, to energize the spectator into keener awareness of the vigor, the mystery, the humor, the variety, and the wonder of life." – Martha Graham

When is the last time you danced like no one was watching, sang a song like no one could hear you or did anything that you wanted to do without the extra baggage of thinking what someone might think about it? Life isn't meant to be taken sooo seriously. Get out of your rigid ways, loosen up and free yourself from the shackles that you have bound to your feet. Get LIVING! If what you are doing doesn't bring happiness to your life then stop doing it and just dance!

The sun is shining, the air is warm. Why not throw some fun into your routine? You never know what kind of happiness you will bring to every-one around you, including yourself, if you just remember how to play now and again.

Think about it…

Love and Sunshine,
Tracy

Check in on your attitude

"I discovered I always have choices and sometimes it's only a choice of attitude."
– Judith M. Knowlton

"Today I will do what others won't, so tomorrow I can accomplish what others can't." – Jerry Rice

How has your attitude been lately? How have you been taking on the things that are not so much fun? Have you been grumbling about it or have you gone about your business and just kept smiling? Maybe you are "thinking" too much and not "feeling" your way through your life. What would you be able to create in your life if you gave your attitude a bit of a tune-up and just smiled your way through and lived each moment with joy instead of complaining about it?

Think about it…

Love and Sunshine,
Tracy

Learn to ask for help

"Men are anxious to improve their circumstances, but are unwilling to improve themselves; they therefore remain bound." – James Allen

Why is it that you are still wanting to blame others for what happens in your life and then complain that nothing is the way you want it to be? Have you ever thought that the first place to look for anything that doesn't or isn't going so well in your life is in the mirror? Learn to ask for help. You were not born with every answer but somewhere there is someone who has the answer to the question you are asking. You just need to learn to ask the questions and be ready and open to where or who might have an answer for you.

What would you be able to create in your life if you committed to at least ten minutes every day to improving and enlightening yourself, or just learned to ask for help?

Think about it…

Love and Sunshine,
Tracy

Are you wasting your time?

"We act as though comfort and luxury were the chief requirements of life, when all that we need to make us really happy is something to be enthusiastic about." – Charles Kingsley

"Doing what you love is the cornerstone of having abundance in your life." – Wayne Dyer

"Find something you love to do and you'll never have to work a day in your life." – Harvey MacKay

Why do we go about our business like the world owes us something? When is the last time you contributed to your own happiness? Someone once told me: "If it doesn't make you happy then don't do it." Wise words. Have you ever felt at the end of your day that you haven't done anything, yet it seemed like you were constantly running around attempting to get things done? Or if you are going to work just so you can say you are busy, what kind of accomplishment is that? What truly makes you happy? Do you even remember? Or are you so stuck in what you think society wants you to do that you have lost hope and are resigned to the fact that this is as good as it is going to get? Well…I'm here to tell you, that that is a bunch of HOOHOCKEY!

Your life is as good or as happy as you are allowing it to be—end of story! If you are not happy in your job then find one that you love! If you are not happy in your career then find the one that you love! If you are not happy in your home then find one that you love! If you are not happy in your anything it is, as it always has been, up to you to find your *own* happiness! No one else is to blame or is responsible for your life…ever! What would you create in your life if you actually did something that you loved to do *every* day?

Think about it…

Love and Sunshine,
Tracy

Remember your spiritual side

"The function of prayer is not to influence God, but rather to change the nature of the one who prays." – Soren Kierkegaard

"Spirituality is the sacred center out of which all life comes, including Mondays and Tuesdays and rainy Saturday afternoons in all their mundane and glorious detail…The spiritual journey is the soul's life commingling with ordinary life." – Christina Baldwin

"It is not my business to think about myself. My business is to think about God. It is for God to think about me." – Simone Weil

If you can let go and let your Divine, whatever that is for you, handle all the not-so-fun stuff that happens instead trying to control everything and everyone around you, where do you think you would be in your life? If you had nothing to bog down your thoughts and stress you out, where do you think you would be in your happiness? It may be as simple as having faith that your Divine already has a perfect plan for you, knowing that there is an infinite supply of all that you desire, and that it is up to you to just BE happy!

"I am a perfect idea in Divine Mind and I am always in my right place doing my right work at the right time for the right pay!"

Think about it…

Love and Sunshine,
Tracy

July 29th

Let go your need to control

"Life does not happen to us, it happens from us." – Mike Wickett

"The willingness to do creates the ability to do." – Peter McWilliams

Are you still waiting for someone else to do something in order for you to move forward or just BE happy? Haven't you realized by now that you are the only one responsible for how you feel about your life? Or even what happens in it? You want to control everything and everyone else— except the only one who can ever affect and effect your *own* life—you! What would you create in your life if you just accepted the things you cannot control and actually did something about the things that you can?

Think about it...

Love and Sunshine,
Tracy

Why so violent?

"There are three kinds of violence: one, through our deeds; two, through our words; and three, through our thoughts... The root of all violence is in the world of thoughts, and that is why training the mind is so important." – Eknath Easwaran

"The ancestor of every destructive action, every destructive decision, is a negative thought." – Eknath Easwaran

"We are what our thoughts have made us; so take care about what you think Words are secondary. Thoughts live; they travel far."– Swami Vivekananda

Have you realized that if someone could hear what you say to yourself, they would either run away or call the authorities? Lol...Why have you taken it on yourself to be your own judge and jury? What happened to you in your past that made you think you have to continue punishing yourself over and over day after day? Take some time to sit and think about it. Is what you are saying about yourself the truth? Really? We make things that were said to us or experiences that happened to us as truth. But really, is it? So what if someone told you long ago that you were good for nothing? Why are you continuing to take someone else's perspective on the one subject that you know best...yourself? You are who you are in every given moment because you CHOOSE to be who you are, not because anyone else told you that is the way you should be! Your choice—end of story! Stop engaging in your own personal violence against yourself!

I learned the following from Florence Scovel Shinn:"Happiness is earned through perfect control of your emotional nature! In your Divine Design there is no limitation, only health, wealth, love and perfect self-expression."

Here is an affirmation that Florence shared with her readers that I feel is well suited for you:

"I let go of everything that is not divinely designed for me and the perfect plan of my life now comes to pass. I now fill the place that I can fill and no one else can fill. I now do the things which I can do and no one else can do."

Forgive yourself! Let go of your need to control things that you cannot control. Stop the self-bashing and get back to BEing the perfect you that you were meant to BE!

Think about it...

Love and Sunshine,
Tracy

Have you forgotten the simple pleasures?

"It is our basic right to be a happy person, happy family, and eventually a happy world. That should be our goal." – Dalai Lama

"We can no longer afford to throw away even one unimportant day by not noticing the wonder of it all. We have to be willing to discover and then appreciate the authentic moments of happiness available to all of us every day." – Sarah Ban Breathnach

Have you ever felt like you were walking around with blinders on? There is so much beauty that surrounds us every day that goes unnoticed. It's quite sad really. Life is meant to be full of happiness, not stress and strife. If you are not happy then it's by your choice that you feel however you are feeling. Get out of your slump. Accept what you cannot control. Forgive yourself. Pick yourself up and take those stinkin' blinders off and just move on! What do you think you would be able to create for yourself if at least once a day you slowed down and enjoyed the simple pleasure of smelling a flower?

Think about it…

Love and Sunshine,
Tracy

August 1st

My will or Divine will?

"It is important not to 'need' what you are calling to you but rather to have a certain detachment about it. Let it be all right if it doesn't come, or if it comes in a different form than what you expect. After you have asked for something, surrender to whatever comes as being appropriate." – Sanaya Roman and Duane Packer

"Acceptance says, True, this is my situation at the moment. I'll look unblinkingly at the reality of it. But I'll also open my hands to accept willingly whatever a loving Father sends me." – Catherine Marshall

"This business of hozho. The way I understand it…I'll use an example. Terrible drought, crops dead, sheep dying. Spring dried out. No water. The Hopi, or the Christian, maybe the Moslem, they pray for rain. The Navajo has the proper ceremony done to restore himself to harmony with the drought. You see what I mean. The system is designed to recognize what's beyond human power to change, and then to change the human's attitude to be content with the inevitable." – in Sacred Clowns, by Tony Hillerman

Hozho—this Navaho term which, while encompassing and often explained as harmony, delivers so much more when you plumb the true depth of its meaning.

"Hozho cannot be adequately translated into a single English word. It is the essence of the Navaho way of being, a sense of elemental rightness that is core to their way of living—a way of being that we could do worse than to strive for in our own lives. Hozho is a word of depth and layers, meaning at once harmony and beauty, truth and balance. To be in hozho is to be at one with and a part of your environment and the world around you, in such a way that the notes of your life complement and resonate with the symphony of life all around you. You neither pitch above nor below the thrumming chords of the Universe, but yet at the same time your melody stands on its own merits and is heard with utter clarity: pure in tone and pitch and strength, singular yet subsumed in the whole.

Hozho is not the easiest word to explain, but its essential meaning can be intuited through experience. Think of those times when you felt as if you truly were part of the creation around you, yet clearly a singular being, at once loved by and in love with all that was around you. Perfectly matched, perfectly balanced, perfectly in tune—walking with beauty and rightness and joy in every step and every breath. That is hozho, and I wish you the ability to find it and live it in your life." – Soni Pitts

Hozho and how to achieve it:

Harmony, beauty, balance, tranquility, equilibrium, rightness, present-moment centred awareness, truth, clarity of action, thought and thinking.

Close your eyes. Cease to listen. Be silent. Seek no contacts. Be still. Be gentle. Be patient. Be humble.

Take Action. There is only now. Focus on what you want not what you don't want. Smile, Breathe, Go Slowly. There isn't a road to happiness; happiness is the road. A candle loses nothing if it is used to light another candle. Your soul is dyed according to the colour of your thoughts. Meditate.

Wow, I learned a lot today. Did you?

Think about it...

Love and Sunshine,
Tracy

August 2nd

Visualization...

"It's not your eyes that see. It's your brain that sees." – John Assaraf (from The Secret)

_=_=_=_=_=_=_=_=_

"When I was a kid, my Dad shared with me the power of visualization and positive thinking. He told me if I wanted to accomplish something, I could. All I had to do was set my goal, write down the individual steps to go from start to finish, and give it a go.

And though he never mentioned Napoleon Hill and the quote, "Whatever the mind can conceive and believe, the mind can achieve," that message was still embedded in my childhood teachings. Rarely can we conceive something without first visualizing it in some way—perhaps as words or as feelings (yes you can 'visualize' feelings, even if that feels a bit abstract)± most often as images.

My father also said, "If there's anything you can't do, I'll see what I can do to help you clear that roadblock."

Sometimes those roadblocks were physical obstacles (like I needed to earn more money than I had time to earn, so he loaned me some), and sometimes they were mental obstacles (like when I wanted to quit martial arts because I couldn't learn 'Star Form'). Either way, what followed was a life of great success for me. I accomplished more before I was of voting age than many people accomplish in entire lifetimes. A big part of that is the hidden wisdom within my Dad's approach.

You see, it wasn't just about positive thinking, visualization, or goal-setting. Whether he was consciously aware of this or not, I was receiving a message that said "If you truly set your heart on something, and you take action, there is a really really good chance it's going to happen. And if you can't do it alone, the Universe will send you help."

In my life, help comes in many forms. Sometimes it's an actual person lending a helping hand, sometimes it's a message within a story from a brand-new friend, and sometimes it's in the form of an unexpected email that, for some strange reason, I accidentally opened and found a nugget of timely wisdom in.

Whatever it is, help is always around us if we're open to it.

I actively draw upon many resources to maximize the opportunities for help in my life. I realize that my mind has been 'programmed' since birth. In some cases it was positive programming (like 'visualization works' or 'you can achieve your goals') and sometimes it was negative programming (like 'There isn't enough in the world'). Whatever it was, I recognize that I've been programmed.

And unless I'm able to live totally 100 percent in the present moment, I'm continuing to both add new 'programs' and re-play old ones (regardless of whether or not I want to, or even whether or not they're helpful to me).

Because of that awareness, whenever a new helpful technology comes around that gives me an opportunity to at least choose the new programs I want to embed within me...I pay attention. Not because I am expecting some sort of rapid transformation and having all my goals be instantly achieved, but rather, because of something deeper...something more meaningful.

For me it's this sense that every little piece of the puzzle is contributing to my overall unfoldment. It's not that any single activity is a single answer. It's that when I integrate many different tools, techniques, meditations, passions, fun, and spiritual practices together, what I find is that each piece contributes a little more towards the life I truly want to live.

So when you're receiving lots of hints, clues, and feedback pointing to the same thing, just pause for a moment and ask yourself, "Is this something that might be a piece of MY personal transformation puzzle?" If so, then check it out.

...and not because I or anybody else recommends it, but rather, because there's a part of you that is curious about what opportunities you have to live the life of your dreams. After all...

You never know in what ways the Universe is sending you help. :)

Your Partner In Transformation," – Chris Cade

_-=_-=_-=_-=_-=_-=_-=_

I found the above message to be impactful for me today so I decided to include the whole message rather than take a nugget or two from it.

I, myself, did not get the same kind of help from my parents as Chris did but I find it interesting that today we are sending out the same kind of message(s) so what does that tell you? It does not matter where you come from or who you were yesterday…all that matters is who you are today!

Since I did not receive the encouragement as a child that I can do anything, I did not want my daughter to go through the same experience. I tell her over and over again, "You are a super shining star and you can accomplish anything that you put your mind to…and if you do not know the answer what will you do?" She tells me "Ask!" I tell her, "That is right! If you do not know that answer there is always someone out there who does, so ask…"What I think I will add to our regular conversation is this: "If you cannot do it on your own, your Divine will always send you help…so have faith and be open!"

Think about it…

Love and Sunshine,
Tracy

Learn to let go

"To attain knowledge, add things every day. To attain wisdom, remove things every day." – Lao Tzu

"When guilt rears its ugly head confront it, discuss it and let it go. The past is over. Forgive yourself and move on." – Bernie S. Siegel

This is what I know: If you do not let go and release something, whether it is a thought, a feeling or a constant way of being, to create space for a new thought, a new feeling or a new way of being...nothing will ever change.

Think about it...

Love and Sunshine,
Tracy

August 4th

Hope and disappointment

"It's precisely the disappointing stories, which have no proper ending and there-fore no proper meaning, that sound true to life." – Max Frisch

"Hope is the companion of power, and the mother of success; for who so hopes has within him the gift of miracles." – Samuel Smiles

"The very least you can do in your life is to figure out what you hope for. And the most you can do is live inside that hope. Not admire it from a distance but live right in it, under its roof." – Barbara Kingsolver

Have you ever noticed that when you feel disappointed it is because you expected things to go a certain way and they didn't or you are so attached to the result that it has to be an exact way so if one little thing is off you feel you've been let down? You may be so entangled in the details of things being or going a certain way that you may miss what you are really after. How's that working for you in regards to bringing happiness into your life? Maybe it is why so many people, when asked "What do you want?" answer "I don't know."

Nothing is ever set in stone, and if it is…what did my friend tell me? Oh yeah, you just blow up the stone! Lol…I love it! Beth, it worked for me! I remember thinking that something or someone was set in stone and what I did for myself was to imagine (remember imagine is the operative word here!) going in and wiring up some dynamite to the constant result I was getting and I mentally blew it up into tiny pieces. Then I swept them all up and dumped them in the garbage. The next thing I knew I was getting a different result that brought me happiness instead of disap-pointment. What I learned is that as I became detached from the result, my result changed.

Hope for things. Imagine them like they are already happening. The only thing I can suggest is that you detach yourself from an expected result. Think of it like being a little kid on Christmas Eve and not caring what Santa may bring, just get excited that Santa is going to bring you some-thing! Then instead of being disappointed all the time maybe you will live your life full of happy excited anticipation of the next moment no matter what it brought you.

Think about it…

Love and Sunshine,
Tracy

Who are you?

"Mysterious and intimidating to contemplate, the human brain is the most complex thing there is and the most difficult task it can undertake is to understand itself." – David Noonan

"I don't think God cares where we were graduated or what we did for a living. God wants to know who we are. Discovering this is the work of the soul—it is our true life's work." – Bernie Siegel

When are you going to stop looking to the "whats" that you do for the answers to the "who are you" question? Confused? *What* you are is not anywhere near *who* you are! The simplest example I can think of is when born, every female is a daughter. "Female" and "daughter" both answer the question "What am I?" In that case every woman on the planet is the same. Where we gain our uniqueness from others is in answering the "who are you?" question. Are you a loving daughter? A smart daughter? A supportive daughter? A caring daughter? A friendly daughter? An intelligent daughter? A beautiful daughter? A sensual daughter? A peaceful daughter? A happy daughter? It is in knowing what *kind* of daughter you are that you find out the answer to the "who you are" question.

Think about it…

Love and Sunshine,
Tracy

Need to let go of control?

"The world is not to be put in order; the world is order, incarnate. It is for us to harmonize with this order." – Henry Miller

"Ego believes that it needs to protect us from external dangers. Through control and manipulation, it aims to keep us safe. This need of ego is based in fear." – Unknown

"If we hope to live in love, we must become acquainted with soul. Experiencing soul brings a deep knowing that this is a loving universe. Experiencing soul also builds faith. We learn to trust that we don't have to run the show. And when we do this, we tap the source of true freedom and joy." – Unknown

"It is not action or effort that we must surrender; it is self-will, and this is terribly difficult. You must do your best constantly, yet never allow yourself to become involved in whether things work out the way you want." – Eknath Easwaran

"True spiritual surrender responsibly opens itself to the unknown." – Stephen V. Doughty

The above quotes are just another reminder for us to detach ourselves from our results. By learning to accept "what is", you are more able to let go of ego's controlling fear-based nature therefore it is simple to detach from an expected result. If you do not like something then look to the mirror instead of your finger.

Think about it...

Love and Sunshine,
Tracy

Find your board, learn to surf!

"Just as the tumultuous chaos of a thunderstorm brings a nurturing rain that allows life to flourish, so too in human affairs times of advancement are preceded by times of disorder. Success comes to those who can weather the storm." – I Ching No. 3

Just as things are darkest before the dawn so is the storm before the calm. If you can ride through the waves of your emotions you too will be successful in finding your inner peace. You must learn to ride your emotions out till they lap at the shore of your happiness. This does not mean to never feel your emotions because any surfer knows the more you feel the wave the more you are able to maneuver on top of it. Emotional surfing is about you not letting your emotions drag you under and possibly drown you. Learning to ride out your emotions to find your inner peace will only ever lead you to your happiness. Isn't it about time you got on your board instead of swimming all the time?

Think about it...

Love and Sunshine,
Tracy

Changing consciousness

"Every human has four endowments— self awareness, conscience, independent will and creative imagination. These give us the ultimate human freedom… The power to choose, to respond, to change." – Stephen R. Covey

You can stay ingrained in your story, only see your point of view and live your life wondering why no one ever gets you. Or you can take what has always been yours and live your life with awareness, consciousness, independent will and creative imagination to lead you to happiness moment by moment. It is, as it always has been, up to you to decide.

Think about it…

Love and Sunshine,
Tracy

You get what you prepare for

"If someone wants 'A' to happen, yet they prepare for 'B,' they will always get 'B.' Prepare for 'A.' – The Universe

"Do not pray for tasks equal to your powers. Pray for powers equal to your tasks." – Phillips Brooks

How can I make it any simpler than what the Universe has already said. If you want "A" then prepare for "A."

Think about it…

Love and Sunshine,
Tracy

What happened to your common sense?

"I learned that good judgment comes from experience and that experience grows out of mistakes." – Omar Bradley

"Happiness comes when your work and words are of benefit to yourself and others." – Buddha

"The root of joy is gratefulness...It is not joy that makes us grateful; it is gratitude that makes us joyful." – Brother David Steindl-Rast

If you are still complaining about what is wrong in your life and blaming others for how things are going, how are you ever able to learn from your mistakes and feel joy in your life by being grateful for what you have in this moment? If you are not benefiting yourself or those around you with what is coming out of your mouth then what's that saying? Oh, yeah... "If you do not have anything nice to say, do not say anything at all."

Think about it...

Love and Sunshine,
Tracy

Listen to the quiet voice inside

Listen to the quiet voice inside

"To know how to choose a path with heart is to learn how to follow intuitive feeling." – Jean Shinoda Bolen

"The only real valuable thing is intuition." – Albert Einstein

"Intuition is a spiritual faculty and does not explain, but simply points the way." – Florence Scovel Shinn

"The most decisive actions of our life…are most often unconsidered actions." – André Gide

Have you found that you may have reasoned yourself out of the very thing that you were after? Or maybe you do not even realize that you are doing it? If you have a certain result that you are trying to attain, whether it is manifesting a certain amount of money by a certain date, meeting your perfect love, finding your ideal career or maybe selling a certain possession. What have you done to take action to actually attaining those things? Did you listen to your inner voice when you had a hunch to do or say something or did you reason that thought away? Sometimes your intuitive thoughts sound like crazy things to do, but if you listen you may be pleasantly surprised how well things fall into place. For example, if you are working on manifesting $500 and your intuition tells you to give someone $100, what would you do? Would you reason your intuition away by saying that you need that $100 to get to your desired $500 or would you gladly offer your $100 knowing that by following your intuition, your faith will get you to your desired $500? If you do not give the money gladly you may fall short on your desired $500 but if you gladly gave the money and that person turns around and buys you a lottery ticket in thanks for helping them out and that ticket turns out to gain you $5000, where would you be then?

You never know what will happen unless you stop reasoning yourself out of listening to your intuitive leads. Just something for you to have a look at and see how it relates in your life.

I will leave you with an affirmation from Florence Scovel Shinn that may help you to trust in your intuition:

Tracy Friesen

"I am always under direct inspiration. I know just what to do and give instant obedience to my intuitive leads."

Think about it…

Love and Sunshine,
Tracy

Direct your evolution

"Consciousness is the basis of all life and the field of all possibilities. Its nature is to expand and unfold its full potential. The impulse to evolve is thus inherent in the very nature of life." – Maharishi Mahesh Yogi

"There is only one thing more powerful than all the armies of the world, that is an idea whose time has come." – Victor Hugo

"We lie in the lap of immense intelligence." – Ralph Waldo Emerson

No one is broken and no one needs to be fixed—we are in a constant state of Self Evolving. We make choices in our lives that create consequences. We are all products of our choices and we all have the possibility to continuously evolve who we are by learning from our consequences. If you want to remain the same, that is, as it always has been, *your* choice. Someone once told me, "If you are not living you are dying." Does that mean if you are not evolving you are shrinking?

Think about it…

Love and Sunshine,
Tracy

You are bigger than you think

"He who would be serene and pure needs but one thing, detachment." – *Meister Eckhart*

"The bird of paradise alights only on the hand that does not grasp." – *John Berry*

"It's best not to get too excited or too depressed by the ups and downs of life." – *Dalai Lama*

Why is it that we get so attached to certain results in our lives that we lose focus on BEing happy with what we have in our present moment. For me, right now I am so concerned about my future that I have gotten myself in a funk. Even my daughter has picked up on it. She said to me this morning: "Mom? Are you OK? You look unhappy." I told her that I was feeling unhappy because I have so much swirling around my head from recent events that I am only thinking about what I have to do in the near future, regarding future decisions, future conversations, future interactions with my family, my friends, my hobbies, my career. She said to me, "Why don't you just think about happy things?" She is right. I haven't been thinking about happy things at all. I have been so attached to the results in my life that I haven't even felt gratitude in the last few days. No wonder I am in a funk. (Btw…that is just a story I am telling myself, too.) I've even affected my fun time, my release time—why? So I get to be right that people are against me? So I get to play a victim? So I can have a right to be mad and angry? So I get to make every story that runs through my head true? Maybe?

Being on the defensive only works in sports games and/or driving. It never has a place dealing with your emotions and feelings. As soon as you go on the defensive with your own feelings and emotions you make someone else wrong for the way they are feeling, and how well does that go over? Yeah I know…not good—ever. There is no right or wrong when it comes to your feelings, emotions and/or your perceptions. What I am seeing for myself is that I need to detach from getting an expected result and start preparing for "A" instead of moping around losing valuable time, and just BE happy with all the great things that I have in my life right now in this moment. The first thing I am going to do is SMILE! Ahhh, that feels better already.

If you related to my story at all today maybe you too just need to detach from your results, stop trying to force them and just have faith because if you prepared for "A" then you'll get "A."

Think about it…

Love and Sunshine,
Tracy

Hmmm…silence…

Think about it…

Love and Sunshine,
Tracy

August 15th

Not knowing is a gift

"It's not knowing what to do, it's doing what you know." – Anthony Robbins

"Not knowing anything is the sweetest life." – Sophocles

Yesterday when I attempted to write my message I just stared at the empty screen for like an hour. I finally just left my computer, perplexed. Why wouldn't my fingers just start typing? I left the blank message screen open and every time I passed my computer I stopped and attempted to write it again. It wasn't that I had nothing to say; it was more that I had sooo much to say that I didn't know what to say or how to say it. By the end of the day I still hadn't written anything. I wanted to just hit send with the empty message but then I thought that maybe you wouldn't get it. But who am I to think I know what you will understand or not understand? What I know is this: Not knowing is a gift! In saying "I don't know" you can then immediately think or say what you do know. It's like magic. It also allows you to get beyond your preset way of BEing. Not knowing is the perfect place to be, because all possibilities are open to you. You are not attached to the result because you have no idea what *is* going to happen. Isn't that great?

If you approach everything in your life with "not knowing" as a beautiful glorious place to be, you may just start living more in the present moment!

Think about it…

Love and Sunshine,
Tracy

Finding contentment

"When the sun rises, I go to work. When the sun goes down, I take my rest. I dig the well from which I drink. I farm the soil which yields my food. I share creation. Kings can do no more." – Chinese proverb

"If we have not quiet in our minds, outward comfort will do no more for us than a golden slipper on a gouty foot." – John Bunyan

"Try to be like the turtle—at ease in your own shell." – Bill Copeland

If you are never happy with what you have and who you are in this moment, you will find it hard to be happy with anything in any moment. Even if you are given the very thing that you are seeking, you will always find something to be unhappy about. Trust me. The way to BEing happy is to be grateful for everything that you do have in *this* moment, because all you are doing is making more room for more things to be grateful for. This is the kind of never-ending story that you want.

Think about it…

Love and Sunshine,
Tracy

Just because it's your opinion it doesn't make you right

"Fight for your opinions, but do not believe that they contain the whole truth, or the only truth." – Charles A. Dana

"The recipe for perpetual ignorance is: be satisfied with your opinions and content with your knowledge." – Elbert Hubbard

"A great many people mistake opinions for thought." – Herbert V. Prochnow

"All empty souls tend toward extreme opinions." – William Butler Yeats

"Arguments only confirm people in their own opinions." – Booth Tarkington

You, like everyone else, has a point of view. If you get caught in thinking that just because you have one it means that there never is any other possibility, then you may live your life in struggle and strife. Taking another's point of view personally may only leave you with upset feelings because their point of view doesn't match yours. Also, just because someone expresses their own opinion or point of view doesn't mean that you need to express yours as well. Sometimes people just want to be heard or vent what's on their mind, without having to be concerned about what's on your mind.

If you see your opinion or point of view as the only opinion or point of view, or feel you have to justify your opinion or point of view, then you may find that you will remain in an unhappy state in all aspects of your life. It is just an opinion and everyone has one, so why would you want to waste any of your precious time asserting that yours is a possible one to have?

Think about it…

Love and Sunshine,
Tracy

The source of anger

"Anger is that powerful internal force that blows out the light of reason." – Ralph Waldo Emerson

"At the core of all anger is a need that is not being fulfilled." – Marshall B. Rosenberg

"How much more grievous are the consequences of anger than the causes of it." – Marcus Aurelius

Anger is not a bad thing. It is not even at the lowest of all the lower vibrational energies. But anger used for your own personal release may not be such a great thing for you or for anyone else in your path. Oh, you might think that it is a good thing to scream, yell and maybe throw things but honestly, if you really think about it, how do you feel after you engage in such activities? Being angry is one thing. It is an emotion that we should honor just like any other emotion that we are having. When you feel angry it does not give you the right to unleash your wrath on anyone or anything just because you are angry. It is something to recognize, acknowledge and maybe just accept.

When you feel anger you could say to yourself, "Oh look, that stirred up a feeling of anger in me…wow…interesting." The next step would be to go within and figure out for yourself why a certain incident, whether it is words, actions, or even just the mere presence of someone, would create feelings of anger in yourself? It *never* has anything to do with anyone else—ever! If you think it does then you are using it as an excuse to not to be responsible for your own feelings. It is always up to you to find out why you create the feelings of anger and allow yourself to act in the ways that you do when you are feeling that way.

Think about it…

Love and Sunshine,
Tracy

Being mindful

"It is the mind that makes one wise or ignorant, bound or emancipated." – Sri Ramakrishna

"If a pickpocket meets a Holy Man, he will see only his pockets." – Hari Dass

"Minds are like parachutes; they work best when open." – Lord Thomas Dewar

How are you looking at yourself in this moment? Are you full of hope? Are you looking at yourself like you can take on anything and everything that comes your way or are you looking at yourself as being *so* small and insignificant that nothing you do makes any difference? How are you selling yourself short in this instant, which prevents you from living an extraordinary life? The biggest change in the world ALWAYS comes from you first creating it in yourself. There is nothing that you cannot do if you first think that it's possible, because without the belief that it is possible nothing will ever happen.

Have you ever found yourself stuck in your opinion and it frustrates you so much that you feel that you are spinning in circles? Maybe all you need to do is find the rip cord?

Think about it…

Love and Sunshine,
Tracy

An Angel says...

A good friend sent this to me in an email. When I read it, it made me smile so I thought it may do the same thing for you. Be kind to yourself and others today, you never know what's going on in someone's life to give them an off day.

-=-=-=-=-=-=-

An Angel says…

Never borrow from the future. If you worry about what may happen tomorrow and it doesn't happen, you have worried in vain. Even if it does happen, you have to worry twice.

Go to bed on time.

Get up on time so you can start the day unrushed.

Say No to projects that won't fit into your time schedule or that will compromise your mental health.

Delegate tasks to capable others.

Simplify and unclutter your life.

Less is more. (Although one is often not enough, two are often too many.)

Allow extra time to do things and to get to places

Pace yourself. Spread out big changes and difficult projects over time; don't lump the hard things all together.

Take one day at a time.

Separate worries from concerns. If you can't do anything about a situation, forget it.

Live within your budget; don't use credit cards for ordinary purchases.

Have backups; an extra car key in your wallet, an extra house key buried in the garden, extra stamps, etc.

K.M.S. (Keep Mouth Shut). This single piece of advice can prevent an enormous amount of trouble.

Do something for the Kid in You every day.

Get enough rest.

Eat right.

Get organized so everything has its place.

Listen to a tape while driving that can help improve your quality of life.

Write down thoughts and inspirations.

Every day, find time to be alone.

Take your work seriously, but not yourself at all.

Develop a forgiving attitude (most people are doing the best they can).

Be kind to unkind people (they probably need it the most).

Sit on your ego.

Talk less; listen more.

Slow down.

Remind yourself that you are not the general manager of the universe.

Every night before bed, think of one thing you're grateful for that you've never been grateful for before.

_=_=_=_=_=_=_

My favorites: "Remind yourself that you are not the general manager of the universe," "K.M.S" and "Write down thoughts and inspirations."

Think about it . . .

Love and Sunshine,
Tracy

Is your past in the present again?

"If you accept a limiting belief, then it will become a truth for you." –
Louise Hay

"There are no limitations to the self except those you believe in." – *Seth*

If you say it is true in your mind then it WILL be true in your outward world, no matter what! Whether you are saying something positive about yourself or whether it is a not-so-positive thing, you will create actions and experiences to validate the belief that you have about yourself or anyone else for that matter. Honestly, why would you want to limit yourself in any way? How does it feel to be bound by your own thoughts? Isn't *that* a great image to have—your thoughts and beliefs wrapped around you like a straight jacket! Are you comfortable? Really? Well, the only reason I can think of for you to be OK with limiting yourself is that you may not want to be responsible for your life in how you feel and act, perhaps? It is your choice to believe whatever you want—ALWAYS. What do you think you would be able to create in your life if you released yourself from any limitations that you have put upon yourself? The possibilities are endless!

Think about it…

Love and Sunshine,
Tracy

You are only as strong as your word

"The highest courage is to dare to be yourself in the face of adversity. Choosing right over wrong, ethic over convenience, and truth over popularity…these are choices that measure your life. Travel the path of integrity without looking back, for there is never a wrong time to do the right thing." – Michael Moore

"Character is doing the right thing when nobody's looking. There are too many people who think that the only thing that's right is to get by, and the only thing that's wrong is to get caught." – J.C. Watts

"If you have integrity, nothing else matters. If you don't have integrity, nothing else matters." – Alan Simpson

What does integrity mean to you? This is what I know about integrity. It is doing what you say you are going to do. In my opinion, that's it, when it comes to your character that is. Not a complex thing at all. Sometimes life gets in the way of your integrity but did you know that you can still honor your word even if you do not keep it? Hmmm… How, you say? Honoring your word is being able, in the moment that you realize that that you are not able to keep your word, to notify all those who will be impacted. Let them know that you are not able to keep your word and then let them know when you will be able to fulfill what you said you were going to do. If you are no longer able to do what you said you were going to do then take responsibility for the consequences that may arise from you not keeping your word. This is integrity.
You are only as strong as your word—ever.

Think about it…

Love and Sunshine,
Tracy

It takes un-reasonable action

"Action may not always bring happiness, but there is no happiness without action." – Benjamin Disraeli

"You've got to love what you do to really make things happen." – Philip Green

"If you don't take charge of shaping your own destiny, others will apply their agenda to you." – Eric Allenbaugh

If you are sitting there saying that you want something in your life yet you bring out reasons and excuses when someone asks you why you haven't attained it yet, maybe it is something that you really do not want? Because if it is really something that you want to create in your life, first of all you'd be happy about where you are in creating it and secondly you would be saying and doing things in a progressive way to attain it rather than explaining why you do not have it yet

Think about it…

Love and Sunshine,
Tracy

August 24th

Build up your awareness muscle

"It is difficult to see the picture when you are inside of the frame." – Unknown

"What is necessary to change a person is to change his awareness of himself." – Abraham H. Maslow

Awareness is the key to your happiness! Once you become aware of something it will always be known to you. You gain the knowledge of it and you can never pretend that you do not know about it anymore. If you ignore it then it is by your choice and it is your responsibility to deal with the consequences. Have you ever used the quote "Ignorance is bliss?" I am sure you have, especially when you become aware of certain behaviours you may have that are not so progressive to getting you what you want in your life. You see, being aware of things doesn't mean that you cannot do them anymore. It means that you do them by choice, therefore accepting all the responsibility of your actions and the impact on others that they may create. There is no good or bad, right or wrong, or positive or negative—just "what is."

Awareness is freeing yourself to live true to yourself no matter who you are BEing. If you do not like the consequences of your behaviours it is, as it always has been, up to you to choose a different behavior to create a different result or consequence. It is not *ever* in the actions of someone else.

Think about it…

Love and Sunshine,
Tracy

Tracy Friesen

Knowledge is different for everyone

"…conflict is the primary engine of creativity and innovation. People don't learn by staring into a mirror; people learn by encountering difference." – Ronald Heifetz

"Homogeneity makes for healthy milk but anemic friendships. We need relationships that cross culturally imposed lines to enlarge our hearts and expand our vistas." – Dan Schmidt

People may have different perceptions and points of view than you, but really are they that much "different" from you? Think about someone who may rub you the wrong way or you have a not-so-uplifting feeling when you are around them. What is it really that you do not like about them? If you really want to take on your life, write the traits down. Now go to your mirror and look at the list. After you read each one look at yourself. Once you are finished the list—OK, brace yourself—every one of those traits that you listed about the other person are qualities you do not like about yourself. (Gasp! Oh my goodness, did she say that out loud?) I did.

This may sound contradictory to Ronald's quote. What I get out of what he is saying is that if you are just staring at yourself in the mirror and thinking that everyone should be like you, you may not learn anything about yourself or anyone else for that matter. People are the most different in their cultures, colors, and beliefs but underneath it all we are not that different in the way we perceive and interpret our environment based on our experiences. Our experiences create our knowledge. If we are never given a certain bit of information to create a knowledge base about something, are we any less of a person than the person who was given the information? Knowledge doesn't make us smarter. You are as smart as you will ever be and ever have been. Someone just has a different knowledge base than you. That's all. Let's say you are a waiter/waitress working in a large, busy restaurant and you took a brain surgeon with no prior food service training and put them in the middle of rush hour and said to them, "OK, you are responsible for tables 25 to 34—go! Do you think the brain surgeon would even have a clue where to begin? Do you not think that they might have a whole lot of questions? Like maybe...uh, where are tables 25 to 34? Or maybe where are the menus? Or even where is some paper and a pen? Because they were asking, in your opinion, silly questions and didn't have your knowledge of your environment and surroundings, would you look at them like they were, for a lack of a better word, stupid? Hmmm...It is all in the information that someone holds as knowledge. Knowledge is different for everyone. It does not make anyone any better than or greater than anyone else—ever.

Think about it....

Love and Sunshine,
Tracy

How do you work with anger?

"Character isn't inherited. One builds it daily by the way one thinks and acts, thought by thought, action by action. If one lets fear or hate or anger take posses-sion of the mind, they become self-forged chains." – Helen Douglas

"Too often we underestimate how quickly our feelings are going to change because we underestimate our ability to change them." – David Gilbert

How *do* you work with anger, anyway? Or any emotion for that matter? If you are still in a state of pointing your fingers at someone else when you are feeling angry, I am sorry for bursting your bubble, but it is, as it always has been, only *you* that makes yourself angry and not someone else—EVER! In the moment it may feel good to unleash your rage on someone else but do you really feel all that good afterwards, when all is said and done and you have calmed your emotions and thoughts? Really? By doing this you are just cheating yourself of BEing the true you that you are. If you accepted responsibility for who you are at all times, whether you are a happy you, a sad you, a joyful you, a mad you or even a furious you, you would be comfortable in all your emotions and you wouldn't have to blame someone else for BEing your true authentic self. You are a powerful being with the ability to instantaneously change your thoughts and/or emotions. It's just as simple as it is to flick a switch.

Think about it…

Love and Sunshine,
Tracy

Honesty—freedom from deceit or fraud

"Truth stood on one side and Ease on the other; it has often been so."—
Theodore Parker

"An honest answer is the sign of true friendship." – Proverbs 24:26

*"No one can lie, no one can hide anything, when he looks directly into some-
one's eyes." – Paulo Coelho*

"Do not do what you would undo if caught." – Leah Arendt

At one time I thought integrity and honesty were the same thing but they are not. Being honest is telling the truth and having integrity is keeping your word. Telling the truth may leave you with feelings of unease, but wouldn't it be better not to hold things in and possibly create a gap where there was once a space full of love and freedom? Not telling the truth binds you in place, puts blinders on and potentially leaves you in a standstill and this is never a good place to be.

There is no such thing as a willingness to be honest. Either you are or you are not. Being willing to be honest is like a blind man being willing to see. Why not take on your life and be honest, not only with those you hold most dear in your life but with everyone that you encounter?

What kind of happiness and freedom would you create in your life if you did not feed your fear and just told the truth?

Think about it…

Love and Sunshine,
Tracy

Open your hands

"More than any other part of the body, our hands reveal our inner state." – Omraam Mikhaël Aïvanhov

"What is always speaking silently is the body." – Norman Brown

One thing I learned from my brother, who teaches life skills to kids through sports instruction, is that you gain the most power running when your hands are open and relaxed. So when you are in your "stuff" check your hands. If you are clenching your fists maybe, just maybe, your mind is closed too.

Think about it…

Oooh, I love my brother!

Love and Sunshine,
Tracy

August 29th

Half-step back

This is taken from a personal email that I sent to my husband when we going through a difficult time contemplating divorce. I trust that you will take from it what you need.

Love and Sunshine,
Tracy

‗=‗=‗=‗=‗=‗=‗

Sunday November 8th 2009

> *"Human history is the sad result of each one looking out for himself." –*
> *Julio Cortazar*

> *"But life lived only for oneself does not truly satisfy men or women. There is a*
> *hunger in Americans today for larger purposes beyond the self." – Betty Friedan*

I find it interesting that I would receive this message on Sunday. That is the day I had my life-altering experience with Beaver (Beaver was a horse that help me learn, in my Energy Medicine course for animals, to take a half-step back in my life). Also it is the anniversary of my Dad's suicide. I get the above statements. To me, it means there is sadness in selfishness because for me true happiness is only felt when shared with another.

This is impactful for me because it makes me remember my decision-making process and why I chose the path I am on [to be able to go through with this separation]. I wish for you nothing but truth because it is in your truth that you will find the guiding light. Taking responsibility for your own actions is the most freeing experience that one can live through. A lack of BEing completely real with all around you is a form of control. When one is able to release that need to be in control true life happens. Otherwise, one can live in a false sense of living through justification of what is "right" for them. There is no meaning behind any decision. Remember…"Chocolate, Vanilla choose?" "I choose Vanilla because I choose Vanilla." "Ok then, Chocolate choose." (Just to clarify a bit…my husband and I took the same course that taught us if you are only given one choice it is up to you to accept it without giving it meaning or reason.)

You do not change yourself by changing. Things change by accepting your "Chocolate" (or the "what is") that you are presented with. You cannot stop yourself from changing. You do not even have to want to change to change. By wanting to change it means bringing your past into your future. Life is an ever-evolving choice. It is 100 percent OK to make a choice, then in the next minute make a different choice.

Awareness is the key to your success. Denial of the truth will only create more untruths in your life that you will have to justify. When one hears their own inner voice say, "I do not like it when…" this may be a time to go look in the mirror and ask, "What am I not willing to look at?" Also if, a person makes a statement of justification or a rationalization after revealing a truth about themselves, it also may be a time to look at themselves to find out where they are not BEing their true authentic self. Playing games of tit for tat is draining and leaves everyone feeling yucky and icky in the end.

I realize my own truth and I am ENOUGH. I do deserve HAPPINESS and I do deserve the LOVE of my LIFE. No restrictions, conditions or boundaries. I am open and free to ALLOW whatever is to come. I have found that if you are in need to hide something then you are living in guilt that you are doing something wrong. This would be a perfect time, perhaps, to fully look at your actions and question where the truth may lie for you and really look at why you are doing the things you are doing without justification.

Nothing is permanent and EVERYTHING is possible. If you got rid of the story you created in your life you might realize that you are living a completely different life. Get to the source of what you are chasing in life. If you take care of your roots your fruits will always be lush and plenty and never-ending.

All My Love,
Tracy

August 30th

What depletes your soul?

"Certain activities, attitudes, foods, and persons support the cultivation of an unconscious life. They draw us away from our center. They throw us off-balance. They deplete the soul." – Patricia Lynn Reilly

"Enlightenment is not about imagining figures of light but of making the darkness conscious." – C. G. Jung

I had a good chuckle when I first read Jung's quote. What instantly popped into my head was a room full of people trying to imagine figures of light and there was an "Enlightenment Within" sign on the door. Lol… Well, maybe it loses something in translation but I thought it was funny. But seriously, Jung makes an excellent point that I do not want to take away from. A way to get to enlightenment is to acknowledge our own darkness. If you are continually denying your dark side you may never see your light within. Perhaps one thing to get past is making yourself wrong for being a certain way. It is never wrong to be any way, ever. If you acknowledge even your not-so-positive side and accept it with love you may find it easier to keep your soul full of love and therefore live your life a bit more…enlightened.

Think about it…

Love and Sunshine,
Tracy

Tracy Friesen

You are responsible for your life

"Doubt can only be removed by action."– Johann Wolfgang von Goethe

"One of the many fringe benefits of having sneaky, pushy, and demanding people in your life, comes when you realize—usually at the end of a long day, deep in thought, with a pot of warm cherry Kool-Aid by your side—that in spite of all the drama, huffing, and puffing, no one can keep you from yours."
– the Universe

"A successful life is one that is lived through understanding and pursuing one's own path, not chasing after the dreams of others." – Chin-Ning Chu

Have you been caught lately in "this person makes me feel this way or that way?" Did you know that no one ever can make you do or feel any way? At the end of the day you, and only you, make the final choice to do, say or feel the way you do—end of story. Oh, it's nice to live in the story that you have no control over your own thoughts, feelings and emotions. But you are missing out on so much of your happiness by not taking on your life and getting that it is, as it always has been, your choice. I am not saying that you cannot ever be mad, sad, angry, frustrated, impatient, irritated, or any of the lower vibrational feelings. What I am saying is that it is your choice to feel that way based on past experiences that you have had, and over time you have made a decision that it is always going to be that way when certain circumstances arise. Hey, it is OK. I am just saying do not point your finger at someone else because you feel a certain way. When you take responsibility for your life, your actions, your thoughts, your feelings, and/or your emotions you have the power to do anything that you put your mind to.

Think about it…

Love and Sunshine,
Tracy

Feeling disconnected?

"People are lonely because they build walls instead of bridges." – Joseph F. Newton

"We have to decide for ourselves what's nourishing to our souls, and do those things over others." – Thomas Moore

You may think that building a wall around you is protecting you from letting all the bad get in. This may be true, but what you are also doing is keeping all the good out. If this is the case how can you be surprised that you are so lonely?

If you feel disconnected from people do you really think that the wall—that barrier—you have put up is ever going to help you establish any kind of connection? Try this. Go stand six inches away from but facing a wall. Now pretend there is someone that you really like and trust standing in front of you on the other side of that wall. Now shake their hand. Hmmm…You see what I mean? With the barrier that you have created around you, you cannot even shake the hand of someone who is there to bring you love and support, so are you really surprised that you feel disconnected from the people that you care about? It's not their fault—EVER! It was and is your choice on a daily basis to create your wall. What do you think you would be able to create in your life if one day you decided to tear down the confines of your wall and allow yourself to be loved?

Think about it…

Love and Sunshine,
Tracy

Why wait?

"Create a definite plan for carrying out your desire and begin at once, whether you are ready or not, to put this plan into action." – Napolean Hill

"Waiting is a trap. There will always be reasons to wait. The truth is, there are only two things in life, reasons and results, and reasons simply don't count." – Robert Anthony

"Whatever we are waiting for—peace of mind, contentment, grace, the inner awareness of simple abundance—it will surely come to us, but only when we are ready to receive it with an open and grateful heart." – Sarah Ban Breathnach

"Do not wait; the time will never be just right. Start where you stand, and work with whatever tools you may have at your command, and better tools will be found as you go along." – Napolean Hill

If you want something to happen and you are just sitting there waiting for it, thinking about all the reasons you do not have it yet, are you really surprised that it isn't in your life? You are the only one who can make the choice to create the things you want in your life. If you want happiness then be happy. If you want peace then be calm. If you want love then be loving. If you want money then be resourceful. If you want *anything* in your life, it is, as it always has been, up to you to be the very thing that you are looking to create in your life.

Think about it...

Love and Sunshine,
Tracy

Open communication

"Silence is one of the hardest arguments to refute." – Josh Billings

"Lying is done with words and also with silence." – Adrienne Rich

"The most important thing in communication is hearing what isn't said." –
Peter F. Drucker

Are you open in your communication? Or are you leaving things unsaid, hiding things or flat out lying about them? In my opinion, they are all the same. No matter if you decide to not speak the truth because you think it may hurt someone's feelings, or if you are fearful that someone else might find out what you are up to, it is still being dishonest. It brings up the quote I used last week: "Do not do what you would undo if caught." – Leah Arendt. It's all in the realm of not being complete and open in your communication. Who are you to decide what information is appropriate information to give someone? Maybe the truth you have to say is the missing piece that that other person has been searching for and needs in order for them to make an educated decision?

Communication IS the bridge to your relationships. If the only thing you have in your tickle trunk of ideas to build a strong trusting relation-ship is communication, and you choose to hide things—whether they be thoughts, ideas, feelings, emotions or actions—isn't that like removing a brick from your bridge with every lie you tell or for every thought or action not said? And what will happen to that bridge over time if you continue to lie about things or if you leave things unsaid? Hmmm, inter-esting... What kind of happiness and freedom would you create in your life if you did not feed your fear and just told the truth and were open in your communication—ALWAYS?

Think about it…

Love and Sunshine,
Tracy

September 4th

When do you give more than you can afford?

"Generosity is another quality which, like patience, letting go, non-judging, and trust, provides a solid foundation for mindfulness practice. You might experiment with using the cultivation of generosity as a vehicle for deep self-observation and inquiry as well as an exercise in giving." – Jon Kabat Zinn

Being generous doesn't mean that you have to go to your pocket book and just mindlessly write a cheque to some random charity. Have you ever thought that you could just be generous with yourself? Maybe you could be generous with your time, generous with your actions, generous with your thoughts, generous with your feelings, generous with your emotions, generous with your BEing. If you are looking to create a happy, loving relationship full of open communication and solid trust, maybe starting with being generous with all that you are and not hiding anything might possibly create exactly what you are looking to produce in your life. If you do not have what you want, then maybe you might want to look at where you are not being generous with some part of you?

Think about it…

Love and Sunshine,
Tracy

Health and help

"More tears are shed over answered prayers than unanswered ones." –
Mother Teresa

"God answers prayer in His own way, not ours." – Mohandas Gandhi

Why is it that you will pray and pray and pray and wish and hope for something and then, when you get it, you are disappointed and realize that it wasn't something that you wanted after all? Maybe, it is because you didn't pray for the "right" thing for you? You may have put it in your mind but never put in your heart to see if it is really what you want. Our minds can play tricks on us and make us "think" what we want but your heart will never turn you astray. If it hurts your heart, well then, it's not for you.

If you ask for the perfect "thing" to arrive at the perfect "time" and to receive it in the perfect "way," you may be pleasantly surprised that you are supplied in infinite ways. Your Divine is looking out for you, has your best interest at heart and will present to you what is, by Divine right, yours.

Think about it...

Love and Sunshine,
Tracy

What is important to you?

"My ultimate freedom is the right and power to decide how anybody or any-thing outside myself will affect me!" – Stephen R. Covey

"Faced with the choice between changing one's mind and proving that there is no need to do so, almost everyone gets busy on the proof." – John Kenneth Galbraith

When you make a choice are you still at some level blaming someone else for a consequence of that choice? For any choice that you make, whether it be deciding to end a friendship or deciding to paint your kitchen fuchsia, someone may not be happy with your choice—but isn't it better to be honest with someone rather than create upsets in other parts of your life just to avoid saying something to someone that you feel might hurt their feelings? Did you know that you are not responsible for their reaction to your request or actions? If they feel hurt, that is how they choose to react to your request. If they do not like your request or action, it is their responsibility not yours for their own feelings. They do not have to like it. They do not have to understand it either. Just accept it. It really is that simple. Why would you want to carry around someone else's reaction as personal to you? It is their story and does not have anything at all to do with you—ever!

What do you hold important in your life? What are you working to create for yourself in the now? Are you willing to feel a little bit of personal discomfort in order to have what you want? In the end you are still the only one making the decision to do anything, and/or feel any way that you do.

Think about it…

Love and Sunshine,
Tracy

Ch-ch-ch-changes...

"They always say time changes things, but you actually have to change them yourself." – Andy Warhol

"Know what's weird? Day by day, nothing seems to change, but pretty soon… everything's different." – Calvin from Calvin and Hobbes

"There is nothing like returning to a place that remains unchanged to find the ways in which you yourself have altered." – Nelson Mandela

"It is not necessary to change. Survival is not mandatory." – W. Edwards Deming

No one ever said that you "have to" change. If you like what is happening in your life and how you are feeling about it, then don't do anything. If you do not like what is going on in your life and how you are feeling about it, you still do not have to do anything, except, not complain about it. As soon as you start to complain about anything that is going on in your life you are pointing your finger elsewhere and blaming others for what only you can control. What you really need to do is go look in a mirror and accept "what is" and then change it if you want to. It is, as it always has been, your choice!

Think about it…

Love and Sunshine,
Tracy

Believe in your own success

"What you believe yourself to be, you are." – Claude M. Bristol

"It is better to believe than to disbelieve; in so doing you bring everything to the realm of possibility." – Albert Einstein

"Believe it can be done. When you believe something can be done, really believe, your mind will find the ways to do it. Believing a solution paves the way to solution." – Dr. David Schwartz

It is better to be in a state of belief rather than disbelief. Not only do you raise your vibrational energy, your overall outlook on life shifts. It may seem that all the planets get into perfect alignment and everything goes your way. You get everything that is by Divine right yours and you are perfectly HAPPY in every moment! Yippppeeee!!! Haven't felt like that? Hmmm…Maybe it is because you are stuck in disbelief? It is always your choice.

Think about it…

Love and Sunshine,
Tracy

Give to yourself first

"First say to yourself what you would be; and then do what you have to do."
– *Epictetus*

"Let the waters settle you will see stars and moon mirrored in your Being."
– *Rumi*

Sometimes people keep the waters rough so they do not have to see how beautiful they are. It is a way for them to deprive themselves of self-love and to not be responsible for their own lives. All in all, when you give to yourself first you'll have endless ways of giving to others.

If you always give to others first before yourself, are you really surprised that you may be left thinking that there is no one there to support you?

Think about it…

Love and Sunshine,
Tracy

Are you missing out to be right?

"Don't Make Assumptions. Find the courage to ask questions and to express what you really want. Communicate with others as clearly as you can to avoid misunderstandings, sadness and drama. With just this one agreement, you can completely transform your life." – Miguel Angel Ruiz

"Assumptions allow the best in life to pass you by." – John Sales

"We simply assume that the way we see things is the way they really are or the way they should be. And our attitudes and behaviors grow out of these assumptions." – Stephen R. Covey

If you find yourself not having the experiences and/or the relationships in your life that you want, have you ever thought that it may be due to the way you communicate with the people around you? If you are living your life under the impression that your point of view is the only point of view out there and that only you know the proper way to do anything or behave in the right way or react properly to a certain outcome, how are you ever surprised that you often find yourself angry, alone, frustrated, justifying your position and/or caught in a place of misunderstanding? Maybe next time, to avoid the drama, you could say to yourself "I may be wrong." (Yikes!…that must have been hard to hear!) You could then start to ask clarifying questions. Instead of getting angry at everyone because they are not responding the way you would, by asking questions you may be surprised at how easy it is to communicate and create an environment of peace, love and happiness whereever you go.

Think about it…

Love and Sunshine,
Tracy

You can't change what's not in your control

"The ease of change, everyone, is directly proportional to one's willingness to reconsider what's best for themselves.

I say let it be easy.

Because, when change comes it always means there's something better." – *the Universe*

Why fight and struggle with something that is out of your control? You never know—the very thing you are struggling against may be the best thing for you in the end.

Think about it...

Love and Sunshine,
Tracy

What if ?

"The universe is full of magical things patiently waiting for our wits to grow sharper."– Eden Phillpotts

"The greatest discovery of my generation is that a human being can alter his life by altering his attitudes." – William James

"Sometimes I've believed as many as six impossible things before breakfast." – Lewis Carroll

Hmmm…What if…?

Think about it…

Love and Sunshine,
Tracy

Are you serving?

"You may be good, but what are you good for? You've got to be good for something. You've got to be about some project, some task that requires you to be humble and obedient to the universal principles of service." – Stephen R. Covey

"We had to learn ourselves, and furthermore we had to teach the despairing men, that it did not matter what we expected from life, but rather what life expected from us. We needed to stop asking about the meaning of life but instead to think of ourselves as those who were being questioned by life, daily and hourly. Our answer must consist not in talk and meditation, but in right action and in right conduct. Life ultimately means taking the responsibility to find the right answer to its problems and to fulfill the tasks which it constantly sets for the individual." – Victor Frankl

"If you think you're too small to have an impact, try going to bed with a mosquito in the room." – Anita Roddick

Whether you think you can or you can't...you are right! If something doesn't create happiness for you, then do not do it! We all have a life purpose that is a perfect fit for us, no matter what it is. It is up to you to find out what that purpose is and just go with it whereever it may take you.

Think about it...

Love and Sunshine,
Tracy

For richer or poorer...

"Prosperity is a way of living and thinking, and not just money or things. Poverty is a way of living and thinking, and not just a lack of money or things."
– Eric Butterworth

Being rich and prosperous has nothing to do with material things. It all lies within the realm of your own thoughts.

Think about it...

Love and Sunshine,
Tracy

September 15th

It's OK to quit

> "Employ the power of positive quitting. Most of us view quitting as something negative, but it's not. Winners never quit, we're told, when, in reality, winners quit all the time: choosing to stop doing things that aren't creating the results they desire. When you quit all the things that aren't working for you, when you quit tolerating all the negative things that hold you back, you'll create a positive charge in your life as well as create the space in your life for more positive experiences." – Jim Allen

> "I like thinking of possibilities. At any time, an entirely new possibility is liable to come along and spin you off in an entirely new direction. The trick, I've learned, is to be awake to the moment." – Doug Hall

Are you remaining in unhappiness and hardship because you do not want to be quitter? Did you know that it takes someone with courage, strength and determination to say enough is enough and make a change for the betterment of their own life? Quitting something because it doesn't create happiness in your life is far more positive and productive for your well-being than continuing to do something because you are concerned about how others view you. Why not take on your own life, and see where quitting something that isn't working for you could possibly be the positive change that you've been looking to create the happiness that you've been seeking all along.

Think about it…

Love and Sunshine,
Tracy

Co-manifestation

"[Manifestation is] the art of fashioning a co-creative, synchronistic, and mutually supportive relationship between the inner creative energies of a person's own mind and spirit and their counterpart within the larger world in order to bring a new and desirable situation into being.

We must see ourselves as co-manifestors—partners in manifestation—all engaged in the primal act of unfoldment and emergence. Each act of manifestation may be directed toward a specific outcome, but it also contributes to the greater manifestation of the wholeness, love, compassion, and creativity of the primal source from which we all come." – David Spangler

Where have your thoughts been lately? In your thoughts are you creating a world of hardship and woe or are you creating a world of Happiness and Love? It is *your* choice. In the end, wouldn't you rather live in a world of joyous fun, laughter and love?

Think about it…

Love and Sunshine,
Tracy

September 17th

Conquer fear with action

"Your fears are not walls, but hurdles. Courage is not the absence of fear, but the conquering of it." – Dan Millman

"Many of our fears are tissue-paper-thin, and a single courageous step would carry us clear through them." – Brendan Francis

Have you ever been so fearful that you just stop doing everything? Brendan is right. Our fears are so paper-thin that all it takes is a single step of faith and your fear will disappear. Why? Because you have made up every single fear that you have; they only exist in your mind and do not ever enter the real world. It is only through your actions that you create the experience of your thoughts, and the one always comes before the other. With that being said, wouldn't you rather create happy, joyous, loving experiences full of passion, laughter and fun?

Think about it…

Love and Sunshine,
Tracy

Fear lives in the future

"We can't fear the past. Fear is a future thing. And since the future's all in our heads, fear must be a head thing." – Tom Payne

"I have not ceased being fearful, but I have ceased to let fear control me." – Erica Jong

Since fear lives in the future and the future hasn't happened yet, isn't that proof enough that you are making it up in your head? What does fear stand for again? Oh yeah: False Evidence Appearing Real! Hmmm...

Think about it...

Love and Sunshine,
Tracy

What message do you need most to hear?

> *"One word frees us from the weight and pain of life; that word is love."*
> *– Sophocles*

> *"Oh the comfort, the inexpressible comfort of feeling safe with a person, having neither to weigh thoughts nor measure words, but pouring them all right out, just as they are—chaff and grain together—certain that a faithful hand will take and sift them, keep what is worth keeping, and with the breath of kindness blow the rest away." – Dinah Mulock*

Maybe the message you need to hear the most is already being spread all around you. Maybe you've been looking so hard for it that you may be missing it. Or maybe you are just trying to hear it only in the way that you want to hear it, and not how the message is actually being given? If you stop trying to control it then maybe, just maybe, you'll realize that it has been in your life all along?

Think about it…

Love and Sunshine,
Tracy

Believe you are a creator

"Every moment of your life is infinitely creative and the universe is endlessly bountiful. Just put forth a clear enough request, and everything your heart desires must come to you." – Shakti Gawain

"By believing passionately in something that still does not exist, we create it. The non-existent is whatever we have not sufficiently desired."– Nikos Kazantzakis

If you haven't realized by now that you are the creator of your life then are you surprised that you are living in a state of want rather than just BEing happy? If you do not have something in your life it is either not meant to be there or you do not have the faith that it belongs there. Continue to create what you will but do not be blaming others for what only you can control.

Think about it…

Love and Sunshine,
Tracy

Love and hate

"If you hate a person, you hate something in him that is part of yourself. What isn't part of ourselves doesn't disturb us." – Herman Hesse

"The price of hating other human beings is loving oneself less." – Eldridge Cleaver

"Hatred paralyzes life; love releases it. Hatred confuses life; love harmonizes it. Hatred darkens life; love illumines it." – Dr. Martin Luther King Jr.

I may have said this before but the opposite of love is not hate. When you go from one extreme to the other you are just as bound to that person as if you were a part of them, so why are you surprised that when your love turns sour, you still cannot stop thinking about that person and they still infiltrate your life? Well for one, you let them and two, something about them still works for you. The opposite of both love and hate is indifference. When your emotions turn from love to hate it is more about you than the other person, anyway. It is like drinking poison hoping the other person will die. When you hate all you do is lose yourself. That's why a philosophy of mine I like to follow is that "love is the answer to everything!"

Think about it…

Love and Sunshine,
Tracy

Decide, commit, move on...

"Better to do something imperfectly than to do nothing flawlessly." – Robert H. Schuller

"Your only limitations are those you set up in your mind, or permit others to set up for you." – Og Mandino

"Life is like riding a bike. It is impossible to maintain your balance while standing still." – Linda Brakeall

Are you feeling like you are out of balance in your life? Did you ever think that it may be due to the fact that you are not making a decision; therefore you are remaining in a voluntary stationary position? To me the only way to get anywhere in life is to: Decide, Commit, and Move on.

Think about it…

Love and Sunshine,
Tracy

Have you already decided?

"The gesture is the thing truly expressive of the individual—as we think so will we act." – Martha Graham

"An avoidance of true communication is tantamount to a relinquishment of my self-being; if I withdraw from it I am betraying not only the other but myself." – Karl Jaspers

If you have already made up the ending to your story in your head why are you disappointed when it actually turns out that way?

Think about it...

Love and Sunshine,
Tracy

Look in the mirror

"No man has a chance to enjoy permanent success until he begins to look in a mirror for the real cause of all his mistakes." – Napoleon Hill

"In my beginning is my end." – T.S. Eliot

In *your* life, why is it that you are still looking for someone else to blame when things do not go the way you want them to? What are you getting out of not taking full responsibility for your own life and its interactions? Still get to be the victim, eh? How's that working for you in creating happiness in your life? Oh yeah, right, when you are a victim there is no happiness and nothing is your fault. Silly me, I forgot. If you are not willing to be true to yourself and honor yourself why are you surprised when someone else doesn't do it either? You are the only person standing in the way of your own happiness and getting exactly what you want in life. The only place to be looking when things do not go your own way is into the mirror, not across the table.

Think about it…

Love and Sunshine,
Tracy

September 25th

Be true to yourself

"In the final analysis, we count for something only because of the essential we embody, and if we do not embody that, life is wasted." – C. G. Jung

"A true knowledge of ourselves is knowledge of our power." – Mark Rutherford

When you are denying your own abilities—to avoid looking like you are better than someone else or the Rock Star that you really are—how are you ever surprised if you are continually coming across people who either do not pay you what you are worth or do not give you the respect you deserve in your chosen profession or day-to-day life? If you continue to deny your true feelings and your true power you may end up getting seriously sick. If you believe in yourself and honor your own abilities everyone else will have to follow suit.

Think about it...

Love and Sunshine,
Tracy

September 26th

Everyone has a point of view

"When you talk, you repeat what you already know; when you listen, you often learn something." – Jared Sparks

If, at this moment, you are stuck in something in your life, have you ever thought that it may be due to the fact that you have blinders on? Are you only willing to see things from your own point of view rather than being objective and seeing that there are at least two points of view to any situation? Did you know that both points of view are right? If you are upset because you want someone else to see things your own way, how's that working for you in creating happiness and joy in your life? Hmmm., interesting...Are you really surprised that you are upset, feel hurt or angry at someone else when you are already justifying that you have the right to feel the way you do? Have you ever thought that you may not have all the information regarding the situation and that you may be making up your own endings in order for you to justify your own feelings? If you are in a situation like this, honestly, no matter what anyone ever tells you it will not matter. Even if you get every detail of every step that has lead to that particular situation, it will not matter. Why? Because you have already made up your mind to be upset and only see things from your own point of view.

When you find yourself justifying your feelings maybe this is the place for you to stop and look to see where you may be able to take responsibility for any part of the situation. Seeing where you, yourself, may be responsible for any occurrences, although this may be harder than justifying your own point of view, it is the only thing that you can control. If you came from nothing going on in your mind rather than from a preset way of already feeling or BEing in this situation, do you not think that you might end up seeing things from the other person's point of view and realize that the endings you've already created in your mind may be different to how the situation really is? Wouldn't you rather be happy than be right, anyway?

Think about it...

Love and Sunshine,

Tracy

Ask for what you need

"Maybe we give to others what we wish others would give to us..." –
Beth François

Hmmm, interesting...A few things come up for me when I read that statement. Although the statement may be more true than not, are we then just perpetuating more of not getting what we want by doing so? If you give with the expectation of receiving the same is it really still giving? Isn't giving suppose to be selfless? If you are giving to someone—whether you are giving something physical like a bouquet of flowers, an emotional response or an action of deep intimate love—should it not be what they want instead of what you want? Maybe it's just a way for us to get good at asking for what we really need instead of playing a guessing game with the people we care about.

Just something to think about...

Love and Sunshine,
Tracy

Never stop learning, never stop growing

"The great thing in the world is not so much where we stand, as in what direction we are moving." – Oliver Wendell Holmes

"We can learn to be the catalysts for our own change." – Sarah Ban Breathnach

My daughter received a DS as a gift this year and along with it I got the game "*Brain Age*." In the opening introduction of the game the cartoon doctor told me that our brain stops growing at age twenty. If you do nothing to intrigue it your brain continually gets older and older *way* past your true physical age. When I took my first "*Brain Age*" test I found out that my brain has aged to that of an eighty year old brain. That's over twice my real age! Yikes! It got me thinking…If my brain gets older the less I use it then would it not be the same for the rest of my body too? What I found out is that if you are continually learning or studying you are growing consciously but it also keeps you active and thinking young. Maybe it's the reason your creative juices may have become like molasses, maybe all you need to do to jump start you into life is to do some simple math equations…lol. Needless to say on my last "*Brain Age*" test I was marked as having the brain of a twenty-seven year old. Yippee! Now my brain matches my looks…lol. My point is, it is up to you to decide to do something to help yourself remain young, fit and active whatever that may be. Maybe try brushing your teeth with your opposite hand, read some motivating books, research and study a new concept and/or learn a new language. It doesn't matter what, just DO something! What do you think the difference is between what an eighty year old thinks about and what a twenty-seven year old thinks about? Hmmm, interesting… get cracking!

Think about it…

Love and Sunshine,
Tracy

Challenge yourself

"We have a tendency to make assumptions about everything. The problem with making assumptions is that we BELIEVE they are the truth." – Unknown

Why is it that when something happens we instantly go to making it so personal that it creates for us nothing but upset and drama—when in reality it has nothing ever to do with us because the other person most likely wasn't thinking about us at all. It may sound harsh but it is true. People do things that are best for them and rarely think about how it will impact anyone else because it is not about you, the other person—ever!

This reminds me of something I recently read in a book called *The Four Agreements*. When we take things personally we create a belief about the situation and we assume we are right about it to the point that we will destroy relationships in order to defend our position. And how's that working for you in creating a life full of joy and happiness? Still want to be right, eh? Well through clear communication, like asking specific questions regarding what you make up in your mind instead of assuming you already have the answer, your relationships may start to change.

Here's a challenge that a good friend of mine brought forward to me and I thought that you, too, may get something out of it:

Challenge: Take on every conversation or upset as an opportunity to train yourself in just being with others' thoughts, opinions and actions without having to have one yourself! It really is all a choice!

Think about it…

Love and Sunshine,
Tracy

Joy always follows forgiveness

"The greatest evil that can befall man is that he should come to think ill of himself." – *Johann Wolfgang Von Goethe*

"If we don't forgive ourselves for our mistakes, and others for the wounds they have inflicted upon us, we end up crippled with guilt. And the soul cannot grow under a blanket of guilt, because guilt is isolating, while growth is a gradual process of reconnection to ourselves, to other people, and to a larger whole." – *Joan Borysenko*

If you do not make mistakes how are you ever to learn and grow? And forgiving another doesn't necessarily mean forgetting; it just means you let go of the emotional attachment you've created around what happened and you no longer are taking it personally. When you forgive you allow yourself to be you and honor yourself for being the best you that you are! And hands down you are nothing less than AMAZING! Once you forgive, especially yourself, and free yourself from that icky preset way of feeling you'll find that there is nothing left for you to do but to BE happy.

Think about it…

Love and Sunshine,
Tracy

Tracy Friesen

Continuous effort

"The only thing even in this world are the number of hours in a day. The difference in winning or losing is what you do with those hours." – Woody Hayes

"Continuous effort—not strength or intelligence—is the key to unlocking our potential." – Frank A. Clark

If you ever want to get from here to there or if you have ever wanted to get something in life, all that is required of you is to continuously put one foot in front of the other—nothing more.

Think about it…

Love and Sunshine,
Tracy

October 2nd

Do you give to get?

If you give looking to receive some sort of reward in return, whether it is praise or some sort of monetary value, are you still giving? If you give your time and/or your services and expect something in return isn't that called getting a paycheck?

Think about it…

Love and Sunshine,
Tracy

Appreciate the mystery

"The mystery of life is not a problem to be solved but a reality to be experienced." – *Aart Van Der Leeuw*

"I believe there is no source of deception in the investigation of nature which can compare with a fixed belief that certain kinds of phenomena are impossible." – *William James*

"Your theory is crazy, but it's not crazy enough to be true." – *Niels Bohr*

"To know that we know what we know, and to know that we do not know what we do not know, that is true knowledge." – *Copernicus*

If you live your life from the story in your head, are you really surprised that you experience it exactly how you think it is?

Think about it…

Love and Sunshine,
Tracy

October 4th

Create happiness right now

"It is our basic right to be a happy person, happy family, and eventually a happy world. That should be our goal." – Dalai Lama

"…we can no longer afford to throw away even one unimportant day by not noticing the wonder of it all. We have to be willing to discover and then appreciate the authentic moments of happiness available to all of us every day." – Sarah Ban Breathnach

Y ou are the only one who can look at your own life and find something to be grateful for and just BE happy that you have it. If you cannot find anything to be grateful for, how are you ever surprised that you are lonely, angry, sad, mad, frustrated, depressed, and /or you feel disconnected? It is, as it always has been, *your* choice to feel however you want to feel, so why wouldn't you want to continually create happiness?

Think about it…

Love and Sunshine,
Tracy

Create balance

"Many people like to think that they'll find balance AFTER they find success. But in reality, achieving balance IS success." – Brian Koslow

"It is literally true that you can succeed best and quickest by helping others to succeed." – Napolean Hill

Finding that perfect balance in your life truly is a success worth celebrating. And it is as easy as flicking a switch.

Think about it...

Love and Sunshine,
Tracy

Take your blinders off!

"Have you ever noticed, running head first into a brick wall usually doesn't change the fact that it is a brick wall. You must find a way to maneuver around it or you really will end up hurt!" – Miss Tammy Gunn

This goes for etheric walls too!

Think about it…

Love and Sunshine,
Tracy

In love's light

"The feminine is more powerful than the masculine, the soft is more powerful than the hard, the water is more powerful than the rock." – Osho

"The moment you enter into the world of words you start falling away from that which is. The more you enter into language, the farther you are away from existence." – Osho

Have you ever realized how many different stories you make up in your head every day to justify your frustration, your aggravation, your resentments and/or your anger about the things in your life that are not going the way you want them to go? This all stems from our language and is triggered every day by the words "once upon a time." No matter what *has* happened or what *is* happening in your life, you can choose to make it mean whatever you want. Like it or not it is "what is", and nothing can change the factuality of it. The more you tell a story about that fact the more you lose your power and you may create the very thing that you are trying to avoid. Instead of using force or your aggression, why not take the more gentle approach and allow your power to flow from within you from within your heart? What's that saying, again? "You can catch more flies with honey than with vinegar." The more confrontational you are the bigger the story you are going to have to tell yourself to justify your actions in the end. Just keep in mind, LOVE is the answer—always—and you'll do just fine!

This reminds me of an inspirational story that happened to a friend of mine while we were taking a communications course together. Just to set up the scene imagine this small petite woman in her twenties wearing a hijab, walking along in downtown Toronto. She sees this man across the street yelling at his friends. He is obviously very angry. His friends get in a cab and leave and he goes into a convenience store. She impulsively runs across the street and into the store where the man went and she sees the man now yelling angrily at the person behind the counter. She then acts on what we had been learning in our course about how to communicate with others. She says to the man, "Excuse me, sir…" The man turns to her, looking scary and mean, and with a scowl on his face he yells at her, "What do you want?" She in turn says, "I am sorry for whatever is going on in your life that you feel you have to act this way but I wanted you to know that I care." The man starts to walk towards her and says, "You do not know me; I am a very BAD man!" My friend, now frightened, continues, "I just want you to know that I care and that I love you for who you are and I thought you could use a hug…" She said that the man's energy changed and he became softer. She reached up and gave him a hug and she said that the man started to cry, and after a moment he said, "Thank you" in soft innocent voice. She said, "You are welcome," and left the store.

Wow…I know…powerful. Now this woman went to an extreme but holy cow, can you imagine the impact she had on that man and how he may continue to live his life because she acted on the love from within her heart? You see, LOVE really is the answer! The soft feminine power is *so* much stronger than the masculine aggression. My friend was able to melt that man's heart by a few kind words and a loving gesture. What would you be able to create in your life if you stayed out of the "once upon a times" in your head, stuck to the facts and just plain used your heart instead of your head once in a while? What if you were able to see everyone, including yourself, in love's light? I believe that we would all be living in a different world…don't you?

Think about it…

Love and Sunshine,
Tracy

Are your beliefs holding you back?

"There's nothing to stop any human being other than what they're believing."
– Byron Katie

"The only time we suffer is when we believe a thought that argues with what is…" – Byron Katie

Our beliefs are something that make us who we are, but have you ever thought to examine them to see if it is through them that you are holding yourself back from what you really want in life? Our beliefs are extremely powerful tools to guide us on our daily path. Most people do not question their own beliefs, but have you ever challenged yourself to question whether just because *you* believe something to be true, it actually is true? Oh, in believing that it is true you get to be right about everything, that's for sure, but that still doesn't make it true. If you feel that you are suffering in your life maybe it is time to check in on what you hold as a belief about yourself, the people you care about, the people you interact with, your work, your community, your city, your country, and/or the world. Maybe, just maybe, it is time to put those old beliefs aside and start to look at yourself with no judgment and see what happens from there. You never know what you will be able to create in your life if you show up to every conversation and to every event with a blank slate about yourself, those you interact with, those you know, those you don't know, those you just met, those you care about, those you don't care about, everyone and/ or everything that you once held a belief about.

Think about it…

Love and Sunshine,
Tracy

Love, love, love...love is all you need

"Love is not only something you feel. It is something you do."– David Wilkerson

If you are just sitting there in a state of "loving" someone, what are you actually *doing* that ensures that they too know that you love them?

Think about it…

Love and Sunshine,
Tracy

Are we feeling stuck?

"This too shall pass." – King Solomon

"Difficult times have helped me to understand better than before, how infinitely rich and beautiful life is in every way, and that so many things that one goes worrying about are of no importance whatsoever..." – Isak Dinesen

"If you can find a path with no obstacles, it probably doesn't lead anywhere." – Frank A. Clark

Maybe it is time to slow down and just be grateful for what you have in your life at this moment. PAUSE—if for nothing else, you *are* still breathing...

Slow down...reflect...rejuvenate...Your creative mind will thank you for it and just maybe you'll have something new to think about...

Love and Sunshine,
Tracy

October 11th

Choose wisely

"A decision today changes tomorrow forever." – John Di Lemme

And it's up to you what that tomorrow will be, so choose wisely.

Think about it…

Love and Sunshine,
Tracy

You are a product of your choices

The following is taken from an email Song Chengxiang sent promoting a hypnotherapy program to help you boost your confidence as well the use of Emotional Freedom Techniques (EFT) for helping you with your emotions. I am not promoting either but I enjoyed reading the prelude to the program and found its information helpful. I thought you too may find some insight in its information:

_=_=_=_=_=_=_=_=_

If you are not one hundred percent satisfied with the current status of your life as it is right now in terms of anything including relationships, finances, career, parenting, etc. there is only one thing that you need to assess and that's your decision making process.

You see, our lives are shaped by our experiences and all experiences are the result of a decision. If you decide to touch a burning stove, the result will be that you get burned. If you decide to jump in a pool of water, the result will be that you get wet.

Sometimes however, the result that we experience from a decision isn't so clearly visible prior to making that decision. In other words, we think that by making a certain decision, we will achieve a certain result but somehow that result turns into something else. And that's when things get tricky. And this is why if areas of your life aren't moving along as planned, you must assess your decision making process.

Decisions are driven by two things; the confidence in one's ability to achieve a certain result and more importantly, emotions. The reason why I say "more importantly" is because emotions ultimately guide every decision and will always override one's confidence.

For example, if you decide that it's time to lose weight or quit smoking, you can have all the confidence in the world in your ability to achieve those goals but if your emotions point you in the opposite direction, you will ultimately never achieve those goals. Therefore, to truly enhance any areas of your life, you must work on both your confidence and your emotions.

_=_=_=_=_=_=_=_=_

It's one thing to have all the confidence in the world but if you do not have your emotions in check you may just be spinning your wheels and wondering why you are not going anywhere. When your emotions are involved it may be as simple as just releasing what isn't working for you any longer.

Think about it...

Love and Sunshine,
Tracy

What's in your way really?

"The question isn't who is going to let me; it's who is going to stop me." –
Ayn Rand

When you believe in yourself and your own abilities there is nothing that you cannot accomplish—ever! The answer to Ayn's question is and always will be YOU!

Think about it...

Love and Sunshine,
Tracy

October 14th

You are in control!

"All the breaks you need in life wait within your imagination, Imagination is the workshop of your mind, capable of turning mind energy into accomplishment and wealth." – Napoleon Hill

When are you going to realize that your life is the way it is because you and only you made it that way? When you finally *do* take responsibility for your entire life it is like winning the lottery!

Think about it...

Love and Sunshine,
Tracy

Why suffer any longer?

"Forgiveness does not mean that we suppress anger; forgiveness means that we have asked for a miracle: the ability to see through mistakes that someone has made to the truth that lies in all of our hearts.

Forgiveness is not always easy. At times, it feels more painful than the wound we suffered, to forgive the one that inflicted it.

And yet, there is no peace without forgiveness. Attack thoughts towards others are attack thoughts towards ourselves. The first step in forgiveness is the willingness to forgive." – Marianne Williamson

When we do things out of vengeance and vindictiveness, it's like taking poison and expecting the other person to die. Continually having anger and attacking thoughts towards another individual is the doing the same thing. How's that working for you so far? You will never be at peace until you first forgive. Why would you ever want to bog yourself down with such nastiness and be defined by your anger and hateful thoughts? There is *so* much in life that you can show gratitude. You are fooling yourself to believe that by hanging onto your insufferable thoughts that you are doing yourself any good. In the end no one cares if you were "right" about the story that goes on in your own head. It only matters to you—ever! On any given day, I would rather be HAPPY than right. What about you?

Think about it…

Love and Sunshine,
Tracy

What is regret?

"You can't go around being what everyone expects you to be, living your life through other people's rules, and be happy and successful." – Wayne Dyer

"If only. Those must be the two saddest words in the world." – Mercedes Lackey

"When one door closes, another opens; but we often look so long and so regretfully upon the closed door that we do not see the one which has opened for us." – Alexander Graham

I read this article the other day about regret and it is still with me today. The article said that regret is all about fear and I disagree so much with this statement that I had to stop reading the article halfway through.

The first thing I did was go look up regret in the dictionary. As a verb the first definition was: 1. to feel sorrow or remorse for.

I then looked up remorse: 1. deep and painful regret for wrongdoing; compunction.

I then looked up compunction. Since the first definition used both regret and remorse in it I choose the second definition: 2. any uneasiness or hesitation about the rightness of an action.

None of these definitions, to me, say anything close to being fearful. It just reminded me that we need to wary of the things we read and see. Even you, don't believe a word I say because maybe regret to you *is* about fear!

In the end both the article and I agree that regret is a time waster. No matter what you believe about it, that fact still remains true. It happened. You can waste your whole life regretting something that happened or didn't happen or you can just accept what is and live your life with joy and happiness in this moment! It's your choice.

Think about it…

Love and Sunshine,
Tracy

Direct your evolution

"Consciousness is the basis of all life and the field of all possibilities. Its nature is to expand and unfold its full potential. The impulse to evolve is thus inherent in the very nature of life." – Maharishi Mahesh Yogi

WAKE UP!!!

Think about it . . .

Love and Sunshine,
Tracy

Perception defines our reality

"The eye sees only what the mind is prepared to comprehend." – *Henri Bergson*

"There is no reality in the absence of observation." – *The Copenhagen Interpretation of Quantum Mechanics*

If you reread the first quote the operative word is "prepared." That means that you've already made up your mind how you are going to perceive things no matter what happens. Hmmm…How's that working for you so far? What if you came to every situation, every conversation and/or every encounter with a clear mind, without any preconceived notion of how things are going to go? Yeah that's right, leave your baggage at home. What kind of communication would you be able to create then? What if every single person out there left their baggage at home and we all came to every conversation, every situation, and/or every encounter with a clear empty mind, without any preconceived notions from our own personal stories of how things are going to go? What kind of world would we all create then? It is from our own perception that we mold our world and whatever you perceive you believe. And if *you* believe it then it *must* be true, right?

Think about it…

Love and Sunshine,
Tracy

Heal the past

"What you bring forth out of yourself from the inside will save you. What you do not bring forth out of yourself from the inside will destroy you." – Gospel of Thomas

"Letting go of our suffering is the hardest work we will ever do. It is also the most fruitful. To heal means to meet ourselves in a new way—in the newness of each moment where all is possible and nothing is limited to the old." – Stephen Levine

In order for you to ever have anything new or different in your life you first must make room for it. If you do not release or let something else go then you'll have exactly what you have right now and just a hope for something different. Letting go is the easy part. It is the wanting to be right about something that makes it hard. You do not believe me? OK then, bring into your mind something that isn't working for you. Now just release it with unconditional love. Thank it for its message and its medicine, for you do not need it anymore. If you find yourself going to a justification of why you need to hold onto it, then you just want to be right about that feeling or emotion that it creates for you. Hmmm, interesting…Wouldn't you rather be happy than right anyway?

Think about it…

Love and Sunshine,
Tracy

Growing through awareness of money

"What is [the role of money] in the search for meaning? Is our relationship to it one of the chief factors that keeps us in our prison, or could it also be a tool for breaking out, for awakening to a life filled with intensity of purpose?" – *Jacob Needleman*

"What we're after in Prospering is nothing less than a major shift in consciousness in the attitudes, beliefs, and ideas you have about yourself and your relationship to money."– *Jerrold Mundis*

If you think that money is not an important part of your life, how are you ever surprised that you do not ever have any? The amount of money that you have is in direct proportion to your attitude towards it. If you do not believe me then look at your bank account and then be honest how you feel about money. As I said, your relationship with money is reflective of your attitude about it. If you think you are poor you will be living in lack. If you think you are rich and abundant money flow is not and will not be a problem. If you are unsure of your attitude towards money I highly suggest taking a look at your bank account and then taking some time to jot a few things down about what you think about money. Do you think money is hard to come by or do you think money comes to you easy and often? Do you work hard for your money? Does money grow on trees? Do you need to save for a rainy day? (Insert belief here...)

You really can turn around your month-to-month, paycheck-to-paycheck living style. You just may have to start with your attitude. One should love people and use money and never the other way around. It's in your attitude that will show you how your relationship with money is affecting you attaining the things you really want in your life.

Think about it...

Love and Sunshine,
Tracy

Explore and experience

"I do not accept any absolute formulas for living. No preconceived code can see ahead to everything that can happen in a man's life. As we live, we grow and our beliefs change. They must change. So I think we should live with this constant discovery. We should be open to this adventure in heightened awareness of living. We should stake our whole existence on our willingness to explore and experience." – Martin Buber

That sounds so exciting! So many people get caught in thinking that they know exactly what is going to happen because they live from the story in their head instead of exploring new experiences called life. Why not just be open to "what is" and live your life with freedom and happiness instead of thinking your life is nothing but a big pile of poo? Wouldn't you rather be wrong on this one? I know I want you to, because you are getting kinda stinky.

Think about it...

Love and Sunshine,
Tracy

It's time to get out of the way!

"When the issues of someone else's life have you tied in knots, it usually means it's time to start focusing on your own life.

Of course it's easier to solve other people's issues, that's why you chose more challenging ones." – the Universe

Have you ever found yourself so wound up in someone else's troubles that you have been able to forget all about your own strife? It may feel good for a while but in the end, even if you help the other person out of their situation, you are still left with your own unhappiness and discord. Maybe you would be more effective, not only for yourself but for others too, if you took responsibility for your own life first because when you take responsibility for your own life something amazingly unexpected happens. You start to become happy with what you have and you are able to be who you already are and nothing or no one stands in your way to your own happiness. Right now you are the only person who is standing in your way—so MOVE will ya!

Think about it…

Love and Sunshine,
Tracy

Mind control

"The successful man is the average man, focused." – Unknown

"Concentration is the ability to think about absolutely nothing when it is absolutely necessary." – Ray Knight

"Eventually, meditation will make our mind calm, clear, and as concentrated as a laser which we can focus at will. This capacity of one-pointed attention is the essence of genius. When we have this mastery over attention in everything we do, we have a genius for life itself: unshakable security, clear judgment, and deep personal relationships." – Eknath Easwaran

These are not the droids you are looking for (she waves her hand, using the Force...) Lol...OK, this is not the kind of mind control that we are talking about here but I think the Force still plays a part. The day I was able to sit and think of nothing was the day that things came into a different perspective for me. I was able to stay present without thinking of the past or the future. I was truly able to think of nothing and just sit in appreciation of all that was around me in that moment. It *is* a fabulous feeling just to BE present with nothing bogging you down. We get to that point by controlling our own mind.

Think about it...

Love and Sunshine,
Tracy

Embrace your life

"If there is a sin against life, it consists perhaps not so much in despairing of life, as in hoping for another life, and in eluding the implacable grandeur of this life." – Albert Camus

"Recognize that life is what you get when you're born…living is what you do with it." – Jim Allen

It's up to you to shape your own life. It is, as it always has been, your choice to do or not do anything. Whether you think so or not, you are the one who is choosing the life that you are currently living and it is up to you to change it if you do not like how it is laying out for you. The only time you have to live is right now in this moment—and wouldn't you rather live it BEing happy?

Think about it…

Love and Sunshine,
Tracy

Journey home

"Everything seeks its source." – *a Universal Principle*

"Two people have been living in you all your life. One is the ego, garrulous, demanding, hysterical, calculating; the other is the hidden spiritual being, whose still voice of wisdom you have only rarely heard or attended to—you have uncovered in yourself your own wise guide." – *Sogyal Rinpoche*

Using the universal principle that "everything seeks its source," I find it interesting that people will still send out negative or lower vibrational energy in their thoughts and actions knowing full well that in the end everything comes back to them, some say tenfold. Still they claim that they are victims and have no responsibility for how their lives are less than satisfactory in this moment. If it is true that "everything seeks its source," then you know that I am going to send out as much peace, love, happiness and prosperity as I can so that when it is time for that energy to start its journey home it will permeate my whole essence and BEing with ten times the power that I sent it out with! WHOO!! Come on peace, love, happiness and prosperity!

Isn't it time you put that voluble ego to rest and start listening to the voice of your infallible intuition, your Divine-power within, that is unfailing in its effectiveness to keep you on your rightful path, gaining you nothing but the best of what is meant for you in your Divine plan?

Sending out peace, love, happiness and prosperity…peace, love, happiness and prosperity…peace, love, happiness and prosperity…peace, love, happiness and prosperity…peace, love, happiness and prosperity…peace, love, happiness and prosperity…peace, love, happiness and prosperity…peace, love, happiness and prosperity…peace, love, happiness and prosperity… peace, love, happiness and prosperity…peace, love, happiness and prosperity…peace, love, happiness and prosperity…peace, love, happiness and prosperity…peace, love, happiness and prosperity…

Think about it…

Love and Sunshine,
Tracy

October 26th

Valuing all work

> *"We honor life when we work. The type of work is not important: the fact of work is. All work feeds the soul if it is honest and done to the best of our abilities and if it brings joy to others." – Matthew Fox*

> *"Now in order that people may be happy in their work, these three things are needed: They must be fit for it; they must not do too much of it; and they must have a sense of success in it—not a doubtful sense, such as needs some testimony of others for its confirmation, but a sure sense, or rather knowledge, that so much work has been done well, and fruitfully done, whatever the world may say or think about it." – John Ruskin*

> *"People rarely succeed unless they have fun in what they are doing." – Dale Carnegie*

We all have a life's purpose, whatever that may be for you. You will know if you found yours if you are truly happy with what you are doing on a daily basis. Your Divine meant for you to be abundantly happy and prosperous—to have fun with your life—so why don't you?

Think about it…

Love and Sunshine,
Tracy

Are you stuck again?

"Everyone who got to where they are had to begin where they were." – Richard Paul Evans

"Give the world the best you have and the best will come back to you." – Madeline Bridges

Have you ever had the feeling that you were stuck in place? I am sure I am not the only one. One thing I have realized is that when I feel in that "stuck" state it is most likely because I am not willing to see that what I am looking for may be right in front of me or all around me. Also, it is not showing up in the exact package that I want it to and I find myself spinning in circles. It's so simple to get past. All I have to do is remove my expectations and my path is opened up for me. Remember you get what you give, so if you are in a state of resisting all you will be met with is resistance.

Think about it…

Love and Sunshine,
Tracy

October 28th

Use the force

"There is a vitality, a life force, a quickening that is translated through you into action, and there is only one of you in all time, this expression is unique, and if you block it, it will never exist through any other medium; and be lost." – Martha Graham

"Life has its own hidden forces which you can only discover by living." – Soren Kierkegaard

The rhythm to your life force exists where it exists for you. If it is in dance then dance! If it is in music then sing! If it's in collecting garbage then collect garbage! We all have a unique connection to the life force that runs through everything and everyone. Find yours and you will find your happiness!

Think about it…

Love and Sunshine,
Tracy

Patience, trust and faith

"Patience is waiting. Not passively waiting. That is laziness. But to keep going when the going is hard and slow—that is patience." – Unknown

"None of us knows what might happen even the next minute, yet still we go forward. Because we trust. Because we have Faith." – Paulo Coelho

All it takes is patience, trust and faith. Oh, and maybe get rid of your expectations too and voila! You may have all that you have ever wanted laid out at your feet. If you follow your intuition, listen to your inner Divine and continue to have faith that all that is meant to be Divinely yours is already available to you, you cannot go astray. You will be living in your happiness, grateful for all that you have and joyous to be alive!

Think about it…

Love and Sunshine,
Tracy

Trust in abundance

"Once, when we were discussing a world peace project with my teacher, Maharishi Mahesh Yogi, somebody asked him, Where is all the money going to come from? And he replied without hesitation, From wherever it is at the moment." – Deepak Chopra

"Manifestation is an act of trust. It is the soul pouring itself out into its world, like a fisherman casting a net to gather in the fish he seeks; with each cast properly made, we will bring what we need to us, but first we must hurl ourselves into the depths without knowing just what lies beneath us." – David Spangler

If you have no trust in your abundance how are you ever surprised that it isn't there?

Think about it…

Love and Sunshine,
Tracy

Purpose brings joy

"Our purpose is hidden in our joy, our inspiration, our excitement. As we act on what shows up in our life our purpose shows up." – James King

"There is no more important step you can take than to define your life's purpose. It develops your sense of belonging to our universe." – Arnold Patent

If you are sitting back and waiting for your purpose to fall in your lap, how can you be surprised that you are overwhelmed with a sense of no purpose? If you do not act on your Divine guidance you may be missing all the signs that are pointing you to your own life's purpose, and how sad would that be, when all your Divine wants for you is for you to be abundant and happy.

Think about it…

Love and Sunshine,
Tracy

What is your body telling you?

"There are times when we may fool ourselves. There are times when we can fool others. But we can never fool our body. It is the most sensitive barometer of our inner world." – Sherrill Sellman

"Instead of frittering away your vibrancy with worry or distraction, realize your mind and body are inextricably united. What calms and tones up one, soothes and improves the other." – Marsha Sinetar

"When you are saying that you are happy and you are not, there will be a disturbance in your breathing. Your breathing cannot be natural. It is impossible." – Osho

"Your body is the ground and metaphor of your life, the expression of your existence. It is your Bible, your encyclopedia, your life story. Everything that happens to you is stored and reflected in your body. In the marriage of flesh and spirit divorce is impossible." – Gabrielle Roth

"If you don't take care of your body, where will you live?" – Unknown

If you are not listening to what your body is telling you, how are you ever surprised that you feel unbalanced, unfocused, out of shape, tired, pulled, overwhelmed, sluggish, anxious, tight, sore, and/or stressed all the time?

Think about it . . .

Love and Sunshine,
Tracy

Just let it go . . .

"To attain knowledge, add things every day. To attain wisdom, remove things every day." – Lao Tzu

"When guilt rears its ugly head confront it, discuss it and let it go. The past is over. Forgive yourself and move on." – Bernie S. Siegel

I think I have said this before: How are you ever to add the things you really want in your life if you do not first make room for them by letting something else go? Letting go is the best activity that you could be engaging in on a daily basis because if you do not learn to let go, how are you ever surprised that the same sh*t keeps showing up in your life?

Think about it…

Love and Sunshine,
Tracy

A hot tub for the mind

"Imagine a hot tub for the mind. That is what meditation is; it can bathe your mind in relaxing thoughts." – Eknath Easwaran

"Sometimes the most important thing in a whole day is the rest we take between two deep breaths, or the turning inwards in prayer for five short minutes." – Etty Hillesum

Oooh...I love the idea of a hot tub for the mind. A luxurious spa bath that soothes and calms your mind...ahhhh...I can just imagine the serenity...the peacefulness...the feeling of being safe and secure... ahhhh...blissful. What could be any better way of keeping your monkey brain quiet?

Think about it...

Love and Sunshine,
Tracy

Being alone

"Man's loneliness is but his fear of life."– *Eugene O'Neill*

"I celebrate myself, and sing myself." – Walt Whitman

We are all made of the same energy. It flows through each and every-one one of us. Move beyond your fear (it doesn't exist anyway). Open your mind and your heart and you may realize that you are never alone.

Think about it…

Love and Sunshine,
Tracy

Anywhere

"The path to enlightenment is not a path at all, it's actually a metaphor for the time it takes for you to allow yourself to be happy with who you already are, where you're already at, and what you already have—no matter what. Just do it." – the Universe

How many of you have been actually looking for the "right" step or the "right" direction or even the "right" road to find your enlightenment? Yet it is not any of those things at all and it's just a feeling of happiness. Wowsers...That means you can find enlightenment anywhere! In a song...in a dance...in taking out the garbage...ANYwhere!

Think about it...

Love and Sunshine,
Tracy

Smile!

"Smile, it's free therapy." – Doug Horton

"Depend upon it that if a man talks of his misfortunes there is something in them that is not disagreeable to him; for where there is nothing but pure misery there is never any recourse to the mention of it." – Samuel Johnson

If you are finding that you have a need to tell someone, anyone and/ or everyone about the woes that are going on in your life, have you ever thought that the more you talk about the crappy things that happen, the more you attract them to you? Since you talk about them sooo much it shows that you actually like them and they work for you somehow. Hmmm…Do not believe me? Then stop talking about them! Stop telling everyone your woe is me story. If you cannot stop, then there is something about what is happening that you like. Maybe you do not have to be responsible for something? Maybe you get to blame someone else? Maybe you get to play the victim? How is that working for you so far to bringing you any closer to BEing happy?

If something crappy happens to you, deal with it. Instead of calling the first person you think of and saying, "You'll never guess what happened to me!" and then going on and on in every detail about how crappy it is/ was, maybe you just need to accept it and move on! There is never any need to tell anyone about the woes in your life—ever!

Think about it…

Love and Sunshine,
Tracy

Do you suffer from SIARs?

"If you do what you've always done, you'll get what you've always gotten." – Anthony Robbins

"Low days exist to remind you that you still have choices." – the Universe

"We either make ourselves miserable or we make ourselves strong. The amount of work is the same." – Carlos Castaneda

"Action springs not from thought, but from a readiness for responsibility."– Dietrich Bonhoeffer

Do you spring out of bed with great excitement about what your day is going to bring or are you tired, listless and exhausted because today is going to be just like yesterday? If you relate more to the latter then you may be struck down with SIARs: Stuck-In-A-Rut syndrome. It's happening all around you and you may not even know it. If you keep company with people who love to say things like "*that* will never work" or "why would you want to do *that*?" or "are you sure you want to risk it?" then you are amongst those who suffer from SIARs and may want to keep you down.

Being stuck in a rut is really just a choice you are making because it's working for you somehow to remain stationary—but that's the beauty of being in a rut. You always know where you are and being stationary may be the exact thing you need to propel yourself forward!

Think about it…

Love and Sunshine,
Tracy

Ahhh, success...

"The mark of a successful man is one who has spent an entire day on the bank of the river without feeling guilty about it." – Unknown

The person with the most money is not the most successful. The most successful is the person who lives their life happy from the moment they wake up to the moment and they fall asleep again that night. Your Divine wants you to be happy, why don't you? You are the only shadow standing in the way of your own sunshine.

Think about it…

Love and Sunshine,
Tracy

Is your subconscious running the show?

"Our subconscious minds have no sense of humor, play no jokes and cannot tell the difference between reality and an imagined thought or image. What we continually think about eventually will manifest in our lives." – Robert Collier

"The subconscious is ceaselessly murmuring, and it is by listening to these murmurs that one hears the truth." – Gaston Bachelard

Yesterday I learned something new or maybe I just understood it at a deeper level. Either way, I was struck with one of those light-bulb moments and I was left saying to myself "Huh! No wonder..." about a lot of things.

I followed a link from a friend's Facebook "like" about Emotional Freedom Techniques (EFT). For years I have been aware of EFT tapping and what it is all about but never delved into it before. I found myself watching this 30-minute video featuring Bruce Lipton, a cell biologist, about quantum mechanics and how this powerful science is explaining why many people's lives do not reflect what they really want. There were two specific stories that he told which I found helpful for my own personal growth and understanding and they both involved our subconscious mind.

He talked about how as children we downloaded or pre-recorded ways of being from those around us, like our parents. We picked up behaviours and ways of being that are invisible to us because they are operating from our subconscious mind. That is why it is easy for a 3rd party person to pick up on similar behaviours in family members when you do not see it yourself. Hmmm, interesting...That got me thinking. This is why awareness is such a key factor in helping us change our ways of BEing. The second story he told was about what our subconscious mind really is. He suggested that our subconscious is not a person but a tape recorder. I have heard this before but as he spoke about it I gained a deeper understanding of what that really meant and I was floored with more "no wonder!" thoughts.

He said our subconscious is a tape recorder only able to play back what is has recorded. If you are working on changing your life with positive thoughts, if those new thoughts do not match the recording that your subconscious is playing, nothing will ever change in your life. To illustrate this idea, he said get out a tape recorder and push play. Now go up to that tape recorder and tell it to play something different. Yell at it to change the program that it's playing. You could do this all day and you know that the tape recorder will not change whatever it is playing. Doesn't that sound ridiculous, yelling at a tape recorder? Lol...He said trying to better your life with positive thinking, new psychology or self-help is like yelling at a tape recorder. If the programming of your subconscious doesn't match what you are thinking in your conscious mind that is why nothing ever changes! To change the programming of your subconscious you have to learn how do it while holding down the record button and that, he said, is where the EFT Tapping came into play.

I really enjoyed listening to Bruce. What I got out of it was that if someone is telling me about a behaviour of mine that isn't working for them, instead of getting angry about it and thinking they are crazy for even proposing that I am *that* way, maybe I should listen, take heed and it may be something for me to look at re-recording in my subconscious.

Think about it...

Love and Sunshine,
Tracy

Independent choice

"Freedom of choice is more to be treasured than any possession earth can give."
– David O. McKay

"The truest characters of ignorance are vanity, pride and arrogance." –
Samuel Butler

"What man wants is simply independent choice, whatever that may cost and
wherever it may lead." – Fyodor Dostoyevsky

I find it kind of funny, but not in the ha-ha way, that really, we all have independent choice, but most of us ignore the fact and just lay down, play the victim and kick and scream that we had no choice.

Think about it…

Love and Sunshine,
Tracy

What are you offering these days?

"Never underestimate your own importance in the world today and in worlds to come." – the Universe

"A loving person lives in a loving world. A hostile person lives in a hostile world. Everyone you meet is your mirror." – Ken Keyes

You are the creator of your world. You are the only one responsible for what happens in it on a daily basis. There never really is a set outcome to your world because you are constantly changing it. You are, as you always have been, the only controller in your life. If you want to receive love then BE loving. If you want tranquility in your life then BE peaceful and calm. If you want excitement in your life then BE exciting. It is up to you to create the world that you want to live in for all aspects of it. Just think about the possibilities of it! Wow…Exciting!

Think about it some more . . . Getting goose bumps, yet?

Love and Sunshine,
Tracy

Bring awareness to your generosity

"Generosity lies less in giving much than in giving at the right moment." –
Jean De La Bruyère

"Generosity is another quality which, like patience, letting go, non-judging, and
trust, provides a solid foundation for mindfulness practice. You might experiment
with using the cultivation of generosity as a vehicle for deep self-observation and
inquiry as well as an exercise in giving." – Jon Kabat Zinn

If you think that "giving" is about money then you may be going around living your life with blinders on, perhaps missing out on the best parts in life. Generosity is definitely a timing thing. It may not be the giver that has a timing issue but the person who is receiving the generosity that might, so just be mindful if you get a different result than you thought you were going to get.

You may never know that giving something as simple as your smile to someone at the perfect moment may be the greatest gift that they ever receive but it's so worth it. When you give without expectation of receiving back, you are rarely going to be off in your timing!

Think about it...

Love and Sunshine,
Tracy

Opening the heart

"Everything is made of light; everything is alive. The Great Mystery of life has little to do with intelligence. The universe is not an intellectual process. The intellect is helpful; but our hearts are the wiser part of ourselves." – Mellen-Thomas Benedict

"If you open your heart, love opens your mind." – Charles John Quarto

If only we all could come from our hearts instead of our interpreted egos in our head—wow! What a world we would live in then.

Think about it…seriously…

Love and Sunshine,
Tracy

Are you missing the joy of life?

"Thinking about interior peace destroys interior peace. The patient who constantly feels his pulse is not getting any better." – Hubert van Zeller

"So many people work so hard, to achieve, attain, accumulate and cherish their fortunes. How many of us blissfully fill our days and nights being the Divine expression we are? This is the meaning of life. It is to be. As a result, all of your creations are a natural outflow from the Divine within your being. This is the joy of life." – Barbara Rose

The things in life that you do are supposed to bring you joy and happiness. If you are not smiling the moment you wake up and you realize what you are going to be doing that day, either it is not what you are supposed to be doing or you are trying too hard to achieve it.

Think about it…

Love and Sunshine,
Tracy

Learn to be aware

"You can live a lifetime and, at the end of it, know more about other people than you know about yourself." – *Beryl Markham*

"To be authentic is literally to be your own author, to discover your own native energies and desires, and then to find your own way of acting on them." – *Warren G. Bennis*

"Self-knowledge is the great power by which we comprehend and control our lives." – *Vernon Howard*

Living unaware of your own self is a way for you to not be responsible for your own life and continue to play the victim. Because you allow yourself to remain in an "I don't know" state you perpetuate not making any decisions and continue to play the woe is me game. How's that working for you anyway? The sooner you open your awareness to self the sooner you can get to BEing the "happy" you that you were always meant to be. The myth to uncover here is that a lot of people think that once you become aware of yourself that you may have to change and become someone different. It's quite on the contrary. The more you become aware of who you are, the more you remain the same. You can remain the same crabby person, if you want, but done with awareness that means there is acceptance there. You continue to do the same things in your life without any sign of complaint or woe, and then happiness is a guaranteed outcome. As soon as you are complaining then you are not living in awareness or acceptance of who you are. I do not think I can say this enough: wouldn't you rather be happy than right?

Think about it...

Love and Sunshine,
Tracy

The way you look at yourself and your world

"Be not afraid of growing slowly, be afraid only of standing still." –
Chinese proverb

"Too many people miss the silver lining because they're expecting gold" –
Maurice Seitta

The way you look at yourself and your world has a powerful effect on every aspect of your life. Your career and your relationships are two areas that are bound to improve as your attitude improves. But that is only the beginning. Your attitude also affects your health, your happiness, your goals, even the quality of your fondest dreams. When you have an attitude of "I'm Worth It!" you'll find that you are willing to do whatever is necessary to improve the quality of your life. Why? Because now you believe that you deserve only the best! There are hundreds of books, audios and videos available that can help you improve the quality of your health, your finances, your ability to reach goals, your career, and your relationships. When you are uncomfortable with yourself in any area in your life, seek the help you need.

Life is a process of continual growth. Growth comes about when we effectively meet the challenges in our lives. Think of the challenges you face in just that way—as ways to grow. The next time you are faced with a situation that looks difficult tell yourself, "Great! Now I can GROW!" The truth of the human condition is that very few of us choose to grow just for the heck of it. Pain forces us into it. You DO have the power to achieve anything you want out of this life. You have the potential for unlimited happiness and opportunity and when life looks tough just remember that a diamond is only a lump of coal that made the best out of a little pressure.

Think about it…

Love and Sunshine,
Tracy

In the end

"In the end, it's not the years in your life that count. It's the life in your years."
– Abraham Lincoln

"In the End, we will remember not the words of our enemies, but the silence of our friends." – Martin Luther King, Jr.

When in doubt, give, let them have it, surrender, make peace.

If you spend your whole life fighting just so that you can say you are right who do you think, besides yourself, will be there in the end to hear it?

Think about it…

Love and Sunshine,
Tracy

Embrace the positive and the negative

"Only when we can love hell will we find heaven." – Unknown

"When you are able to contain both the light and dark together, that is a very enlightening state. It means that you no longer have to choose one experience over another. You do not have to choose love OR hate, blame OR forgiveness, sadness OR joy, anger OR openheartedness. You are no longer polarized; no particular feeling boxes you in and keeps you from the light of true self. You then have access to the full range of human experiences you came into this life to embrace." – Martia Nelson

Acceptance is the key. Accept who you are in every moment, in every thought, in every feeling and in every BEing that you are and you may come to accept everyone else in their own moments, their own thoughts, their own feelings and their own BEing.

What would the world look like if everyone accepted everybody?

Think about it…

Love and Sunshine,
Tracy

Distinguish personality desires from soul needs

"Human history is the sad result of each one looking out for himself." – *Julio Cortazar*

"Selfishness is not living as one wishes to live, it is asking others to live as one wishes to live." – *Oscar Wilde*

"The human being who lives only for himself finally reaps nothing but unhappiness. Selfishness corrodes. Unselfishness ennobles, satisfies. Don't put off the joy derivable from doing helpful, kindly things for others." – *B. C. Forbes*

We only ever get upset over anything because we do not get what we want—end of story. So next time you have the urge to get on your defensive horse and before you commence your full-fledged retaliation on someone else's upset, no matter how hard it may seem, why not take a half-step back, put yourself in their shoes and ask yourself, "What is this person not getting in their life to act this way?" You never know, by giving them what they want you just may receive what it is that *you* want?

Think about it…

Love and Sunshine,
Tracy

Think for yourself

"I think the reward for conformity is that everyone likes you except yourself."
– Rita Mae Brown

"Once in a while it really hits people that they don't have to experience the world in the way they have been told to." – Alan Keightley

If you are not living your life for yourself, how are you ever surprised that you are unhappy, dissatisfied and/or unfulfilled all the time?

Think about it…

Love and Sunshine,
Tracy

Happiness is right in front of you

"The way to get started is to quit talking and begin doing." – Walt Disney

"Discipline is making the choice between what you want now and what you want most." – Unknown

Have you ever noticed that the people who are forever talking are the ones who are not accomplishing very much and usually complaining about their lives? If only they had the discipline to move away from instantaneous gratification and learned to be patient. They may realize that they are closer to what they want than they think they are.

Think about it…

Love and Sunshine,
Tracy

November 22nd

Self-deception

"The first and worst of all frauds is to cheat one's self." – *Phillip James Bailey*

"The longer the excuse, the less likely it's the truth." – *Robert Half*

"When we know deep down that were acting with integrity despite impulses to do otherwise, we feel gates of higher energy and inspiration open inside of us." – *Dan Millman*

At the end of the day you are the only person who will be able to look yourself in the eyes and know that you told the truth and lived your day with integrity and no excuses.

Think about it…

Love and Sunshine,
Tracy

Validation isn't just about parking

"The logic of validation allows us to move between the two limits of dogmatism and skepticism." – Paul Ricoeur

Validating those around you and letting them know the good that they do really has an impact on someone's general health and output of work. It also brings inner warmth that reminds that person of how awesome they really are. Smiles are guaranteed and feelings of happiness along with it. When is the last time you validated someone important to you? Did you ever think that you may be able to turn their frown upside down just by letting them know how great they are and what they mean to you? No? How many smiles do you think you could get out of the people you love and even strangers on the street just by validating them?

Don't just think about it today…DOOO EEET!!!

Love and Sunshine,
Tracy

Is your integrity intact?

"In order to live a rich life, everything about who you are must be one, in alignment, and in pure harmony." – Suze Orman

"Honor your integrity and you will be repaid many times over with increased prosperity." – Sanaya Roman and Duane Packer

You are only as powerful as your word.

Think about it…

Love and Sunshine,
Tracy

We experience what we believe

"You are free to believe what you choose and what you do attests to what you believe." – A Course of Miracles

"Sooner or later, those who win are those who think they can."– Richard Bach

This is such a simple concept yet sooo many of you out there just do not get it and continue to think your life is crap and the world is made of sh★t, then wonder why you are so miserable all the time. Geesh…This may be a great opportunity for you to sit down and write out your beliefs and see where and why your life is the way it is. You may be surprised that you *are* the only one responsible for all your misfortune and see how simple it may be to change things around.

Think about it…

Love and Sunshine,
Tracy

November 26th

Commitment

"Our deepest need is for the joy that comes with knowing we are of genuine use to others." – Eknath Easwaran

"There is no such thing as just existing. Everything is in service to everything else. Existence is giving and receiving. A stone gives and receives no less than a saint." – Jacob Needleman

What is commitment? Commitment is doing the thing you said you were going to do long after the feeling you said it in has gone away. That is commitment.

Think about it...

Love and Sunshine,
Tracy

Conflicts with the kids? Relax!

"Family life! The United Nations is child's play compared to the tugs and splits and need to understand and forgive in any family." – May Sarton

"Those who have children can become masters of patience, endurance, and steadfastness, because children will test you at every turn. The way to make our children patient and loving is to be that way ourselves." – Eknath Easwaran

Oh boy, is this ever a good one for me to take heed. When I was discussing the issues I was having with my eight-year-old daughter a good friend of mine told me to stop getting triggered by her. HA! I wanted to tell my friend where to go with that advice because surely what is happening has nothing to do with me, pul-lease…Lol. Wow, how arrogant we can be from time to time and not even realize that all we are doing is pointing our fingers elsewhere when what we should be doing is giving ourselves a good look in the mirror. Here's something that you may or may not be aware of: Your children learned all their behaviours from you and that's why you do not like it when they show you something you do not like in yourself. Hmmm, interesting isn't it?

Think about it…

Love and Sunshine,
Tracy

November 28th

Where do you look for inspiration?

"Consult not your fears but your hopes and dreams. Think not about your frustrations, but about your unfulfilled potential. Concern yourself not with what you tried and failed in, but with what is still possible for you to do.." – Pope John XXIII

"The point is not to pay back kindness but to pass it on." – Julia Alvarez

If you always look at what's not working in your life how are ever to see what is possible for you? And if you can never see what's possible how are you ever surprised that nothing is working for you?

Think about it…

Love and Sunshine,
Tracy

Tracy Friesen

BE genuine

"To be yourself in a world that is constantly trying to make you something else is the greatest accomplishment." – Ralph Waldo Emerson

"Be who you are and say what you feel, because those who mind don't matter and those who matter don't mind." – Dr. Seuss

"What you must dare is to be yourself." – Dag Hammarskjold

If you choose to be someone you are not for the benefit of someone else how are you ever surprised that you feel that no one knows you or takes you seriously?

Think about it...

Love and Sunshine,
Tracy

November 30th

Life getting you down?

"When everything seems to be going against you, remember that the airplane takes off against the wind, not with it." – Henry Ford

"So if something still hurts, baffles, or confuses, it only means a miracle has occurred, the pendulum is mid-swing, and that soon you'll know exactly what I'm talking about." – the Universe

The only way to get from one point to another is to take action and move and in the process you may possibly grow. The best thing you can ever do when faced with life's hardships is to have patience, accept what is, have faith that everything happens for a reason and in the end everything is OK. If it's not OK, then it's not the end.

Think about it…

Love and Sunshine,
Tracy

Tracy Friesen

Still sitting there?

"The purpose of life is to discover your gift. The meaning of life is to give it away." – David Viscott

"You don't have to get it right, you just have to get it going." – Unknown

If you are stuck in a mindset that you must be perfect, you may be forgetting that even the most expensive diamonds in the world have their flaws and that is what makes them sooo valuable.

Think about it...

Love and Sunshine,
Tracy

December 2nd

Who's responsible?

"The best years of your life are the ones in which you decide your problems are your own. You do not blame them on your mother, the ecology, or the president. You realize that you control your own destiny." – Albert Ellis

"You are not responsible for the programming you picked up in childhood. However, as an adult, you are one hundred percent responsible for fixing it." – Ken Keyes, Jr.

As soon as you blame another for something that has happened to you in your life, you give up your power to change. Even though we are all connected by the same energy we are all individuals acting out our own lives. There are no sides and no one is ever against you. Everyone out there acts, chooses and lives each day for themselves no matter what happens. No one owes anyone anything, especially you—no matter what has taken place. It is up to you in every moment in every day to act and choose for yourself to bring joy and happiness to your own life.

Think about it…

Love and Sunshine,
Tracy

Be willing to repeat

"Change is the constant, the signal for rebirth, the egg of the phoenix." –
Christina Baldwin

"It all depends on how we look at things and not on how they are in them-
selves." – C.G. Jung

For us it comes down to a choice of who we are going to BE and how
we choose to perceive the world around us. No burning required—lol!
The phoenix is one of my favorite symbols. Such a magnificent represen-
tation of something that doesn't have to be sooo dramatic.

Think about it...

Love and Sunshine,
Tracy

December 4th

Travel with awareness

"…focus on the journey, not the destination. Joy is found not in finishing an activity but in doing it." – Greg Anderson

"Slow down and enjoy life. It's not only the scenery you miss by going too fast—you also miss the sense of where you are going and why." – Eddie Cantor

Slowing down and enjoying your life is one of the best things that you can do for your happiness. Whether you are just going to the grocery store or you are traveling along your life's path, a great thing to always have with you is your trusted friend awareness.

Think about it…

Love and Sunshine,
Tracy

Tracy Friesen

Why stop searching?

"Remember not only to say the right thing in the right place, but far more difficult still, to leave unsaid the wrong thing at the tempting moment." – Benjamin Franklin

"As long as one keeps searching, the answers come." – Joan Baez

It is never in the "how" that things get done. It is in your unrelenting desire and possibly your knowingness—your inner faith—that you already have what you want, that your answers show up for you. If you stop searching your answer is always no. Why not give yourself a chance at yes and just keep searching?

Think about it...

Love and Sunshine,
Tracy

December 6th

Opportunity

"We are continually faced with great opportunities which are brilliantly disguised as unsolvable problems." – Margaret Mead

"A wise man will make more opportunities than he finds." – Francis Bacon

"What is opportunity, and when does it knock? It never knocks. You can wait a whole lifetime, listening, hoping, and you will hear no knocking. None at all. You are opportunity, and you must knock on the door leading to your destiny. You prepare yourself to recognize opportunity, to pursue and seize opportunity as you develop the strength of your personality, and build a self-image with which you are able to live—with your self-respect alive and growing." – Maxwell Maltz

It is up to you to make the choice and take action to find your own opportunities—always. If you are stuck in thinking that nothing comes your way, what have you done to bring it about?

Think about it…

Love and Sunshine,
Tracy

Lose the baggage

"Promise Yourself…to be so strong that nothing can disturb your peace of mind…. To be too large for worry, too noble for anger, too strong for fear, and too happy to permit the presence of trouble." – Drawn from the Optimist Creed of the Optimist International Club

"If you wish to travel far and fast, travel light. Take off all your envies, jealousies, unforgiveness, selfishness, and fears." – Glenn Clark

Maybe the reason that you are sooo tired and overwhelmed all the time is that you haven't taken the time to leave your baggage at home. You know if you leave it by the curb you can always pick it up on your way home, if you want to that is. Just imagine how freeing it would be to remove the shackles of your past? The past is gone. It isn't happening again. You are consciously choosing it in every moment to make it seem real. Instead of living the same ol' same ol', why not try something different, break away from your past and just BE who you want to be? What kind of happiness can you create if you are from this day forward, always doing something that *you* want to do?

Think about it…

Love and Sunshine,
Tracy

December 8th

No regrets...

"Never regret. If it's good, it's wonderful. If it's bad, it's experience." — Victoria Holt

"What lies behind us and what lies before us are small matters compared to what lies within us." – Ralph Waldo Emerson

The second quote is one of my all-time favorites because when you really get that you are the only person responsible for your life, then you really get that nothing else that happens around you matters because you are in complete control of your own happiness—always.

Think about it…

Love and Sunshine,
Tracy

Imprisoned by your thoughts?

"Problems exist only in the human mind." – Anthony de Mello

"Don't water your weeds." – Harvey Mackay

How many times have you felt that you had no control over your thoughts? I'll let you in on a little secret. You do have the power to control your own thoughts and emotions! There, I said it! It all comes down to a choice—your choice. If you were a gardener would you want to water the weeds or pull them out instead? We are all gardeners of our own mind. It is up to you what you decide to let grow and flourish—always!

Think about it…

Love and Sunshine,
Tracy

December 10th

What are you feeling?

> *"We know too much and feel too little. At least, we feel too little of those creative emotions from which a good life springs."* – Bertrand Russell

> *"With just a little education and practice on how to manage your emotions, you can move into a new experience of life so rewarding that you will be motivated to keep on managing your emotional nature in order to sustain it. The payoff is delicious in terms of improved quality of life."* – Doc Childre

When is the last time you actually felt something rather than just thinking you felt it? Have you ever noticed how many people think their way through their own lives? You miss out on so much, because all the fun and happiness is in the feeling! It's no wonder that your life may seem dull, boring and lifeless. How about every time you catch yourself saying the words "I think," change it to "I feel" instead. You never know what kind of feelings or emotions that you may bring up that you actually had no idea you were feeling.

Think about it...

Love and Sunshine,
Tracy

It's always you...

"Everything that happens to us is a reflection of who we are." – Deepak Chopra

Reread Deepak's quote. If you really get what he is saying, then how can you ever be surprised if your life isn't going the way you want it to go?

Think about it…

Love and Sunshine,
Tracy

Bring your awareness

"It is difficult to see the picture when you are inside of the frame." – Unknown

"What is necessary to change a person is to change his awareness of himself." –
Abraham H. Maslow

How many times have you been stuck in trying to see the whole picture from the middle of the scene? Doesn't work very well, does it? When you bring your awareness to the picture you can broaden your view and just maybe you will be able to see that you are not the only person with a point of view.

Think about it…

Love and Sunshine,
Tracy

Success is imminent if you just keep going

"Gratitude makes sense of our past, brings peace for today, and creates a vision for tomorrow." – Melody Beattie

"You won't be happy with more until you're happy with what you've got." – Viki King

"Never look back unless you are planning to go that way." – Henry David Thoreau

"There is only one way to succeed at anything and that is to give everything." – Vince Lombardi

If you are at a crossroads in your life. the best thing for you to do is Decide, Commit, and Move on.

Think about it…

Love and Sunshine,
Tracy

Lost and Found

Until you are lost you cannot be found.

Think about it...

Love and Sunshine,
Tracy

Tracy Friesen

Getting down to essentials

"Besides the noble art of getting things done, there is the noble art of leaving things undone. The wisdom of life consists in the elimination of non-essentials."
– Lin Yutang

"The ability to simplify means to eliminate the unnecessary so that the necessary may speak." – Hans Hofmann

W hat have you been dragging behind you all this time that really isn't necessary anymore? If you haven't looked in a while I bet you'll be surprised to see that your handbag of "I'll deal with it later" has become a gynormous trunk that should take three people to carry. Geesh…No wonder you are so tired all the time. Maybe it's time to deal with these weights one at a time and deem what is essential and what is not—or just cut the cord entirely and release all that isn't serving you for your better good. It's your choice and whatever you choose to do is the perfect choice. Wouldn't you rather be FREE than right, anyway?

Think about it…

Love and Sunshine,
Tracy

Obstacle or building block:
What do you see?

> *"We can throw stones, complain about them, stumble on them, climb over them, or build with them."* – William Arthur Ward

> *"If you are patient in one moment of anger, you will avoid one hundred days of sorrow."* – Chinese Proverb

> *"Good judgement comes from experience; experience comes from bad judgement."* – Mulla Nasrudin

No matter what happens to us I believe that everything happens for a reason and it is how you react to it that determines your level of happiness—always. If something happens and you react with anger, resentment, distain and/or rage, do you really think that anyone, especially you, will be anywhere near happy?

Another year is coming to an end. Do you really want to spend another minute complaining, stumbling or griping that your life isn't what you want? WAKE UP!!! It's up to you and only you to make your life what you want it to be. A good place to start is to accept that it is OK to be where you are today. Then take one step in front of the other, expect good happy things, and good happy things will come your way.

Think about it…

Love and Sunshine,
Tracy

Let your love flow

"Character isn't inherited. One builds it daily by the way one thinks and acts, thought by thought, action by action. If one lets fear or hate or anger take posses-sion of the mind, they become self-forged chains." – Helen Douglas

"Too often we underestimate how quickly our feelings are going to change because we underestimate our ability to change them." – David Gilbert

Around this time of year some people seem to get angrier and angrier as the year comes to an end. This is learned behaviour. As easy as it is to let loose the rage, it is just as easy to take a deep breath and let your love flow. It all comes down to a choice—your choice. Do you want to be right or do you want to be happy?

Think about it…

Love and Sunshine,
Tracy

Send out love and happiness!

"In every area of our lives, we get back what we send out." – Marshall Sylver

If you are not experiencing the life you want to live, have you ever thought to look to how you feel about it? What kind of signals or messages are you sending out? Are you sending out strife or love and happiness?

Think about it…

Love and Sunshine,
Tracy

Love your shadows

"There is that part of ourselves that feels ugly, deformed, unacceptable. That part, above all, we must learn to cherish, embrace, and call by name." – Macrina Wiederkehr

"The first step toward change is acceptance. Once you accept yourself, you open the door to change. That's all you have to do. Change is not something you do, it's something you allow." – Will Garcia

Acceptance is the key to your overall happiness. So many people think that because you accept something it means you *have* to like it. Well, I am here to tell you that nothing could be farther from the truth! Accepting "what is" is just that—accepting it. No one asked you *anything* about how you *feel* about it! It's just plain and simple. Accept it or do not accept it there's nothing more to do. There is no liking or not liking involved. It's no wonder to me that things go the way they do when people are constantly confusing the point that their opinion matters to the acceptance of anything that goes on in their life. It's exactly what Will says above: Change is something you allow. Is it really worth wasting your life just so you can say, "I am right!"?

Think about it…

Love and Sunshine,
Tracy

December 20th

Where are your priorities?

"You always have time for the things you put first." – Unknown

If you think that you have your priorities straight, yet the first thing you do when you wake up is worry and stress about your life I would really think twice about where you are putting your energy. Reread the above quote. What really comes first in your life?

Think about it…

Love and Sunshine,
Tracy

Where's your state of mind?

"It's not that some people have willpower and some don't. It's that some people are ready to change and others are not." – James Gordon

"When you judge another, you do not define them, you define yourself." – Wayne Dyer

Lately have you found yourself right in the middle of the hustle and bustle and just as angry as everyone else? Or is everyone else just as angry as you, perhaps? Hmmm…Instead of fighting to be right all the time why not take it from Ghandi and "BE the change you want to see in the world?"

Think about it…

Love and Sunshine,
Tracy

The path to wholeness

"When we are conscious of our personal uniqueness and our universal nature we express ourselves creatively. In this way we fulfill our dreams and our life purpose." – Andrew Schneider

What I get out of this statement is that when we acknowledge our behaviours (the good, the bad and the ugly, for lack of better words) and accept them and ourselves for who we are; when we understand that how we personally feel is just our own point of view, that everyone has a point of view and that no one (ourselves included) is "wrong" for it; when we can live our lives fully self-expressed with happiness in everything that happens to us, around us and in everything that we do—then and only then will we see and feel our own light within and feel whole.

Think about it…

Love and Sunshine,
Tracy

Why are you doing that?

"What we see depends mainly on what we look for." – *Sir John Lubbock*

"The great thing in the world is not so much where we stand, as in what direction we are moving." – *Oliver Wendell Holmes*

You may have been doing something or reacting the same way for sooo long that you do not even remember why anymore. Perhaps it is time to take a half-step back and be objective. It is time to get out of your story of how you think your life is, and find out how your life *really* is. You may be pleasantly surprised to realize that your life is pretty wonderful after all.

Think about it…

Love and Sunshine,
Tracy

December 24th

Stop being so hard on yourself

"In the confrontation between the stream and the rock, the stream always wins, not through strength but by perseverance." – H. Jackson Brown

"It is by what we ourselves have done, and not by what others have done for us, that we shall be remembered in after ages." – Francis Wayland

Have you ever stopped and taken some time to reflect on all that you've done? Wow…Look at how much you've accomplished in the last five years, the last year, the last month, just yesterday or even in the last few hours for that matter. Has anyone else been through what you've been through? Accomplished what you've accomplished? Survived what you've survived? Well? Has anyone? It's time you slowed down, took some time to look back for a bit and realize that you are something SPECTACULAR to pull off what you've done in your life thus far. Remember that no matter what happens, it happens for a reason. Even if you do not know why in this moment, just have faith that the good will come. Whereever you are in your life it is the best most perfect place to start the rest of your life.

Think about it…

"It is time for us to stand and cheer for the doer, the achiever, the one who recognizes the challenge and does something about it." – Vince Lombardi

YIPPPEEEEEEE!!!   HOOORRAYYYY!!!   WAY   TO   GO!!! YOU ROCK!!!

Love and Sunshine,
Tracy

You were meant to be happy

"Have you noticed, that sadness in your life has never, ever, not even once, lasted? It's impossible." – the Universe

Contrary to your belief, perhaps, all your Divine wants for you is for you to BE prosperous, happy and abundant—always!

Think about it…

Love and Sunshine,
Tracy

A new look at old attitudes

"I can change. I can live out my imagination instead of my memory. I can tie myself to my limitless potential instead of my limiting past." – Stephen Covey

"Change. It has the power to uplift, to heal, to stimulate, surprise, open new doors, bring fresh experience and create excitement in life. Certainly it is worth the risk." – Leo Buscaglia

I can change. I can live out my imagination instead of my memory. I can tie myself to my limitless potential instead of my limiting past. I can change. I can live out my imagination instead of my memory. I can tie myself to my limitless potential instead of my limiting past. I can change. I can live out my imagination instead of my memory. I can tie myself to my limitless potential instead of my limiting past.

What is it going to take for you to make the decision to change?

I can change. I can change. I can change. I can change. I can change.
I can change. I can change. I can change. I can change. I can change.
I can change. I can change. I can change. I can change. I can change.
I can change. I can change. I can change. I can change. I can change.
I can change. I can change. I can change. I can change. I can change.
I can change. I can change. I can change. I can change. I can change.
I can change. I can change. I can change. I can change. I can change.
I can change. I can change. I can change. I can change. I can change.
I can change. I can change. I can change. I can change. I can change.
I can change. I can change. I can change. I can change. I can change.
I can change. I can change. I can change. I can change. I can change.
I can change. I can change. I can change. I can change. I can change.
I can change. I can change. I can change. I can change. I can change.
I can change. I can change. I can change. I can change. I can change.
I can change. I can change. I can change. I can change. I can change.

Think about it…

Love and Sunshine,
Tracy

Stop the battles

"When you fight something, you're tied to it forever. As long as you're fighting it, you're giving it power." – Anthony de Mello

"What you resist persists. And only what you look at, and own, can disappear. You make it disappear by simply changing your mind about it." – Neale Donald Walsch

Only through your acceptance of the situation will you ever be able to get to a place where you can change your mind about it. I never said you had to like it, just accept it.

Think about it...

Love and Sunshine,
Tracy

I dare you!

"The future is not some place we are going, but one we are creating. The paths are not to be found, but made. And the activity of making them changes both the maker and their destination." – John Schaar

"Let him who would enjoy a good future waste none of his present." – Roger Babson

Instead of using your imagination to continuously bring you down, why not use it to create the life of your dreams? Go on, I dare you!

Think about it…

Love and Sunshine,
Tracy

Feeling overwhelmed?

"Life does not happen to us, it happens from us." – Mike Wickett

"When we know that the cause of something is in ourselves, and that we (ourselves) are one of the few things in the universe that we have the right and ability to change, we begin to get a sense of the choices we really do have, an inkling of the power we have, a feeling of being in charge…of our lives, of our future, of our dreams." – John-Roger and Peter McWilliams

When you really get that you are responsible for your own life and that you can change it whenever you want a sense of excitement can overwhelm you. That giddy night before Christmas feeling you had as a child…that "I've won the lottery!" feeling…that I am invincible feeling…that sense of your own power feeling! Wouldn't you rather be overwhelmed with joy and excitement than self-pity and strife? As Mike says, "Life does not happen to us, it happens from us."

Think about it…

Love and Sunshine,
Tracy

Did someone ask for help?

"The strong individual is the one who asks for help when he needs it." –
Rona Barrett

"Asking is the beginning of receiving. Make sure you don't go to the ocean with
a teaspoon. At least take a bucket so the kids won't laugh at you." – Jim Rohn

If it seems that you have been a little light on the receiving end of things
lately maybe it is because you have forgotten how to ask for help? If you
are not sure why things are happening the way they are in your life it
could possibly be because you think you do not ever need help. Not only
the wise but the successful when asked what is the secret to their success
they will often tell you that it is in asking for help when they know that
they do not have the answer. Contrary to your possible belief, there is
nothing weak about asking for help. It is often the most courageous event
in someone's life. Get good at asking for help and I can guarantee you
that your life will not only be less stressful but you will be so much more
happy . . . and isn't that the point anyway?

Think about it…

Love and Sunshine,
Tracy

Out with the old and
in with the new...

"Cheers to a New Year and another chance for us to get it right." –
Oprah Winfrey

"Be always at war with your vices, at peace with your neighbors, and let each
new year find you a better man." – *Benjamin Franklin*

So it is here—the end to another year. If you think that you are in the
same place as you were last year, then maybe you might want to take
some time tonight, before the clock strikes midnight, and reread some
of the messages that were brought to you this year. I believe everything
happens for a reason and you received those messages for a reason. It is up
to you to figure out if you are going to let yourself be brave and courageous and heed them.

Remember, everything is OK in the end. If it's not OK, then it's not the
end. With that I will leave you this year with the words of William Arthur
Ward to think about:

"Another fresh new year is here…Another year to live! To banish worry,
doubt, and fear, To love and laugh and give!

This bright new year is given me To live each day with zest… To daily
grow and try to be My highest and my best!

I have the opportunity Once more to right some wrongs, To pray for
peace, to plant a tree, And sing more joyful songs!"

Happy New Year!!

Love and Sunshine,
Tracy

Contributors

Note: The author of "the Universe" quotes is Mike Dooley.

Front cover photograph "Peace Within" taken by Julie Anne Gardiner "Jules" of wishlistinteriordesign.com enhanced by Kevin Friesen of Kreative Design Fabrication.

End of the month graphic design by Kevin Friesen of Kreative Design Fabrication

CPSIA information can be obtained
at www.ICGtesting.com
Printed in the USA
LVOW07s0536190917
549241LV00001B/1/P